Monks and Bishops

Robert Hay is the Archivist for Lismore Historical Society/Comann Eachdraidh Lios Mòr. His other books include *Lochnavando No More: The Life and Death of a Moray Farming Community 1750–1850* (2005); *Lismore: The Great Garden* (2009, 2024); *How an Island Lost its People: Improvement, Clearance and Resettlement on Lismore, 1830–1914* (2013, 2023); and *The Story of Lismore in Fifty Objects* (2018). He was a contributor to the *Farming and the Land* volume of the Scottish Life and Society series (John Donald, 2011) and has contributed several articles to *Review of Scottish Culture*, *History Scotland* and *Sources in Local History* (Regional Ethnology of Scotland). He has lived full-time on Lismore since 2006.

St Moluag: detail from a stained-glass memorial window in the east gable of Lismore Parish Church, by the leading Scottish designer of her era: Mary Isobel Wood (1886–1975).

Monks AND Bishops

LISMORE
560–1560

ROBERT HAY

ORIGIN

First published in Great Britain in 2025 by
Origin, an imprint of Birlinn Ltd

West Newington House
10 Newington Road
Edinburgh
EH9 1QS

www.birlinn.co.uk

ISBN: 978 1 83983 086 0

Copyright © Robert K.M. Hay 2025

The right of Robert K.M. Hay to be identified as the author
of this work has been asserted by him in accordance
with the Copyright, Designs and Patents Act, 1988

All rights reserved. No part of this publication may
be reproduced, stored, or transmitted in any form, or
by any means, electronic, mechanical or photocopying,
recording or otherwise, without the express written
permission of the publisher.

British Library Cataloguing-in-Publication Data
A catalogue record for this book is available on request from the British Library

Typeset by Initial Typesetting Services, Edinburgh
Printed and bound in Britain by Ashford Colour Limited, Gosport, Hampshire

Contents

List of Plates, Figures and Tables	vii
Acknowledgements	ix
Timeline: 560–1560	xii
1 Introduction: One Thousand Years from Moluag	1
2 The Insular Church and Lismore	3
3 The Making of the Medieval Church in Scotland	13
4 Foundation and Early Years of the Diocese of Argyll (1190–1249)	26
5 The Coming of the Dominicans	55
6 The MacDougall Bishops during the Wars of Independence: Laurence (1262–1299) and Andrew (1300–1342)	66
7 The Cathedral of Argyll	81
8 Martin – the Contumacious Bishop (1342–1387)	93
9 Into the Fifteenth Century: The Last Dominican (1419–1426) and the First Bishop Without Gaelic (1427–1462)	112
10 The Last Days of Argyll Diocese (1475–1560)	131
11 How the Cathedral Affected the People of Lismore	140
12 Epilogue: After the Reformation	149
Bibliography	153
Further Reading	159
Index	165

Plates, Figures and Tables

Plates

p. ii	St Moluag: detail from stained-glass memorial window in Lismore Parish Church
1	Drone image of the parish church and its surrounds
2	Excavation of the monastic site, May 2022
3	Excavation of the cathedral nave
4	Medieval details of the parish church/cathedral choir
5	Charter (1256) from the Bishop of Durham to Alan, Bishop of Argyll
6	Lismore Parish Church, photographed by Erskine Beveridge in 1882, before the major remodelling of 1896
7	Bishop Lauder arrives in state at his cathedral on 29 August 1452 (scene from a performance on 7 August 2015)
8	Seal of George Lauder, Bishop of Argyll, attached to a letter to the Vatican, 5 April 1454

Figures

2.1	Distribution of Insular Church structures in Argyll diocese	7
2.2	Sketch map of the monastic site	9
3.1	Scottish church dioceses, *c*. 1300	21
4.1	Parish churches, diocese of Argyll, *c*. 1300	36
7.1	Tracings of the mason's marks on the sedilia and piscina	84

| 7.2 | Reconstruction of the Cathedral of Argyll by Edward Odling | 86 |
| 8.1 | Family tree of the Royal Stewarts | 98 |

Tables

4.1	Silgrave's list of religious houses in Scotland, annex to his *Chronicle*, *c.* 1272	32
4.2	The mainland medieval parishes of the diocese of Argyll	37
4.3	Compilation of the general or provincial statutes of the Scottish Church, *c.* 1240	44

Acknowledgements

Writing this book has been a long journey. It started a quarter of a century ago, when I first looked into Lismore Parish Church and discovered that it was the choir of the medieval Cathedral of Argyll, albeit knocked about by insensitive remodellings in the past. This started me pondering about the generations of Catholic priests who had sat on the sedilia and washed their chalices after Mass in the piscina. These features had survived the enthusiasm of the reformers, the ruining of the building and the manhandling of the modernisers; and they raised so many questions about how the permanent presence of a community of senior clergy, including bishops – some of whom had studied at English or Continental universities and even travelled to Rome or Avignon – could have affected the life of the island. Later, the success of community archaeology confirmed the national importance of the wider area round the church, including the site of the Early Church monastery, with its associated craft workers.

There has been another long journey for someone raised in the Presbyterian tradition in a country where society has tended to ignore the realities of pre-Reformation Scotland (apart from its kings, queens and wars) – in spite of the fact that the Church was involved in every aspect of medieval life. I must thank my friends raised in the Catholic Church for their help in this journey, not least my neighbour Jennifer Baker. I learned a great deal of relevant background when four of us walked and talked the Camino Frances to Santiago.

The aim of the book is to draw on generations of scholarly work to tell the story of the Early and later Catholic Church on the Isle of Lismore for the general reader, and to start to try to understand how the presence of the cathedral could have affected lives on the island. Telling the story would not be possible without the dedicated work of historians over the last 200 years, in recording information about Scotland from the various papal archives; the resulting records, many now freely available on the internet, have been invaluable in unconsciously revealing details about the Church and people in Argyll.

So many people have helped me on the journey, not least Iain MacDonald, whose book *Clerics and Clansmen* (2013) is the authority for the second half of the history of the diocese. The appendices of his book, drawing on the work of his colleagues at Glasgow University, have been invaluable in tracing the many medieval clergy in Argyll. Recent research by Megan Meredith Lobay and Caroline McNamara on the Early Church in Argyll has advanced our knowledge of the importance of Lismore. Iain, Megan and Caroline have each provided generous support to the project. I cannot thank Douglas Breingan enough for his tireless pursuit of the history of both the cathedral and the monastery, and for his resolute (and justified) criticisms, when I have committed errors of fact or interpretation.

I am particularly grateful to David Caldwell and Kenneth Veitch, who read advance drafts of the book and provided welcome encouragement; and to Richard Oram for advice on the Dominicans in Scotland. His seminal work on the interactions between climate and society have expanded my view of medieval Scotland. I am also grateful to Ronnie Black for information from the Dewar manuscript, and for his support of my writing; and to Donald Meek for his insightful analysis of 'Celtic' Christianity as well as his continued interest in Lismore.

At the start of this project, most of what we knew about the Early Church on Lismore depended on oral tradition, although an obituary in the Irish Annals did confirm that the Irish missionary Moluag had been active on the island. As explained in Chapter 2, understanding of the monastic site has now been transformed by six years of community archaeology, led by Clare Ellis of Argyll Archaeology. None of this could have been achieved without her steady inspiration and the enthusiastic work of the team of volunteers from the island and further afield, sometimes in the most challenging conditions. We had a lot of fun as well as hard work.

I have to record again my gratitude to staff members at the National Library of Scotland and the National Archives of Scotland for their patient help in my search of their collections; to Alison Diamond for her hospitality in my exploration of the Argyll papers in Inveraray; and to Diarmid Campbell for access to his unpublished archive of papers relating to Campbell holdings on Lismore. My thanks to those who generously provided images: Rab Woods (Plate 1) and Pauline Dowling (Plate 7). It is a pleasure to acknowledge the continuing support of the Board of Trustees of Lismore Historical Society/Comann Eachdraidh Lios Mòr in so many aspects of the work on the church and monastery.

As before, I really appreciate the support of Andrew Simmons, for so long my editor at Birlinn. He has the gift of combining a high degree of professionalism with genuine friendship. It has been a pleasure to work this time with Mairi Sutherland and Helen Bleck, and I am grateful to Hugh Andrew for his faith in this project and the encouragement to widen its scope to include the monastery.

The history of the Early Church and Early Medieval Scotland is the subject of active research, with changing perspectives in several important areas – for example, the relative importance of the many Irish missionaries; and the roles of the different MacSorleys in the thirteenth century. In this context, any errors of fact, judgement, interpretation or transcription in the text must be my responsibility alone. There is scope for much deeper and wider research.

As always, none of this could have been done without the continued support of my wife, Dorothea.

Timeline
560–1560

560/2	Arrival of Moluag on Lismore
592	Death of Moluag
1190/1200	Founding of the diocese of Argyll on the Isle of Lismore and the appointment of the first bishop, Harald
1230/35	Death of Bishop Harald
1239	Appointment of William, chancellor of the diocese of Moray, as bishop
1242	Drowning of Bishop William
1249	Death of King Alexander II on Kerrera. Abandonment of the policy to move the diocese of Argyll to the mainland
1250–62	Bishop Alan de Carrick
c. 1250	Start of work on the Cathedral of Argyll on Lismore
1262–99	Bishop Laurence de Ergadia, the first Dominican bishop
1300	Bishop Andrew de Ergadia
1308/9	Battle of the Pass of Brander, followed by the flight of Bishop Andrew and the MacDougalls to the protection of Edward II of England
1314	Return of Bishop Andrew to Scotland
1342	Death of Bishop Andrew. Appointment of Martin de Ergadia (Bishop 1342–87)

TIMELINE

1387–97	Bishop John Dugaldi
1397–1419	Bishop Benedict Johannis
1419	Appointment of Bishop Finlay de Albany
1425–6	Involvement of Bishop Finlay in the rebellion against James I, and his flight to, and death in, Ireland
1427/8–73/5	Bishop George Lauder
1452	Assault of Bishop Lauder on Lismore recorded in the *Auchinleck Chronicle*
c. 1455	Parish church of St Mary the Virgin in Dunoon fulfilling the role of cathedral for the diocese of Argyll
1462	Indult from the Pope permitting Bishop Lauder to live away from Lismore
1473/5	Death of Bishop Lauder
1475–94	Bishop Robert Colquhon
1497–1523	Bishop David Hamilton
1512	Papal letter from King James IV indicating that the cathedral was in ruins
1525–38	Bishop Robert Montgomery
1531	Investiture at Lismore confirms that the choir of the cathedral was still usable
1539–53	Bishop William Cunningham
1553–80	Bishop James Hamilton
1560	The Reformation in Scotland. Abolition of the jurisdiction of the Pope by the Scottish parliament
1750 onwards	Reconstruction of the choir of the cathedral as a Reformed parish church
1896	Major remodelling of the parish church

1

Introduction

One Thousand Years from Moluag

In the afternoon of 9 February 1567, four of Scotland's earls (Argyll, Bothwell, Huntly and Casillis) joined Mary Queen of Scots at James Hamilton's house in the Edinburgh Canongate for a banquet in honour of Count Moretta, the Ambassador of Savoy. By seven o'clock they had moved on to Kirk o'Field to keep company with Mary's husband, Lord Darnley, only a few hours before he was murdered. James Hamilton was able to mix in such exalted company because he was a member of one of the most powerful families in the land: his half-brother, the 2nd Earl of Arran and Duke of Châtelherault, had for several years been Governor of Scotland during Mary's absence in France, and he had a strong claim to the throne.

James Hamilton was also Bishop of Argyll. His illegitimacy, his married status and the fact that he was probably not an ordained priest, had not prevented him from being (unsuccessfully) nominated for the archbishopric of Glasgow in 1547 and being appointed to the Argyll diocese in 1553. Another brother, also illegitimate, was already Archbishop of St Andrews. At the reforming parliament in 1560, James voted for the abolition of the Roman Catholic Church in Scotland and converted to Protestantism, still retaining the position of bishop. It is unlikely that he ever visited his cathedral on Lismore, particularly since the focus of the diocese had moved to Dunoon by the middle of the fifteenth century; his lack of interest in Argyll is shown by the 1556 sale of the Bishop's Castle at Saddell in Kintyre to his half-brother. He was married to Janet Murray, with whom he had three sons and, benefiting from another position as subdean at Glasgow Cathedral, he appears to have enjoyed the high life in the Lowlands until his death in 1580. Thomas Randolph, Queen Elizabeth's confidential agent at the court of Queen Mary, reporting on the licentious behaviour of senior clergy in Scotland in the 1560s, mentions the Bishop of Lismore, who 'now has two women with child besides his wife'.[1]

A thousand years earlier, Moluag, an Irish missionary from the monastery in Bangor, County Down, had arrived with a group of followers on Lismore, full of resolve to bring the good news of Christianity to the island, and further afield on the mainland. There could not be a starker contrast between the austerity of their lives in these early years of evangelism and that of the indulgent James Hamilton. What had happened in the intervening centuries to bring the Church to such a low ebb? This book follows the rise and fall of the Roman Catholic bishopric of Argyll from its foundation around 1200 on Lismore, exploring Lismore's long reputation as a holy island and the continuing veneration of Moluag (later known as St Moluag, although there is no record of canonisation); through the period of building the cathedral (completed before 1400); the roles of the Dominican bishops; the years of prestige, when leading families invested in elaborately carved graveslabs; the lean years when the finances of the diocese were strained; the struggles to keep going through decades of war, civil unrest, despoilation, famine and plague; and the withdrawal of the bishop – but not all of the clergy – from Lismore to Dunoon from the mid fifteenth century. Even at the physical fringes of Scotland and Europe, the diocese was deeply affected by events on the national and international scene.

Before dealing with the cathedral and its clergy, however, the book tells the unfolding story of Moluag's monastery, recently rediscovered by community archaeology. Little has been written about the monastery and the cathedral on Lismore, and this work is timely in view of the proposal of the Church of Scotland to dispose of Lismore Parish Church (the surviving choir of the medieval cathedral), possibly to community ownership.

---

1 Bain (1898), Vol. 1, p. 592.

2

The Insular Church and Lismore

Christianity reached Ireland in the mid fifth century, traditionally by the mission of St Patrick from Cumbria or Wales in the last years of the Roman occupation of Britain, although there may have been a role for St Palladius. Speculation abounds about the reasons for the successful advance of the Church throughout the island, while northern Britain beyond the Forth–Clyde line remained pagan, in spite of the activities of the shadowy St Ninian/Nynia. These include the Church's willingness to adopt pre-Christian sites, practices and saints; the identification of Christ with the warrior gods of the Celtic world; the decline of existing religious practices; and the suggestion that the new religion, with its well-developed hierarchy, suited the ambitions and world view of the ruling class. Christianity offered a coherent narrative of life and death, a rich tapestry of ritual and seasonal festivals, and a structure for the support of society, but, as it evolved, it also facilitated the exercise of authority and the concentration of power. The priests of the Early Church may have preached peace, notably Adomnán's Law of the Innocents, which aimed to protect non-combatants, but history shows that this had little effect in curbing the violence of the times.

The collapse of the Roman Empire in western Europe and the movement of pagan Anglo-Saxons into England did not cut Ireland off from continental Europe, because people and cultures had moved freely by sea along the Atlantic fringe for thousands of years. New monastic ideas were an important factor in the development of Christianity in Ireland, and they may well have arrived there directly from important centres of monasticism around the Mediterranean or from the west coast of Gaul or Iberia, as had aspects of language and culture.

There is no evidence that the Early Church in Ireland was particularly heterodox in terms of belief and theology, and there were no accusations of heresy. Indeed, before the end of the sixth century, Irish missionaries were encouraged to spread across northern Europe, even into Italy. Although not isolated from the continent, the Church in Ireland (the Insular Church) evolved its own particular structure, liturgy and ritual. For the Roman Church, at that time absorbed in survival in the face of incursions by Germanic tribes and Lombards, and pressure in the east from Byzantium, dictating uniformity at the margins of the Christian world was not yet a priority.

The organisational structure of the Insular Church in Ireland and, particularly, the relative importance of bishops and abbots, has been the subject of considerable debate. Abbots had a secular role, with responsibility for the management of the assets of the monasteries, which were the towns of pre-Viking Ireland. They were commonly from the ruling class, and their position (as coarbs) could be hereditary. Bishops were consecrated priests, with primary responsibility for the sacramental activities of the monastery (baptism, marriage, confirmation, the Mass, penance, anointing the sick and dying, and ordaining priests). Uncertainties may have arisen where individuals abused their positions and, in some cases (e.g. later in Iona), the roles may have been combined. It is not clear to what extent, if any, the Pope was able to influence the appointment of senior clergy in these early years.

A little is known about the distinctive characteristics of the Insular Church (the tonsure of the clergy; the degree of celibacy; methods of calculating the dates of religious festivals from the lunar calendar; forms of dress and ritual, including fasting and the celebration of Mass; acceptance of extreme austerity by monks in pursuit of the rules of poverty, chastity and obedience; and the veneration of a constellation of local saints), but it had five lasting impacts on Christendom and European culture: an early promotion of literacy; the preservation of documents, including records of events (annals – invaluable to modern scholars, as no contemporary documentation from what was to become Scotland has survived); a strong tradition of biblical scholarship; a very substantial body of artwork, notably illuminated manuscripts, but also carving and metalwork; and a revolution in dealing with penance. Until then, there had been an emphasis on the public humiliation of repentant sinners ('sackcloth and ashes'), but the Irish Church promoted a new approach involving confession to a priest in confidence, and the private performance of the appropriate penance.

With Christianity established across Ireland in the sixth century, energetic priests of the Insular Church began to show an interest in mission fields overseas, in pagan England and Wales as well as the northern part of Dalriada, and Pictland (covering more than half of the mainland of modern Scotland). The monastery at Bangor in the east of Ulster, founded by Comgall (c. 510/520–597/602), was active in this mission work, although there is uncertainty about whether this included the dispatch of Moluag and his team to Lismore around 560. Towards the end of the century, Columbanus left Bangor on a mission to revive Christianity on mainland Europe, living an adventurous life full of controversy in Burgundy, the Alps and Lombardy, before founding a new monastery at Bobbio in Italy in 614. Maelrubha, another priest educated at Bangor, was responsible for establishing the Insular Church monastery at Applecross in 673.

Columba (originally Crimthan), a high-ranking member of the powerful Ui Neill dynasty, originated in the north-west of Ireland and studied in Leinster. He is said to have left Ireland for Iona for a different reason: as an act of penance for his involvement in the events leading up to the Battle of Cúl Dreimhne in 561 (although the circumstances remain uncertain). He acted effectively as both abbot and bishop of the new monastery on the island, at a daughter house on Tiree, on the unidentified island of Hinba and probably on the shores of Loch Awe. He later founded monasteries back in Ireland. Because of the survival of a biography, or rather a hagiography, of Columba, written within a century of his death by his kinsman Adomnán, his story, enhanced by a plethora of later legends, has dominated the understanding of the mission activity of the Insular Church in Scotland. Recent research has indicated that this simplifies a complex period. For example, Fraser (2009) explores the idea that Iona concentrated on southern Pictland (Atholl and Perthshire), possibly leaving areas further north to the Bangor-inspired missionaries.

The idea that the outreach of Moluag and his followers was mainly in north-east Pictland, establishing centres of evangelism at Rosemarkie and Mortlach, draws heavily on the sixteenth-century *Aberdeen Breviary*. A review of place names and church dedications to St Moluag, as he became, which appear in the Hebrides (Skye, Raasay, Tiree, Lewis, Harris and Mull), mainland Argyll and several places in Aberdeenshire, tends to present a different picture, indicating that the 'cult' of Moluag may have been more widespread; for example, even as late as 1507, a grant to the

Bishop of Argyll by James IV[2] was made 'on account of the singular devotion which he bore towards the blessed confessor Saint Moloc, patron of the cathedral church of Lismore'.

By the eighth century, Insular Church monasteries had been established across most of the mainland of what would become Scotland, and Christianity was the religion of the ruling classes, at least notionally. Mapping of the early Christian monuments in Argyll (Fig. 2.1) shows that the Church was not isolated at a few monastic sites where the clergy turned their backs on the world. There were hermits, living on isolated islets, but the majority of the contemporary structures that have been recognised were modest churches within an enclosure, distributed densely and evenly throughout the low-lying areas where most of the population would have lived.[3] It appears that a parish structure was established early, close to the people and their needs, both spiritual and practical; indeed, it could be argued that some areas have never since been so well served by the Church.

Meanwhile, the 'Roman' version of Christianity had been advancing rapidly following Augustine's arrival in Kent in 597 with a mission from the Pope to convert the pagan Anglo-Saxons. Faced with a choice between the Roman and Insular Churches, King Oswald of Northumbria invited Aidan from Iona in 635 to establish a monastery on Lindisfarne, as a base for the evangelisation of the north of what would become England. The Insular Church was also influential in Wales and in other parts of Anglo-Saxon England wherever Irish missionaries had been at work. The stage was set for a confrontation that would have a major effect on the development of the Church in Scotland.

At its peak, the kingdom of Northumbria extended from the Humber to the Forth, and included much of modern Lancashire and Cumbria, but the heartland was Deira (loosely, Yorkshire) and Bernicia (Durham and Northumberland). Before Oswald, from the ruling house of Bernicia, reunited these two areas, Edwin, King of Deira, had opted for the Roman Church. Consequently, when Oswui succeeded Oswald and secured peace for a time by marrying a daughter of Edwin, husband and wife worshipped according to different rites. At Easter, the high point of the Christian

---

2   *Origines*, p. 22.

3   The remains of the simple rectangular chapel at Ardtaraig (9m × 4m) within a small walled enclosure on the shore of Loch Striven, Cowal, Argyll, is a clear example of the church buildings of the time.

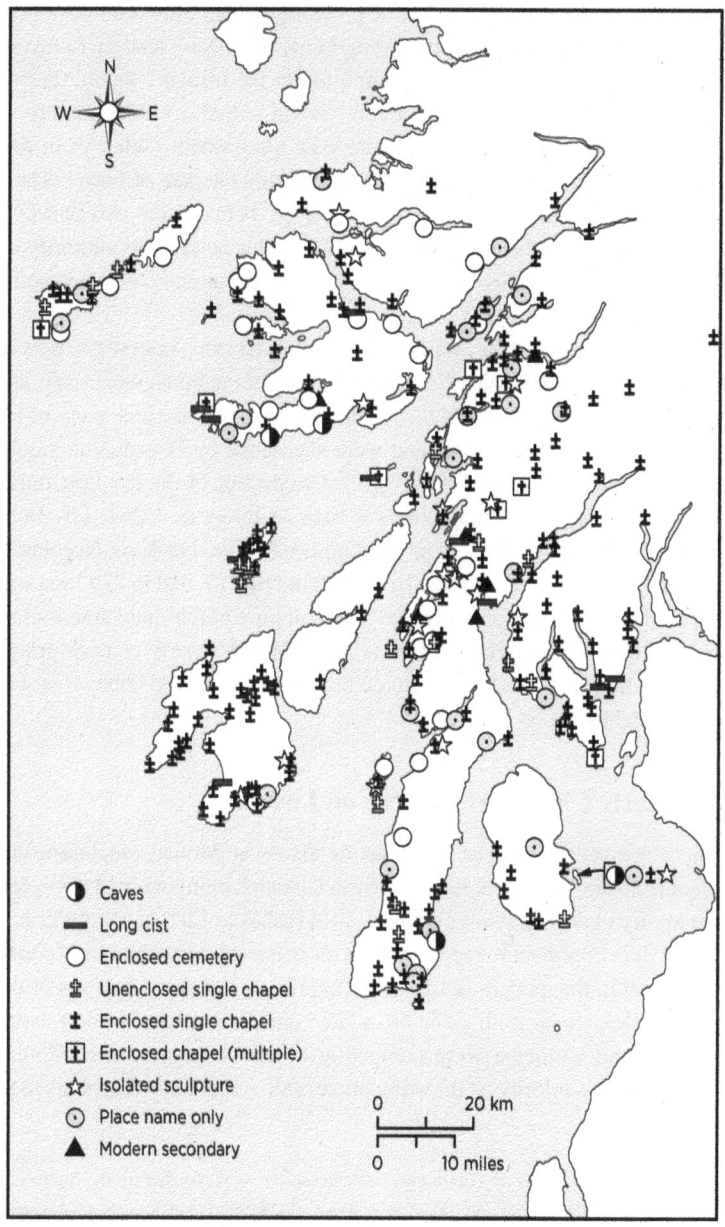

Fig. 2.1 Distribution of Insular Church structures in Argyll diocese.
(Based on a map from Meredith-Lobay, 2009)

calendar, one royal faction would be proclaiming the resurrection of Christ while the other was still fasting during Lent. With Deira tending to favour the Roman rights and Bernicia committed to the Insular Church, tension grew until, after the death of Aidan, Oswui called a synod, mainly of Northumbrian clergy, at the monastery of Streonshalh (Whitby) in 664 to resolve the issue of the method of calculating the date of Easter. There were no fundamental differences of theology between the two parties – it appears to have been mainly a conflict about power and authority, at a time when uniformity across the Christian community was becoming important.

In the resulting debate, Wilfrid, the leading Roman spokesman, proved to be more persuasive than Colman, the abbot of the Ionan monastery, and the synod found in favour of the Roman Church. Colman and many of his supporters withdrew to Iona, and were succeeded by Benedictine monks at Wearmouth (674) and Jarrow (681). The decline of the Insular Church across the British Isles may not have been as abrupt as depicted by Bede in his *Ecclesiastical History of the English People*, but King Nechtan is said to have expelled its clergy from Pictland by 717, and in 729 Iona was persuaded to adopt Roman usage. The Insular Church maintained a last bastion in northern Ireland; even as late as 1200, a party of Irish priests crossed the North Channel to attack the new Benedictine abbey that was being established on Iona.

The Early Church Monastery on Lismore[4]

There are several spectacular legends about St Moluag, including his voyage aboard a stone across the North Channel, along with 12 disciples; his ability to do blacksmithing work with rushes as fuel; and a mission to Thule. It is important to recognise that these miracles were not intended to be factual in the modern sense, but to express favourable attributes of the saint – 'devotional truth'. The oft-related coracle race around 560, when Moluag and Columba were competing to claim Lismore and Moluag established his priority by throwing his severed finger ashore, appears to be

---

4 This section draws on community archaeological work, funded by the Society of Antiquarians of Scotland, the Hunter Trust, the MacDougall Society of America, the MacDougall McCallum Society and a range of other supporters; a preliminary publication of the results is in preparation.

a nineteenth-century myth, possibly concocted by the folklorist Alexander Carmichael and drawing on a range of examples of detached body parts in Irish legends. We would know more about the life and achievements of Moluag if an early hagiography, referred to by later writers, had survived.

Setting aside these myths and legends, Moluag's obituary and the lists of abbots in the Irish records up to around 760 provide reliable evidence of an Early Church presence on Lismore. In spite of this, until recently there was nothing to indicate the actual site of Moluag's monastery or what it was like. Drawing on experience elsewhere in Argyll, and further afield in Scotland, there are several diagnostic signs of the existence of an Early Church monastic settlement on Lismore (Fig. 2.2; Plates 1, 2).

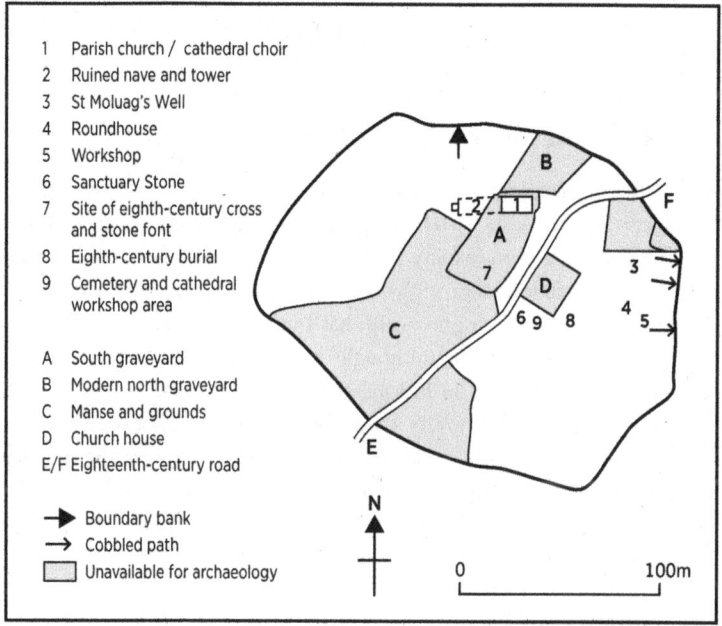

Fig. 2.2 Sketch map of the monastic site, Lismore

Burials

The first real clue to the site of the monastery was provided during the excavations, around 1980, for the foundations of the new church house south of the church, which encountered a great deal of human bone. It was not until nearly 40 years later, in 2018, that community fieldwork, led by Dr Clare Ellis of Argyll Archaeology, with modest funding, began to follow up this clue in the low-lying glebe field east of the church. Tackling persistent flooding of trenches, and with the campaign punctuated by the Covid pandemic, the team at last began to uncover the monastic site, recovering more than 1,500 significant finds over three seasons of digging. Their full relevance will not be understood until professional analyses are complete and published. Excavation of the slightly higher ground around the church house revealed extensive human burials, with excellent bone preservation owing to the lime-rich soils. A first radiocarbon date of an intact skeleton, within an earlier cemetery wall, gave a broadly seventh/eighth-century date, which takes occupation of the site back to within a generation of the proposed arrival of Moluag on Lismore around 560.

Stone Markers/Crosses

Before the archaeological investigation, three relevant monuments had been recorded (Fig. 2.2). Two fragments of a *c.* eighth-century cross, found near the church, are on display in the museum of the Lismore Historical Society, and a crude granite cross, known locally as the Sanctuary Stone, standing below the south graveyard, has traditionally been considered to be a church boundary stone (although recent excavation indicates that it may have been relocated in historic times). Living rock near the top of the graveyard, with a carefully excavated depression (not a cup mark), is known as the baptism stone or font. Excavation across the site has now yielded three separate fragments of richly carved stone cross slabs, with decorative styles that match stones from northern Pictland (at Portmahomack, Applecross, Nigg and Rosemarkie).

Buildings

Before 2018, it was speculated that the monastic chapel was probably *under* the medieval cathedral, although it was recognised that there must have been more than one building, including at least basic accommodation for the clergy. The wet rushy area below the Early Church cemetery looked very unpromising for a settlement, but a thorough geophysical survey in

2019[5] suggested the presence of buildings, indicating that the area must have been drier in earlier times. Excavation uncovered the foundations of an oval drystone building ('roundhouse', external diameter 8m; Plate 2b), which had been subject to fire, and possibly rebuilt more than once. Radiocarbon-dating has now placed it firmly in the eighth century. It is hoped that the role of this building will be revealed by the post-excavation analysis of the finds but, so far, no traces have been found of the monastic chapel. It is possible that further buildings lie under the areas that were inaccessible for the geophysical survey (Fig. 2.2).

Metal-working Area

The geophysical survey also revealed a rectangular feature to the east of the roundhouse. Recovery of 127 small crucibles from the area, mostly fragments but also some rare intact examples, and 742 fragments of casting moulds, showed that this was the site of fine metal-working, including the manufacture of penannular brooches. X-ray fluorescence studies[6] have revealed that, although most of the crucibles were used for melting copper alloys, some were used for silver or gold. A search of the collection of artefacts in the National Museum of Scotland provided confirmation of the use of gold: a touchstone for assaying gold alloys[7] found near the cathedral in the nineteenth century. The area also yielded fine examples of carving of wood, antler and bone. These initial findings suggest that Lismore could well sit among the other established Early Church monasteries in Scotland (Iona, Portmahomack, Inchmarnock, Whithorn) where skilled craftsmen were attracted to serve both the needs of the church and local patrons of the monks. There are also close parallels with craftwork on the royal site at Dunadd, suggesting that Lismore was a destination in long-distance trading of valuable materials.

Enclosure

Most Early Church foundations that have been investigated in the Highlands and Islands, from isolated chapels to monastic settlements,

---

5   Ovenden (2019).
6   Gemma Cruickshanks, personal communication 2022. Publication in preparation.
7   National Museums Scotland (NMS) X.AL 17.

were placed in an enclosure, defining the limits of their spiritual area. These were normally oval or round, demarcated by a bank and/or ditch (*vallum*) or wall (e.g. at Iona and Portmahomack). As the field boundaries on Lismore are almost uniformly rectilinear, the nearly round boundary surrounding Lismore Cathedral (later demarcating the church glebe: Plate 1; Fig. 2.2) has been proposed as the boundary of the Lismore monastery. Limited excavation of the steep north boundary in 2018 exposed a low turf bank without a ditch, whereas at three points on the level east boundary there was a well-laid cobbled pathway, around 0.8m wide. The preliminary interpretation of these findings is that the shallowness of the soil on Lismore and the presence of so much bedrock prevented the construction of a regular ditched and banked boundary, and that the enclosure would have been defined by a bank where practicable, and elsewhere by a hedge or wall with a paved path along its inner edge.

In conclusion, the location of part of the monastic settlement has been discovered, its importance as a centre of fine craftwork is being evaluated, but no progress has been made on finding Moluag's chapel. The range of activities at the site suggests that, as in Ireland, the monastery formed the nucleus of village development.

From the eighth century to the twelfth century, a profound silence falls on the monastery on Lismore (apart from the existence of ninth/tenth-century burials). Were the Insular Church clergy expelled, as on Iona in 717? How was the monastic community affected by the arrival of the pagan Norse, who attacked Iona several times from 795 onwards, resulting in the relocation of the relics of Columba to Kells in Ireland and Dunkeld? Did a community of Céli Dé monks (Chapter 3) colonise the island after the Norse settlement? Without written records we may never know, but the results of archaeology can give some hints. For example, a burial in the ancient cemetery dated to the later Norse period suggests continuity of a Christian community. It is hoped that analyses of burials by the Crick Institute (DNA and radiocarbon-dating) will shed further light on the community after 800. Chapter 3 charts the progressive decline of Insular Church monasteries, north and west of the Forth–Clyde boundary, with bishops and Roman-style dioceses supplanting abbots and Insular-style monasteries.

3

The Making of the Medieval Church in Scotland

When David I, the eighth child and sixth son of Malcolm III ('Canmore') and Margaret (later to be recognised as a saint), finally became king of the emerging country of Scotland in 1124, he found a Church in transition, affected by two movements for 'reform' across Europe. First, for uniformity and conformity, it was now seen to be essential to have a strict hierarchical structure, with bishops subject to regional archbishops (metropolitans) and overall authority resting with the Pope; as the Church expanded, the structure was deployed to exert firm control over belief and behaviour, and to develop mechanisms for the prompt suppression of heresy. In the future Scotland, some dioceses were led by conventional bishops, while others adhered to traditions that had evolved out of the Insular Church, including administrative control by hereditary lay abbots (the coarbs). With the boundary between Scotland and England fluctuating, and uncertainty over whether the King of England was the feudal superior, the archbishops of Canterbury and York squabbled over who commanded spiritual authority in the north.

Secondly, new ideals of monasticism, emphasising the need to withdraw from the world and prepare for the afterlife, had spread through Europe from the Middle East. On mainland Europe, the first organised order of monks was established under the Rule of St Benedict at Monte Cassino in 529 and the next 500 years saw waves of renewal, as successive orders succumbed to worldly pressures. By the start of the twelfth century, parent monasteries in France and Burgundy were establishing colonies of Cluniac, Augustinian, Cistercian, Tironesian and Premonstratensian monks across Europe (each order with its unique rules), sponsored by kings and feudal lords. In Scotland they encountered another strain of monasticism, the Céli

Dé (the Culdees), which had developed in parallel in Ireland out of the ideals of the desert hermits.

This chapter explores the background to the creation of the bishopric of Argyll on Lismore in the late twelfth century, carved out of the sprawling diocese of Dunkeld, apparently supplanting, or absorbing, a community of Céli Dé. It attempts to place the events in the context of contemporary developments elsewhere in Scotland, the British Isles and mainland Europe, and the underlying motives of kings and other powerful individuals.

The Development of the Roman Church in Scotland up to the Accession of David I (1124)

For around 300 years from the completion of Bede's *History* at the monastery at Jarrow in 731 there is little documentary evidence of the development of the Roman Church in what was to become the kingdom of Scotland. Until the eastern boundary with England was fixed at the Tweed, traditionally associated with the Battle of Carham in 1018, the Church in Lothian was effectively part of the diocese of Durham, under the authority of the Archbishop of York; for the Borders lordship of Teviotdale, this association with Durham continued up to the time of David I. In fact, the shrine of St Cuthbert at Durham remained a popular destination for Scottish pilgrims throughout the medieval period.[8] For example, in 1256 the Bishop of Durham issued a charter to Alan, Bishop of Argyll, relaxing 40 days of penance 'to those visiting the feretory [portable shrine] of St Cuthbert or the Galilee [chapel at Durham Cathedral], for devotion or prayer, and to those leaving gifts to it' (Plate 5). The widespread devotion to St Cuthbert in Scotland at that time is demonstrated by similar charters issued to the bishops of Brechin, Caithness, Dunblane, Dunkeld, Ross and St Andrews.[9] By the mid eighth century, York had also taken over responsibility for the ancient centre of British Christianity at Whithorn, and possibly also in Strathclyde, on the evidence of the distribution of carved stones in the Anglian style.[10] The resulting bishopric of Whithorn

---

8   Note the visits of the MacSorleys, Chapter 4.
9   Charter 811 (Plate 5) and associated charters from other Scottish dioceses. Durham University Special Collections.
10 For example, the Govan Stones (Strathclyde) and the Ruthwell Cross (Dumfries and Galloway).

or Galloway functioned at least until 800 and was resuscitated early in the twelfth century, but the early history of the diocese of Glasgow (Strathclyde) is not well known.

South of the Forth–Clyde line, therefore, in areas formerly controlled by Northumbria, the Church was developing according to the normal pattern of the Roman Church, within its conventional structure. However, in Pictland and Dalriada, and later in the united kingdom of Alba/Scotia, wherever law and order permitted, the Church was effectively Roman but held on to features of the Insular Church, particularly its administrative structure, dominated by abbots. Whatever their ambitions, the archbishops of Canterbury and York could not, in practice, exercise their authority north of the Forth–Clyde line. To the west, the original heartland of the Christian mission in Dalriada was in danger of lapsing into paganism, under the onslaught of the Norse; following a series of raids on Iona, starting in 802, most of the surviving monks and many of the treasures of the monastery were transferred to Kells in Ireland in 807. Other relics went to Dunkeld, which became the principal Christian centre in Alba during the ninth century, with royal patronage. We know nothing of the fate of Lismore in these years, but place-name evidence, confirming extensive settlement by the invading Norse, might suggest that the monastery would have been at least temporarily eclipsed. As we have seen in Chapter 2, the only, equivocal, evidence is the finding of a (possibly Christian) Viking Age burial (dated around the turn of the tenth century) within the Early Church cemetery, without grave goods, orientated north-east/south-west.

Meanwhile another of the distinctive features of the Early Church survived and proceeded to flourish in Alba. In the late seventh century in Ireland, a revival of the monastic ideal led to the establishment of ascetic communities of Céli Dé ('Vassals of God', commonly referred to as Culdees), outside the authority of the heritable abbots or coarbs. Unlike parallel revivals in continental Europe, the Céli Dé did not build great churches and monasteries or accumulate significant wealth, at least in the early years; little is known about their life and work apart from their strict adherence to ascetic ideals, but the movement did migrate to Scotland. It was more widely adopted than in Ireland, and its influence spread across northern Europe with Irish and Scottish missionaries. Until the twelfth century, most of the monastic houses north of the Forth–Clyde line were communities of Céli Dé (at St Andrews, Dunkeld, Dunblane, Loch Leven, Brechin, Ross (presumably Rosemarkie), Caithness (Halkirk or Dornoch), Argyll (presumably Lismore), and Iona) (Table 4.1). Their value and prestige within the Gaelic heartland of the developing kingdom, and their incorporation into the Roman Church structure, were recognised by charters from Queen Margaret and her sons up to the opening years of the twelfth century, in spite of their reputation as champions of Continental orders. The surviving eleventh-century Romanesque tower at Restenneth in Angus indicates that at least some of the communities were beginning to develop more substantial church buildings. Many of the communities had ceased to function by the thirteenth century, but the St Andrews Céli Dé, incorporated into the Augustinian priory in 1140, continued at least into the fifteenth century. There is reason to believe that the influence of a Céli Dé community persisted on Lismore up to the fifteenth century (Chapters 4 and 9).

David I spent his formative years, from the age of ten, as an orphan and refugee at the court of the Anglo-Norman rulers of England but, from 1100, his status was considerably enhanced when his sister Edith (renamed Matilda) married Henry I. He grew up as a thoroughly Normanised nobleman, entirely cut off from the Gaelic culture of much of the country he was later to rule, although he must have been profoundly influenced by the reputations of his parents: the military and diplomatic achievements of his father, Malcolm, and the sanctity of his mother, Margaret, eventually recognised by her canonisation in 1250. The Church David encountered in England was highly organised into dioceses under the two archbishops of Canterbury and York, with strong connections with Rome; and on campaigns with the English army in France he visited great monastic houses, including Thiron, near Chartres, where St Bernard had established his reformed ('Tironesian') order. For the King of England and his nobles, the introduction of monks from Benedictine and reformed orders, and the endowment of their houses, was seen both as a Christian duty and a badge of prestige.

The Church was prominent in all spheres of life: law, education, medicine, social control. Senior clergy played central roles in the running of the state, and some even took on the role of leaders in the field of battle. The Church could be involved in the maintenance of infrastructure, as is shown by a papal letter of 16 October 1384:

> To all Christ's faithful. Indulgence of one year and forty days is granted to all who contribute towards the rebuilding of the bridge

across the river Newdach [probably Eachaig] in Cowal, Argyll diocese, which was swept away by floodwaters, causing those who now have to cross the river to be completely submerged and in great danger.[11]

As its body of canon law developed, the Vatican acquired tools to influence the political life of European countries more closely. For example, the need to secure permission from the Vatican for the marriage of members of the highly interrelated ruling classes placed considerable power in the Pope's hands; and, through the act of excommunication, he could dismantle the feudal structure of a state, since vassals were relieved of their obligations to an excommunicated sovereign. This was a major challenge for Robert Bruce, who was excommunicated by Pope Clement V in 1306 for the murder of John Comyn in Greyfriars Church, Dumfries. The papacy was probably at its most powerful between the twelfth and fourteenth centuries, acquiring extensive territory in Italy, and drawing heavily on the finances of the Church across Europe to fund a series of disastrous crusades as well as its continuing conflict with Byzantium. Following a bull of Clement IV in 1265, appointments across the Catholic Church became a 'papal prerogative'; in return for 'provision' to the post, the successful candidate was required to pay a substantial fee (referred to as 'services' in the Vatican records).

Papal authority was undermined in the fourteenth century by schism, with rival popes in Avignon and Rome between 1309 and 1376, each recognised by a powerful group of countries; by the rise of strong national governments, challenging the right of the curia to interfere in internal politics; and by a relentless series of challenges to orthodox theology and clerical abuse of power and resources, which culminated in the Reformation in the early sixteenth century. Nevertheless, many people continued to hold that the Pope had unlimited temporal powers. (It is ironic that under developing canon law, which established primogeniture as the required method of succession, neither Henry I of England nor David I of Scotland might have been first choice as king.)

In 1107, at the death of David's brother King Edgar, the emerging kingdom of Scotland (excluding the Northern Isles and much of the West Highlands and the Hebrides, which were under Norse control) was

11 Burns (1976), p. 103.

effectively in two parts, with yet another brother, Alexander I, ruling Alba/ Scotia and Lothian directly, while David, as 'Prince of Cumbria' held responsibility south of the Forth–Clyde line, excluding Galloway and most of Lothian and Tweeddale, but probably including Lennox, around Loch Lomond. To the south, his territory included modern Cumberland and north Westmorland, excluding an enclave around Carlisle that had been appropriated by the English crown. Much of this territory fell notionally under the bishopric of Glasgow (Strathclyde), which had been vacant and disorganised for many years. When David eventually took over his principality – around 1113 – he moved quickly to revitalise the Church following the European model, at the same time providing himself with trusted councillors and administrators for the area.

He chose, for Bishop of Glasgow, his personal chaplain, John, who had been associated with the enclosed order of monks in France, at Thiron, which he had visited. However, since the consecration of a bishop had to be by an archbishop or more senior cleric, and both David and the Church in his territories refused to recognise the authority of York, John eventually had to travel to Rome for consecration by Paschal II in 1118. With the death of the Pope, the policy changed and the Vatican again insisted on John's submission to York. John, remaining defiant, was subjected to many years of harassment, including suspension, threat of excommunication and an enforced pilgrimage to Jerusalem. As late as 1136 the issue was still not resolved, with Pope Innocent II writing from Pisa to Thurstan, Archbishop of York, 'to pronounce the sentence of anathema against John, pseudo-bishop of Glasgow, until he be healed of his errors and return to the metropolitan right and to subjection to thee'.[12] In that year John was allowed to retire to the quiet life of the monastery. In spite of these diversions from the task of setting the diocese in right order, David and John carried out a full audit of the possessions of the bishopric and were able to raise the finance to make a start on a cathedral for Glasgow, dedicated in the year of John's retirement.

In the same period, Alexander I was facing similar problems in modernising the bishopric of St Andrews, which had eclipsed Dunkeld as the religious centre of the kingdom; this had occurred at least partly because of the widespread endowments St Andrews had accumulated in

---

12 Anderson (1908), Pope Innocent II to Thurston of York, April 1136.

the form of land holdings across the kingdom from Aberdeen to the Merse. Much of the actual diocese, covering Fife, Lothian and the eastern border, had been ruled by Northumbria during the tenth century and had come under the authority of the Archbishop of York, but it had maintained a traditional Gaelic administration and communities of Céli Dé. With the intention of interrupting the line of 'native' bishops and bringing about uniformity with the wider Church, in 1107 Alexander nominated Turgot, Prior of Durham and the former chaplain of his mother Margaret, to be bishop. However, it proved impossible to achieve his consecration without recognising the authority of York. Turgot eventually resigned and returned to the cloister in 1115, to be succeeded eventually around 1124 by Robert, an Augustinian monk from Scone. In a short-lived truce among York, St Andrews and the Vatican, Robert was consecrated at York in 1127 'without profession of obedience'.

Meanwhile, David's astonishing programme of introduction of Continental monastic orders had begun. Until he settled a group of Tironesian monks at Selkirk in 1113, there were two small colonies of Benedictines: at the royal abbey of Dunfermline, established by his mother, and at the priory of Coldingham in Lothian (re-established around 1100 after destruction by Vikings in 870). Alexander I is credited with the foundation of two other abbeys at Scone and on Inchcolm in the Forth. However, within David's lifetime there would be at least eight more major communities, with the Tironesians moving from Selkirk to Kelso next to the royal castle at Roxburgh in 1128. His motive in introducing this enclosed order must have been to provide exemplars of the virtuous life, but he soon learned the value of other orders, particularly the Augustinians and the Cistercians, who, in different ways, took part in his policies for the economic development of the country.

The Reign of David I (1124–1153)

With the unexpected death of Alexander I in 1124, David I became ruler of Alba/Scotia as well as Lothian and Cumbria, although several lordships (Galloway, Moray, Ross and Caithness) were still semi-independent, and the Northern and Western Isles were under Norse control (ruled formally by Norway from 1152). In his time, most of the mainland would be drawn finally into the kingdom of Scotland, but, from the start of his reign, after dealing with a rebellion by an illegitimate son of Alexander, he devoted most of his attention to the south, based on the royal castle at Roxburgh. He spent prolonged periods in England, where he had extensive landholdings, held from his brother-in-law, King Henry. Towards the end of his reign, he achieved a long-standing ambition of incorporating Northumbria into his kingdom, although this did not last beyond his death.

The task of introducing Roman orthodoxy and non-native clerics to the bishoprics of the Gaelic heartland (Dunkeld, including Argyll, Dunblane and Brechin) proved to be beyond the capability of David's administration; it was only after his death in 1153 that Dunkeld and Dunblane would follow St Andrews in having recognisably 'foreign' bishops. Laurence of Dunblane was appointed in 1155, and Gregory (bishop 1147–69) appears to have been the last Gael at Dunkeld. Meanwhile, Brechin maintained 'native' abbots and bishops well into the thirteenth century, with a strong community of Céli Dé.

The Roman model placed the bishop and his cathedral in a 'city' surrounded by the parishes of the diocese but, before David's reign, there were no urban developments north of the Forth–Clyde line that could be described as cities, very few towns, and the nucleus of a cathedral only at St Andrews. As across most of Europe, the kingdom was essentially rural. Instead, the dioceses of the heartland had developed out of Early Medieval abbeys in the ancient earldoms of Atholl, Strathearn and Abernethy, where the 'native' ruling class had a strong interest in maintaining the status quo and, because of the complex pattern of landholding, the boundaries of the dioceses were far from clear. This was particularly the case for the very extensive diocese of Dunkeld, which covered a huge area to the west with uncertain marches with the dioceses of Glasgow, Dunblane, Moray and Ross. Its western seaboard, from the Clyde to around Lochalsh, was shared with the diocese of Sodor/Sudreyar, or the Isles (hereafter referred to as the diocese of Sodor), under the archbishopric of Nidaros/Trondheim in Norway from 1154; Lismore lay squarely at the boundary between Dunkeld and Sodor (Fig. 3.1).

Events in the north of his kingdom allowed David more scope in modernising the Church. The crushing of the 1130 rebellion by Edward, his constable in the north, and the removal of the traditional rulers of Moray (descendants of the royal line of MacBeth and Lulach) by 1134, provided an opportunity for radical changes. These included the 'Normanisation' of the area by the establishment of royal castles, sheriffs and trading

THE MAKING OF THE MEDIEVAL CHURCH

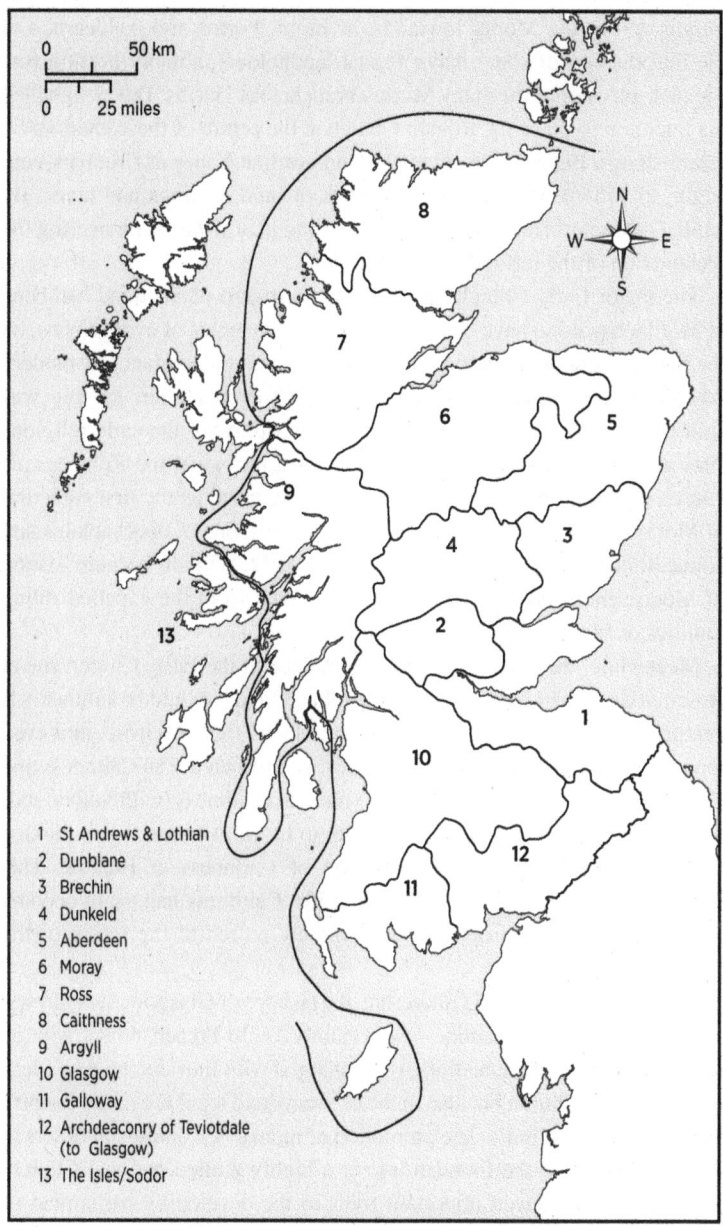

1. St Andrews & Lothian
2. Dunblane
3. Brechin
4. Dunkeld
5. Aberdeen
6. Moray
7. Ross
8. Caithness
9. Argyll
10. Glasgow
11. Galloway
12. Archdeaconry of Teviotdale (to Glasgow)
13. The Isles/Sodor

Fig. 3.1 Scottish church dioceses, *c.* 1300.
(Based on a map from McNeill and MacQueen, 1996)

burghs across the Moray lowlands, at Elgin, Forres and Auldearn, and the introduction of some major feudal landholders, notably Freskin (the Flemish ancestor of the many Murray branches) at Duffus. David signalled his intention to place the Roman Church at the centre of these changes by establishing a Benedictine colony of Dunfermline Abbey at Urquhart, near Elgin, in 1135/6, with rich endowments of land, fishings and taxes. By 1150, Cistercians from Melrose were settling in at Kinloss, pioneering the reclamation of the fertile Laich of Moray.

The major Early Church centre in the north-east of Scotland had been at Mortlach (said to have been one of Moluag's centres of evangelism), on the high ground between the Laich of Moray and the lowlands of modern Aberdeenshire. Some time around 1130, or even earlier, its role was split between the dioceses of Aberdeen and Moray; of the early religious sites at Birnie, Kineddar and Spynie in the Elgin area, the Romanesque church at Birnie, built in 1140, seems to have acted as the first cathedral of Moray. By 1147, David had installed Edward, one of his chaplains and councillors, as Bishop of Aberdeen, and in 1152, William became Bishop of Moray, endowed with extensive lands taken from the expelled ruling families of Moray.

Meanwhile, the bishopric of Ross remained at the Early Church site at Rosemarkie (possibly established by Moluag), and it would be another half century before a foreign bishop was introduced from Melrose, and even longer before the move to Fortrose. However, turbulence in Caithness and Orkney gave David the opportunity to reclaim Caithness (with Sutherland) as a Scottish earldom and, around 1146, to install Andrew, a Benedictine from Dunfermline, as the first Bishop of Caithness at Halkirk. This success was to be short-lived; by the 1150s, Caithness had again become a very hazardous environment, and Andrew retired to the safety of the royal court.

At David's death in 1153, therefore, the bishops of Glasgow, St Andrews, Aberdeen, Moray and Caithness were mainly Anglo-French monks, who, as royal chaplains and councillors, were charged with introducing new ideas not only to the Church but also in the economy and legal life of the country (fostering 'civilisation'). The promotion of monks of Continental orders to the bishoprics laid the foundations for a highly unified national Church, and the bishops played important roles in the developing parliament of Scotland. Before long, the last Gaelic bishops of Dunkeld, Dunblane, Brechin and Ross would also be superseded by 'outsiders'. A common source of difficulty for the bishops was the unresolved relationship with the Archbishop of York, causing Scottish clerics to travel continually to Rome for consecration and the resolution of conflict. A partial solution came later, in 1192, when Pope Celestine III issued the bull *Cum universi*, bringing the Scottish bishops directly under papal control; thereafter, until St Andrews was raised to an archbishopric in 1472, new bishops would be consecrated by the Pope or by a papal legate. Meanwhile, during the fourteenth century, the bishopric of Galloway had been released from the authority of York. In general, in 1200, the 'cathedrals' were simple churches; with the exception of Glasgow, St Andrews and Whithorn, it would not be until well into the thirteenth century that the dioceses would embark on major building projects.

Two other developments would be important in the founding of the new bishopric of Argyll at Lismore. First, in reforming the finances of the national Church, David regularised the teind; from that time until the Reformation, a tax of a tenth of all economic production would be the primary income for the Church in Scotland. A quarter of the teind would normally be devoted to the direct support of the bishop and his cathedral. This had the important consequence of encouraging the bishops to identify their parishes, defining their boundaries and potential resources. Secondly, with the penetration of spoken English (Scots) from the south-east with landowners, traders and clerics, Gaelic began its long-term withdrawal to the west and north. Before long, Gaels would begin to complain that they were ministered to by priests and bishops who could not speak their language.

In parallel with this development of the 'secular' branch of the Church, David had been tireless in establishing more monasteries, with major communities of Augustinians at Holyrood (1128), Jedburgh (1138) and Cambuskenneth near Stirling (1140); Cistercians at Melrose (1136), Newbattle (1140) and Kinloss (1150); as well as the Tironesians at Kelso (1128). With the resources and experience of their orders, including access to teams of itinerant masons, they were able to begin work on their great abbeys, following the outstanding Romanesque example of Dunfermline, which had been started in 1124. In a movement that would gain momentum over the century, Hugh de Morville, one of the powerful Anglo-Norman feudal landlords introduced into south-west Scotland by David, founded the Premonstratensian abbey at Dryburgh (1150); and Fergus, the (native) Lord of Galloway, may have been responsible for the arrival of Cistercians at Dundrennan around 1142. More endowments of this kind would follow in the coming century, and they bear witness to the piety of the ruling class, but they also brought them several benefits, some very worldly: assurance of a favourable destination after death for the lord and his family; a stimulation of the economy of the area; career opportunities for younger sons; a steady supply of administrators and lawyers; a stable community, since there were no problems of succession between generations; as well as considerable prestige to the founder and his family during his own life. On the other hand, by acquiring the rights to the income of parish churches, the abbeys posed a serious threat to the economies of the cathedrals; this would be a particular problem for the diocese of Argyll.

Augustinians monks were able, as at St Andrews where they provided the cathedral canons, to serve in church and community, and they were encouraged by the king to foster the urban development of the kingdom. Over time they became major property owners and providers of hospitality. The Cistercians, a closed order, favoured more remote environments, but were useful in introducing new agricultural techniques, providing examples of economic development. The Premonstratensians, originating out of a movement to reform the Augustinians, in practice played similar roles to those of the Cistercians. Although notionally under the authority of the local diocese, most of the direction of the life of the abbeys and priories came from the mother monastery in continental Europe. Together the new churchmen formed a formidable body of uniquely educated, experienced and well-travelled men, whose impact on the development of Scotland was as great as the great feudal landowners.

The scene was set for the founding of the diocese of Argyll. The 'Normanisation' of the Church under David I meant that Gaelic language and culture were beginning to retreat, although claims that the West Highlands were poorly served by the clergy of the diocese of Dunkeld ignore the fact that Gaelic was still the language of Perthshire. At the same time, David and his successors were establishing the modern kingdom of Scotland. The introduction of senior churchmen into the area was an important element in the 'civilisation' and economic development of the west, as in Moray; and the close involvement in Church affairs of the ruling MacSorleys (descendants of Somerled and founders of the MacDougall and MacDonald dynasties, who held land from both Scotland and Norway) tended to draw them firmly into the orbit of the developing kingdom. In turn, they stood to gain prestige from the establishment of a cathedral in their territory. At the same time, the Bishop of Dunkeld would see great advantage in concentrating his efforts on the more affluent heartland of his diocese, which yielded much higher and more reliable teinds.

4

Foundation and Early Years of the Diocese of Argyll (1190–1249)

The reputations and importance of some of those involved in the foundation and early years of the diocese of Argyll, the MacDougalls in particular, have faded over the centuries; this is mainly because of the enduring love affair between the Scottish people and Robert Bruce, fuelled by the writings of Walter Scott, and the corresponding scorn for those who found themselves on the opposing side during the Wars of Independence:

> Robert Bruce was the greatest King who ever wore the Scottish Crown, and so many stories are told of his courage, wisdom and endurance that we have not room to retell them all.[13]

Married into the Comyn/Balliol family network and with a history of direct dealings with the kings of Norway and England, Alexander MacDougall opposed Bruce and, in a famous skirmish at Dalrigh near Tyndrum in 1306, his son John (Baccach – 'the Lame') is reputed to have snatched Bruce's prestigious charm stone, which was later incorporated into the 'Brooch of Lorn'.[14] The triumph of the MacDougalls, however, was short-lived. In 1308 they were decisively defeated by Bruce at the Pass of Brander. Abandoning their homeland, Alexander and his sons entered the service of the King of England.

The resulting shame has entirely eclipsed the earlier reputation of the MacDougalls who, in the second half of the thirteenth century, were one

---

13 Scott (1934).
14 Campbell (2011). The mounting of the stone is definitely later than 1306.

of the dominant families in the emerging Scotland in terms of territory, military strength and wealth. As well as benefiting from their extensive landholdings, the MacDougalls followed their Norse ancestors in being actively involved in trade, sending their fleets of birlinns to ports on the west coast of England, in Ireland[15] and probably further afield. Details of the cargoes have not survived, but it is likely that they were major suppliers of fish (salmon and seafish, meeting the needs of Catholic customers for up to three days a week, as well as fast days) and hides, returning with salt and luxuries such as wine and spices. With their income from land and sea, Duncan MacDougall (d. 1247), his son Ewen (d. 1265) and their successors were able to build a spectacular range of coastal stone fortresses which eventually included state-of-the-art enclosed keeps at Dunstaffnage, Dunollie, Duntrune and Achinduin (Lismore), hall houses at Ardtornish, Aros and Coeffin (Lismore), and island strongholds on the Garvellachs (Dunchonnel) and the Treshnish Islands (Cairnburgh). Across the Highlands and Islands at that time, only the mighty Comyns could match this level of investment in stone and mortar (for example at Lochindorb, Castle Roy and Inverlochy, possibly Urquhart). The fighting strength of the MacDougalls at their peak can be gauged from a 1307 letter from Aymer de Valence, King Edward I of England's military leader in Scotland:

> As John [Baccach] of Argyll and his people are guarding the town of Ayr and parts adjacent, he commands that they be aided with money and victuals when there. That is to say for 22 men-at-arms and 800 foot.[16]

The official history of the clan claims that they fielded 1,000 Argyll men at Dalrigh and 2,000 at the Pass of Brander. At times, kings of Scots found it difficult to muster such numbers and, no doubt, many more were left at home to defend Lorn and the islands. The MacDougalls must have thought that they had the resources to hold their own against all comers, but they underestimated the military genius of Robert Bruce. Meanwhile, other MacSorleys, the MacDonalds of Islay and the MacRuairis of Garmoran,

---

15   Bain (1884), para 63. Alexander de Ergadia's vessel, with goods to the value of 160 marks, captured at Bristol 1275.
16   Bain (1884), para 1957.

gained lasting credit for their role as staunch supporters of the King of Scots in his years of struggle, and for their contribution to the victory at Bannockburn.

The MacSorleys and the Church

Out of the extremely complex history of the Norse-dominated Western Isles, Somerled had emerged by the middle of the twelfth century as 'King of the Isles' (but excluding Man, Skye and Lewis). At his death in 1164 he was the effective ruler over much of the western mainland from Kintyre to Knoydart, and the islands from Islay to the Uists. In theory, he was subject to the King of Scots and the King of Norway, respectively, for these possessions, but they were normally so preoccupied with problems nearer home that Somerled had considerable independence. His importance can be gauged from the fact that his death is recorded in both the *Melrose Chronicle* (mostly concerned with ecclesiastical and royal events) and the *Annals of Tigernach* (mostly events within Ireland). At his death, his lands were partitioned among three of his sons. The consensus of opinion is that Dugald (the eldest, ancestor of the MacDougalls, d. *c*. 1205) gained Lorn, Benderloch, Lismore, Mull, Coll and Tiree; and Ranald had Kintyre, Islay, Jura, Morvern and Ardnamurchan. Somerled's third son, Angus, and all of his male descendants, were dead by 1210, and their inheritance of Garmoran (Moidart, Arisaig, Morar, Knoydart, the Small Isles, the Uists, Barra and Benbecula) passed to Ranald's line. In due course, most of Ranald's territory was acquired by his son Donald (progenitor of the MacDonalds, whose ambitions culminated in the Lordship of the Isles), while his second son, Ruairi, acquired Garmoran (founding the MacRuairi clan).

Although a warlord of mixed Norse and Gaelic (Gall-Gael) ancestry, in the last years of the Viking Age, Somerled was a Christian and he was not slow in following the lead of powerful families on the mainland in establishing a community of Cistercian monks at Saddell in Kintyre around 1160. His greatest legacy to the Church, however, was his children, who were, at least publicly, very devout. Much of what we know of the MacSorleys comes from the records of religious houses, beginning in 1175 with the entry of Dugald into the 'brotherhood' of the monastery at Durham, giving two gold rings to the shrine of St Cuthbert (a popular saint in Scotland), and promising to provide support to the value of one mark each year.[17] Ranald is credited with reviving the abbey on Iona, introducing Benedictine monks around 1200, to the great displeasure of churchmen in Ireland, and a body of Augustinian nuns arrived in 1203, led by his sister Bethoc or Beatrice as the first abbess. Around 1230, the MacDougalls built the impressive chapel at Dunstaffnage adjacent to their principal castle.

MacDonald clan histories lay great emphasis on Ranald's reputation as a war leader but, towards the end of his life, around 1200, he and his wife Fonia made a major commitment to the Cluniac priory and convent at Paisley, apparently joining the community as lay members. At that time, Ranald promised:

> eight cows and two pennies for one year, and one penny in perpetuity from every house on his territories from which smoke issued, and his peace and protection to the monks whithersoever they should go, enjoining his dependents and his heirs in no way to injure them and swearing by St Columba to inflict on the former the punishment of death, and that the latter should have his malediction if they disobeyed his injunction.

and Fonia granted to the monks

> the tithe of all her goods, whether in her own possession, or sent for sale by land or sea [confirming the idea that the MacSorleys were active in trade].[18]

The continuing relationship between the MacDonald branch of the MacSorleys and the monks of Paisley (soon elevated to the status of abbey) and Saddell was to have serious economic implications for later bishops of Argyll because of generous grants to the monks of the rights to draw the income from lands and teinds in fertile Kintyre, which would otherwise have helped to deal with the chronic financial problems of the diocese of Argyll (e.g. Chapter 8). The close involvement with Paisley was also important in terms of the developing struggle for power in the west of Scotland. Somerled was killed at Renfrew in 1164, in a rising that seems to have been in opposition to the advance of Walter, High Steward

---

17 McDonald (1997), p. 72.
18 *Origines*, p. 2.

of Scotland, whose land grants forced a wedge between the independent lordships of Galloway and Somerled. The priory at Paisley, founded by Walter in 1163, was part of the feudal apparatus of a medieval knight, and the fact that Ranald and his successors also supported the priory, later abbey, indicates that a degree of rapprochement had been achieved between the families. Later chapters in this book will chart the complex relationship that developed between Walter's descendants (the Royal Stewarts) and the bishops of Argyll; and the many quarrels and legal battles that developed among the bishops of Argyll, the bishops of Glasgow and Paisley Abbey, over the ownership of Church assets, particularly in Kintyre.

Accounts of the foundation of the bishopric of Argyll, drawing largely on the story presented in *Scotichronicon* (compiled in later centuries), have concentrated on the role of John, Bishop of Dunkeld. However, it seems likely, from their close involvement with Durham, Saddell, Iona and Paisley, that the MacSorleys (Ranald and Dugald or his son Duncan) played a role as instigators. The lack of any records of the activities of the senior branch (Dugald and his successors) before 1230, has been interpreted to mean that Ranald dominated events over this period. There may also have been a role for King William, in encouraging more orderly Church government at the limits of his realm. His son, Alexander II, certainly employed this approach later in 1230/1; after suppressing the MacWilliam uprising in Moray, he established Valliscaulian monks (a new order arising in Burgundy out of the Cistercians) at Beauly and Pluscarden. The contemporary founding of Ardchattan Priory, with its community of Valliscaulian monks from Beauly, attributed to Duncan MacDougall, suggests that the MacDougalls were attuned to the ambitions of the Scottish crown. The priory proved useful to the diocese, for a time taking responsibility for providing the precentor for the cathedral (Chapter 5).

Most of the MacSorley islands lay within the bishopric of Sodor, with its cathedral on the Isle of Man, but under the authority of Nidaros/Trondheim in Norway from 1153. Their mainland holdings (including Lismore) were at the fringes of the extensive bishopric of Dunkeld, and there is evidence to suggest that the diocese had already made progress in managing the existing network of parishes in Argyll (which would have evolved out of the Insular Church establishments, Fig. 4.1). Indeed, the incomes of parishes in Kintyre were sufficient to justify appropriation by Holyrood Abbey.

FOUNDATION AND EARLY YEARS OF THE DIOCESE

The revival of the early centre of Christianity on Lismore as the site of the bishopric is contemporary with the revival of Iona, and both developments would bring honour and prestige to the MacSorleys.

The Bishop of Dunkeld

Under his grandsons (Malcolm IV, King of Scots 1153–65; William I 1165–1214), the Church in Scotland developed according to the pattern established by David I. New monastic communities were settled by the crown and nobles at Cupar (Cistercian in 1164 by Malcom IV), Kilwinning (Tironesian, 1162, de Morville), Paisley (Cluniac, 1163, Steward), Whithorn (Cistercian, replaced by Premonstratensian, 1175, Lord of Galloway), Lindores (Tironesian, 1178 × 1198, Earl of Huntingdon) and Inchaffray (Augustinian, 1200, Earl of Strathearn) (Table 4.1). Apart from St Andrews, Glasgow, Galloway (Whithorn) and Aberdeen, the bishoprics had not started work in earnest on their cathedrals, but several of the sees were in the hands of monks from Continental orders. Around 1180, the incumbents were:

Glasgow: Jocelin, Cistercian

Galloway: Christian, Cistercian

Dunblane: Simon, background unknown, probably Norman

Dunkeld: Gregory, probably a native Gael

Brechin: Turpin, an Anglo-Norman from the court of William I

Aberdeen: Matthew, Anglo-Norman landed family

Moray: Simon de Tosny, Cistercian

Ross: Gregoir, probably a native Gael, succeeded by Reinald Macer, Cistercian

Caithness: Andreas, native Scot, Benedictine

Table 4.1. Silgrave's list of religious houses in Scotland, annex to his *Chronicle*, c. 1272

House	Order	Foundation
Laudian [Lothian]		
Abbatia Newbotle S. Marie [Newbattle]	Monachi Albi [Cistercian]	David I 1140
Abbatia Maylros S. Marie [Melrose]	Monachi Albi	David I 1136
Abbatia Dreyeburgh [Dryburgh]	Canonici Albi [Premonstratensian]	Hugh de Morville 1150
Abbata Kelzho S. Marie [Kelso]	Monachi Nigri de Tyrun [Tironesian]	David I 1128
Abbatia Rokesburgh [Roxburgh]	Canonici Nigri [Augustinian]	
Abbatia Caldestream [Coldstream]	Moniales Nigrae [Augustinian nuns]	Earl Cospatrick before 1166
Abbatia Edeneburgh [Edinburgh/Holyrood]	Canonici Nigri	David I 1128
Abbata Goddewrthe [Jedburgh]	Monachi Nigri [Benedictine]*	
Prioratus Goldingeham [Coldingham]	Monachi Nigri	Edgar 1097/8
Prioratus Hadingtone [Haddington]	Moniales Albae [Cistercian nuns]	Countess Ada 1178
Prioratus Suthberewik [Berwick]	Moniales Albae	David I 1124 × 1153
Prioratus Northberewik [North Berwick]	Moniales Nigrae	Earl of Fife 1216
Prioratus Eccles [Berwickshire]	Moniales Albae	Earl Cospatrick 1154/5

FOUNDATION AND EARLY YEARS OF THE DIOCESE 33

Scocia [Outside Lothian]		
Episcopatus Sancti Andree [St Andrews]	Canonici nigri, Keldei [Augustinian, Céli Dé]	
Abbatia Dunfermelin S. Trinitatis [Dunfermline]	Monachi Nigri	Malcolm Canmore 1070
Abbatia Streuelin [Stirling/ Cambuskenneth]	Canonici Nigri	David I before 1147
Prioratus de May [Isle of May]	Monachi Nigri	David I 1124 × 1153
Prioratus in Insula S. Columbe [Inchcolm]	Canonici Nigri	Alexander I 1123
Abbatia de Lundres [Lindores]	Monachi Nigri de Tyron	Earl of Huntingdon 1178 × 1198
Prioratus de Pert [Perth]	Moniales Nigrae	
Abbatia de Scone	Canonici Nigri	Alexander I 1115
Prioratus de Nostinot [Restenneth, Forfar]	Canonici Nigri	
Abbatia de Cupre [Cupar]	Monachi Albi	Malcolm IV 1164
Abbatia Aberbrothoc [Arbroath]	Monachi de Tyron	William I 1178
Episcopatus Dunkeldre S. Colükille [Dunkeld]	Canonici Nigri, Keldei [Céli Dé]	
Episcopatus de Brechin	Keldei [Céli Dé]	
Episcopatus de Aberde [Aberdeen]		
Episcopatus de Müreue [Moray]	Canonici Seculares	
Prioratus de Hurtard [Urquhart, Moray]	Monachi Nigri	David I 1124

Table 4.1 *continued*

House	Order	Foundation
Scocia [Outside Lothian]		
Abbatia de Kinlos [Kinloss]	Monachi Albi	David I 1150
Episcopatus de Ros [Ross]	Keldei [Céli Dé]	
Episcopatus de Glaschu [Glasgow]	Canonici Seculares	
Abbatia Sancti Kinewini [Kilwinning]	Monachi de Tyron	Hugh de Morville 1162
Episcopatus de Galeweye [Galloway]		
Abbatia de Candida Casa [Whithorn]	Monachi Albi [Cistercian, replaced by Premonstratensian]	Lord of Galloway 1175
Abbatia M [Unidentified]	Monachi Nigri	
Episcopatus de Dublin [Dunblane]	Keldei [Céli Dé]	
Episcopatus de Katenesio [Caithness]	Keldei [Céli Dé]	
Episcopatus de Argiul [Argyll]	Keldei [Céli Dé]	
Abbatia in Insula [Iona]	Keldei [Céli Dé]	

*Actually Augustinian.

Source: A.W. Haddan and W. Stubbs, eds (1873), *Councils and Ecclesiastical Documents relating to Great Britain and Ireland*, Vol. II, Part I. Oxford: Oxford University Press.

From 1178, the bishopric of St Andrews was being contested between John Scotus (a graduate of Oxford and Paris whom historians believe was not actually a Scot), the choice of the cathedral chapter, and Hugh Capellanus, chaplain to William I. The struggle lasted for ten years, culminating in the success of Hugh, and his subsequent fall from grace, excommunication and death from plague in Rome. Meanwhile, John was appointed to the vacant bishopric of Dunkeld (including Argyll) in compensation.

Church records indicate that the separate diocese of Argyll was founded at the close of the twelfth century. John Scotus, Bishop of Dunkeld, is said to have sent his chaplain, Harald, to Rome to ask that the western part of his diocese be transformed into a new diocese, with the Gaelic-speaking Harald[19] as bishop. The petition was timely, as Scotland was enjoying a brief period of favour: in 1182 Lucius III had judged William I to be the most deserving prince of Christendom, sending him the Golden Rose; and, in 1192, Celestine III issued *Cum universi*, which recognised the Scottish Church as independent of York and answerable only to Rome. The Vatican accepted the argument about the problems experienced by clergy lacking competence in the particular vernacular of a populace, but this cannot have been the whole story because, in the twelfth century, the Scots tongue was only beginning to be prevalent in the Lowlands, and the first language of most people living in the diocese of Dunkeld would still have been Gaelic, as in the West Highlands. Furthermore, although consecrated in 1183, John was not free of the struggle over St Andrews until his return from Rome in 1188; the rapidity of his decision to surrender the western part of his diocese might well reflect a wish to concentrate on the more 'civilised' and economically viable part, which delivered significant teinds. He cannot have been unaware of the armed conflict in the area among the sons of Somerled, which culminated in outright warfare between Angus and Ranald in 1192; and, as a highly educated churchman, used to negotiations at court and in Rome, it could be argued that he would have been pleased to be relieved of the responsibility for vast areas of turbulent and less productive land in the west, still barely under the authority of King William. In this he was undoubtedly encouraged by Ranald and Dugald (or Duncan, Dugald's son) MacSorley, and the king, in pursuit of their own, quite separate, objectives. They, certainly, seem to have been able to convince the Church authorities that the new bishop should be based on the Isle of Lismore, continuing the Christian presence established by St Moluag.

---

19 His name suggests that, rather than a Gael, he was of Norse descent, possibly a Gall-Gael.

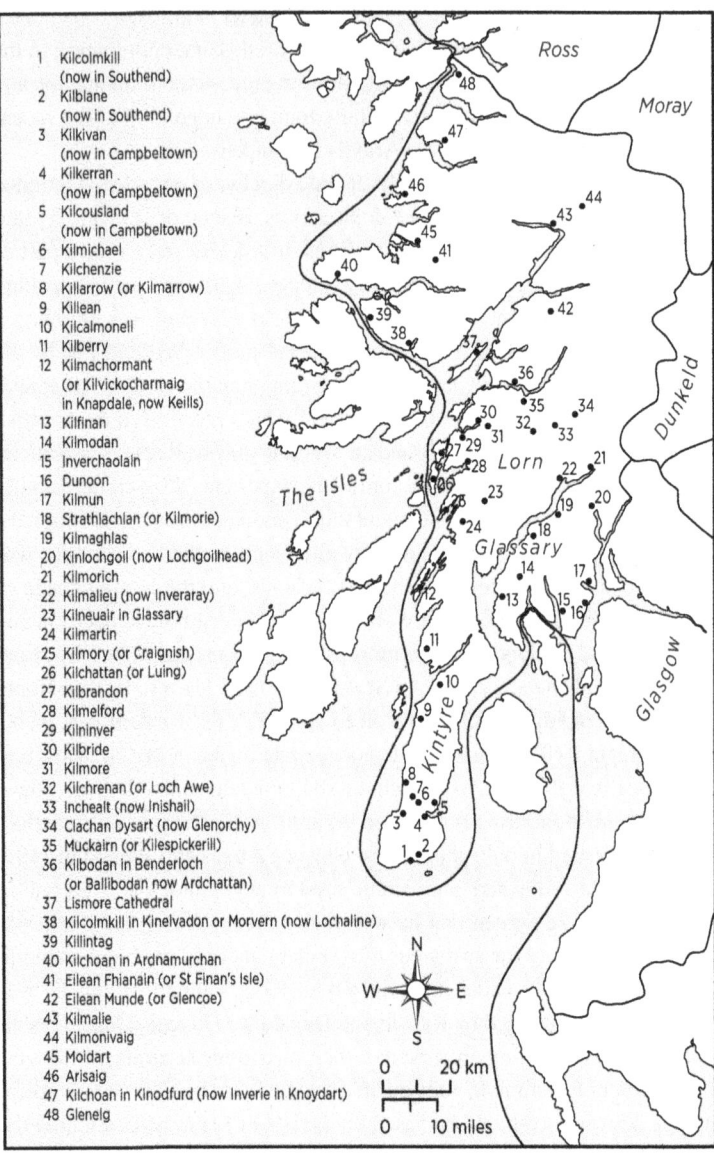

Fig. 4.1 Parish churches, diocese of Argyll, *c.* 1300. Although the three deaneries of Kintyre, Glassary and Lorn existed by 1300, the allocation of some parishes to deaneries is uncertain. (Based on a map from McNeill and MacQueen, 1996)

Harald, consecrated by the Pope, was duly installed as bishop of a vast tract of land, stretching from Cowal to Glenelg, including at least 47 extensive parishes (Table 4.2; Fig. 4.1). Whatever his success in establishing the new diocese, he certainly displayed longevity, serving for around 40 years until his death in the early 1230s, which posed problems for the Church in identifying a successor. There is no record of the endowment of the diocese at its foundation, and it was not until 1228 that Harald, as Bishop of Argyll, was granted permanent possession of three davachs[20] of land in Culkessoch, which may have been in Moray, as the transaction is recorded in the register of its bishop.[21] This was an important endowment because it was directly from the king, Alexander II, and witnessed at Stirling by the chancellor and the two principal law officers (justiciars) of the country, William Comyn, Earl of Buchan, and Walter Olifard.

Table 4.2. The mainland medieval parishes of the diocese of Argyll

Deanery of Kintyre	Deanery of Glassary
Kilcolmkill (Southend)	Glassary (Glassary; Cumlodden)
Kilblane (Southend)	Kilfinan
Kilkivan (Campbeltown)	Kilmadan (Kilmodan)
Kilkerran (Campbeltown)	Inverchaolain
Kilmichael (Campbeltown)	Dunoon (Dunoon & Kilmun)
Kilchousland (Campbeltown)	Kilmun (Dunoon & Kilmun)
Kilchenzie (Kilchenzie & Killean)	Strathlachlan
Kilmarow (Kilchenzie & Killean)	Strachur
Killean (Kilchenzie & Killean; Saddell; Skipness)	Lochgoilhead (Lochgoilhead & Kilmorich)

20 The davach is an ancient land measurement of varying extent, depending on fertility, possibly Pictish. Three davachs represent a significant area, say enough grazing for 180 cattle.
21 *Registrum Episcopatus Moraviensis*, no. 32.

Table 4.2 *continued*

Deanery of Kintyre	Deanery of Glassary
Kilcalmonell	Kilmorich (Lochgoilhead & Kilmorich)
Kilberry (Kilcalmonell)	Inveraray (Inveraray; Glenaray)
Knapdale (N & S Knapdale)	
Deanery of Lorn	**Deanery of Morvern**
Kilmartin*	Eilean Munde† (Lismore & Appin)
Craignish*	Kilmonivaig†
Kilchattan (Kilchattan & Kilbrandon)	Kilmalieu (Kilmallie; Ballachulish; Ardgour)
Kilbrandon (Kilchattan & Kilbrandon)	Kilcolmkill (Morvern)
Kilmelford (Kilninver & Kilmelford)	Killintag (Morvern)
Kilninver (Kilninver & Kilmerford)	Ardnamurchan (Ardnamurchan Sunart)
Kilmore (Kilmore & Kilbride)	Eilean Fhianain (Ardnamurchan)
Kilchrenan (Kilchrenan & Dalavich)	Arisaig (Ardnamurchan)
Muckairn	Knoydart
Inishail (Inishail & Glenorchy)	Glenelg
Glenorchy (Inishail & Glenorchy)	
Ardchattan (Ardchattan & Muckairn)	
Lismore (Lismore & Appin)	

* Lorn or Glassary
† Lochaber, either Morvern or Lorn

Source: *Origines* (modern parishes in brackets).

Bishop Harald's Legacy from the Early Church

In founding the new diocese, the Church needed to decide where to place the bishop's seat in a region entirely lacking in urban development. There were sites of power such as Dunstaffnage, the principal stronghold of the MacDougalls, and there was a small modern monastery at Saddell in Kintyre, but the Church and the MacSorleys (presumably with the blessing of the king) decided on the Early Church site on the Isle of Lismore. After the drowning of Bishop William in 1242, a papal mandate noted that Lismore was 'almost inaccessible from the stormy channel, across which the people could not pass without danger',[22] but in reality, traffic in the west in 1200 was still mainly by sea, by birlinn, even between destinations on the mainland. Lismore occupied an important strategic position on the route north via Loch Linnhe and the Great Glen, and west via the Sound of Mull. It should also not be forgotten that, at that time, Lismore was an arable island, one of the few sources of grain in the west; the later grant of land on the island would have given the cathedral a significant source of food supplies, if not substantial income. With Iona lying within the diocese of Sodor, the lot fell to Lismore, with its long Christian pedigree dating back to Moluag's arrival in the sixth century.

The fact that the mainland adjacent to Lismore is called Appin (abbot's land) has been interpreted to indicate that the Early Church monastery had prospered economically, drawing support from an extensive estate, but following invasions by the Norse and their subsequent occupation of the island there are few traces of the monastery in contemporary records. Tenuous lists of abbots peter out before 1000, but the existence of three place names – Killean (Chapel of Iain/John), Kilcheran (Chiaran/Ciaran) and Kilandrist (Anndraist/Andrew) – has been taken to indicate that, with the return of relative security, the church on the island was represented by cells of Céli Dé, and this is supported by a single piece of surviving documentary evidence. An appendix to Henry Silgrave's *Chronicle of English History*, completed in the mid thirteenth century, lists all of the religious houses in Scotland (Table 4.1), including a community of Céli Dé in Argyll. Around the time of the establishment of the diocese (1200), the Céli Dé at Iona (within the diocese of Sodor) were being displaced or absorbed by incoming Benedictine monks. Although there would have

---

22 *Vetera monumenta*, no. 52, p. 140.

been some prejudice against the Céli Dé among the Continental orders, presumably shared by the Pope, it is likely that Harald accepted them as the founding clergy of his bishopric. In doing this, he was following the pattern of development of the dioceses in the Gaelic heartland (see Table 4.1). The family names of members of the cathedral chapter in 1240 have been cited as evidence for this continuity (see also Chapter 9).

To justify sending Harald to Lismore, there must have been a church and some accommodation for the bishop on the island, however modest. Archaeological investigation of the Early Church site has so far failed to provide conclusive evidence of ecclesiastical structures older than the medieval cathedral (other than the sixth/seventh-century cemetery and associated craft workshops, see Chapter 2). This may be because traces of any earlier church lie under the foundations of the medieval choir, now transformed into the parish church; and the fact that the surrounds of the church have been subject to subsequent development (building and laying-out of gardens of both the old and new church manses; and the extension of the cemetery), without intensive archaeological investigation. At best, by analogy with other Early Medieval churches in Argyll, the 'pre-cathedral' church would have been rectangular, say 15m × 7m, with lime-mortared rubble and a thatched roof. Among the dioceses in Scotland, St Andrews, Glasgow, Aberdeen and Galloway (Whithorn) had begun impressive Romanesque cathedrals in the twelfth century, and the Bishop of Moray had Birnie Kirk, small but beautifully built in sandstone ashlar (*c.* 1140). However, the other dioceses (Brechin, Dunblane, Dunkeld, Ross and Caithness) appear to have been in much the same position as Argyll, with serious building work not starting before around 1220–40.

Bearing in mind the turbulence of the preceding centuries, it is likely that the Church had lost all of its landholdings on the island and the mainland, and it was not until 1240 that the bishop was granted 14 pennylands in the south-west quarter of Lismore by Ewen (MacDougall) of Argyll.[23] The fact that this was not the confirmation of an existing charter from the MacDougalls is surprising in view of their supposed involvement in the coming of the bishopric to Lismore half a century before.

According to tradition, Moluag's crozier (bachuil) did survive the Norse era, and it continues to be held by the hereditary keepers (dewars) on

---

23 Brown and Duncan (1957); Turner (1998). The use of the term 'pennyland' (annual rent one penny) presumably dated from the Norse occupation of Lismore.

FOUNDATION AND EARLY YEARS OF THE DIOCESE   41

Lismore. A charter of 1544 from the Earl of Argyll confirming possession of part of Penybachuil (the pennyland associated with guardianship of the bachuil) to the MacLeas (later Livingstones, known as the Barons of Bachuil), refers to their 'keeping of the great staff of the blessed Moloc, as freely as the father, grandfather and great-grandfather and other predecessors of the said Iain',[24] indicating that this arrangement would already have been in place in 1200. This is consistent with the assertion of Rev. Donald McNicol that the barons held a charter originally from the bishops 'on express condition that they were to preserve the *baculum more*'.[25] Over the years, a wide range of other oral traditions about the bachuil, some conflicting, have been collected, mainly in the nineteenth century. An account in the Dewar manuscripts (MSS) claims that the original baron made the bachuil and gave it to a dean of the cathedral, who responded by granting him *dreuchd anns an eaglais*, 'a position in the Church'.[26] The account collected by Alexander Carmichael also indicates that the baron made the bachuil from a sapling growing overnight next to the Black Cross,[27] but that he sent it to the Pope, who had it 'gilt with gold & gave it to the Baron as a symbol of office'.[28] We will never know the full story of the bachuil[29] but it is likely that, at least in the early days of the diocese, it would have been the focus of an important cult, involved in the blessing of man, beast and boat. It is also likely that Harald had to deal with the persistence of pre-Christian/pagan activities such as fire ceremonies at Beltane and Samhuinn festivals on *Cnoc Aingeal*, the fire cairn near the church.

The other inheritance from the Early Church was its parish structure, arising out of the many small chapels and churches scattered liberally across the diocese. Of the 47 medieval parishes, 26 carry names referring to an early chapel (Kil/*Cille*) devoted to one or other of the familiar Celtic saints (Blane, Bride/Brigid, Brendan, Ciaran, Columba, Finan, Moluag),

---

24 Original charter held at Bachuil House, Lismore. For a full explanation of the role of dewars, see Màrkus (2009).
25 *First Statistical Account of Scotland* (1791), Vol. 1 (Appin and Lismore), p. 492.
26 Argyll Archives, Inveraray, Dewar MS 3, f. 285r. With thanks to Ronald Black.
27 The eighth-century cross slab that stood in the old church graveyard until the Reformation.
28 Carmichael Watson Project, University of Edinburgh. Coll-97/CW106/41.
29 McWhannell (2023).

to a more obscure Celtic saint (Cathan, Colmanel, Comann, Constantine, Findoe the virgin, Fintain (Mund), Kenneth, Maurice) or to the popular international saints of the West Highlands (John, Martin, Mary, Michael) (Fig. 4.1; Table 4.2). A few of the dedications are now obscure. In the lowland areas, the parishes were small (for example the clustering of Kilbride, Kilmore and Kilninver) but, particularly in what became the deanery of Morvern (e.g. Ardnamurchan, Knoydart and Glenelg), the parish priest was responsible for a scattered population over an enormous area.

The Duties of the Bishop

The medieval mind was conditioned to believe that humans were essentially sinful, and that those who committed mortal sins (lust, gluttony, greed, sloth, wrath, envy, pride) were destined for eternal damnation unless the Church intervened through the grace that confession and communion (participation in the sacrament of the Mass) bestowed. Minor or venal sins were more easily forgiven but, by the twelfth century, it was generally accepted that, after death, most people would have to endure a period in Purgatory, experiencing some of the horrors of Hell until their accumulated sins had been purged. Individuals who committed very serious crimes (for example, the murder committed by Robert Bruce in the Franciscan priory at Dumfries in 1306) were excommunicated and considered beyond rescue, unless shown to be truly contrite.

The work of the Church was, therefore, to guide souls to the gates of Heaven and to shorten the time they spent in Purgatory, through its various sacraments, particularly: baptism, marriage, confession and penance, the Mass, and anointing the sick and dying. As it was obligatory to be baptised in order to be granted eternal life, babies had to be christened very soon after birth, so that they weren't consigned to Limbo if death intervened; and marriage was also obligatory, to prevent lust/fornication. Simply attending Mass and repeating the prayers could confer some credit to shorten the time due in Purgatory but the benefits of full participation, consuming the body, blood, soul and divinity of Christ, were not available without prior confession and the completion of the required penance (i.e. achieving a 'state of grace'). This, commonly, involved the saying of prayers, although the eradication of serious sins might require a pilgrimage, for example to the shrine of St Duthac at Tain, St Ninian at Whithorn, St

Kentigern at Glasgow, St Cuthbert at Durham, St Thomas at Canterbury, or overseas to Santiago in Spain. James IV (1473–1513), who made many pilgrimages to Tain and Whithorn, including approaching Ninian's shrine barefoot, famously added a new link each year to the heavy iron chain he wore hidden under his clothes, in penance for his involvement in the rebellion against his father which led to his accession to the throne. His lifelong ambition to complete a pilgrimage to Jerusalem turned out to be incompatible with the demands of kingship. Since it is thought that most people would have completed the full preparation for Mass only once each year at Easter, confession and absolution on the point of death became very important; there was a great fear of dying 'unshriven' at a time when sudden death through disease or violence was common.

This, then, was the primary task for the bishop: to confirm the existence of, or to establish afresh, a network of parish churches, with consecrated priests, to make the sacraments available to each and every individual in his diocese. In particular, Mass had to be said every Sunday and Holy Day in each parish church, and daily in the cathedral (where the officiating priest might have been the only full participant). Until the arrival of the friars, there was no tradition of preaching in either the cathedrals or the parish churches.

Particularly in outlying areas, the parish priest would take responsibility for day-to-day resolution of conflict within the community, an activity that was important in reducing the incidence of serious sins involving violence. There is evidence that the ritual of the Church in Scotland tried to promote harmony in the parish: towards the end of the celebration of Mass, the congregation could be required to kiss the 'pax box',[30] signifying the unity of the community. The priest would also be involved in the support of the old, infirm and orphans within the parish, although the scope for relieving illness in the scattered diocese of Argyll may have been limited. On top of this, the parish priest was expected to provide for travellers: 'according to the custom of Scotland . . . and freely to afford them the necessary food and drink' (the rector of Glassary, complaining about the burdens laid upon him).[31]

In a model province, each bishop would be under the authority of an archbishop who could provide support, or control, as required, but

---

30 For example, on Eigg: Ó hAnnracháin and Armstrong (2014).
31 Munro and Munro (1986).

Scotland was far from being a model province. Its kings and bishops had defied papal authority in refusing to recognise any role for the archbishops of York or Canterbury, to the extent that the entire population had been excommunicated for some years in the late twelfth century. Although partial resolution was achieved in 1192, when Scotland was taken directly under the wing of the Pope as a 'daughter church', the bishops were not permitted to gather together unless called by a papal legate; and it was not until 1225 that the Council of the Scottish Church was established, with the right to run its own affairs within limits set by the Pope. Clearly, in 1200, Harald was very much on his own in establishing and managing his new diocese, although early versions of the statutes of the Scottish Church (the book of rules governing the practical aspects of Church life, generally arising out of a series of Lateran councils in Rome), must have existed before the formulation of the collection laid down in the 1240s (Table 4.3).

Table 4.3. Compilation of the general or provincial statutes of the Scottish Church, *c.* 1240

Subject matter of each statute	
1.	Arrangements for the holding of the Council of the Scottish Churches
2.	Nomination of the convenor (conservator)
3.	Statement of the aim to propagate the Catholic faith
4.	The sacraments to be celebrated according to precise canonical form
5.	Responsibilities for building churches
6.	Chapels not to be built without the consent of the diocese
7.	Masses not to be celebrated in private places without leave of the bishop
8.	Every parish to have its own rector or vicar, qualified to celebrate sacraments, who shall lead a pure and honourable life
9.	Vicars must have sufficient maintenance, to the value of at least ten marks

10.	Clerical attire
11.	Protection of ecclesiastical benefices
12.	Manses of beneficed clergy, and their maintenance
13.	The valuation of churches
14.	Ordination of clergy
15.	Arrangements for priests transferring to monastic orders
16.	Appointment of confessors for parish priests
17.	Letting of Church property
18.	Cohabitation of priests with women
19–21.	Management of Church property
22–23.	Priests not to engage in business or bequeath property to concubines or children
24.	Arrangements for excommunicated persons
25.	Priests not to act as executors of wills
26–28.	Churches as sanctuaries; and arrangements for punishing priests who have broken the law
29.	No secular courts on Sundays or festivals
30.	The liberties of churches to be preserved
31.	Crusaders to be defended
32.	Prevention of arrestment of Church property
33.	Priests not to be tried in secular courts
34–45.	Arrangements for the collection of tithes and punishment of those who prevent their collection
46.	These decrees to be published three times each year
47.	Excommunication for those who plot against the Church
48.	Obedience of priests to the bishop

Table 4.3 *continued*

Subject matter of each statute	
49.	Arrangements for pardoners
50.	Excommunication for those who restrict the liberties of the Church
51–52.	List of crimes that qualify for excommunication
53.	Bishops to support excommunication issued by one of their number
54.	Punishment for fornication by priests
55.	Absolution of excommunication not to be obtained by force

Note. Statutes established in the same period by a synod of the St Andrews and Aberdeen dioceses also include: arrangement of marriage banns; arrangements for penance; visitation of the sick, including lepers; dealing with matrimonial disputes; banning of sports from church and churchyard; exclusion of laymen from the church chancel; annual diocesan visits; arrangements for absence of priests from their parish; and practical details of confession. The St Andrews and Aberdeen statutes also include details of the celebration of Mass but do not refer to a service book.

Source: D. Patrick, ed. (1907), *Statutes of the Scottish Church, 1225–1559*. Edinburgh: Scottish History Society.

On top of all these responsibilities, the Bishop of Argyll would be called upon to provide administrative or legal services to the local nobles; and occasionally to fulfil political roles on the national stage, involving arduous travelling. In principle, all bishops were ex officio members of the king's council.

Financing the Work of the Diocese

To do his work, each parish priest required a church and lodging, in good repair; a glebe to grow much of his food; and a certain amount of resource, as cash or in kind, to pay for his living expenses and outlays on the Mass: wafers of unleavened wheat bread (costly in an area where bere barley was the staple), wine, oil or candles for lighting, service books, vestments. It was the responsibility of the bishop to ensure that each parish priest had the resources to fulfil these duties.

FOUNDATION AND EARLY YEARS OF THE DIOCESE

As noted earlier, from the reign of David I, the parish teind (one-tenth of the annual produce) was, by law, dedicated to the support of the Church:

- the maintenance of each parish church and manse, and the stipends of the rector and his vicar, where relevant;
- the expenses of the bishop, including the costs of his roles on the national scene, the maintenance of the cathedral, the diocese vestments, chalices and service books, his own stipend and those of the diocese dignitaries;
- direct taxation by the Vatican, including the costs of 'provision' of clergy to diocesan posts, but also for special projects such as the crusade planned in 1278, and the payment of David II's ransom.

Some of the payments would have been in cash, but there would have been considerable challenges in conversion from kind, especially in an era when there was chronic shortage of coinage.

The teind was a comprehensive tax, covering all aspects of rural life, and its importance can be gauged from the fact that it features in 13 out of the 55 statutes laid down in the 1240s (Table 4.3). A tenth was due annually of all:

> corn, hay, lint [flax], of gardens, of mills, of fishings, of the young of animals, wool, milk, cheeses at whatever season they are made, butter, fowls, eggs, peats, coppice wood, fruits of trees, trading, hunting, hawking, and other such matters[32]

and there were complex arrangements to apportion the tax where livestock were kept in different parishes (for example, at sheilings); to tax fishing in different parishes; and to evaluate the earnings of day labourers. Recording, collecting, storing and distributing this bewildering array of products must have occupied much of the time of the parish priest, but the fact that vicars (the substitutes for the parish rectors) would have been mainly drawn from the peasantry (see below), with a detailed knowledge of the local economy, must have helped. In some parishes, the situation may have been simplified by awarding the 'garbal' or 'lesser teinds' (e.g. dairy products, wool, young stock, etc.) to the vicar, with the more manageable corn teind delivered to the more senior clergy (see below, Chapter 5).

---

32 Statute 34 (Table 4.3).

At a time when feudal structures were still developing and armed conflict was common, successful collection of the teind must have depended upon the authority and piety of the leading families. Garrisons at Achinduin and Coeffin castles on Lismore may have helped, although there is a tradition that the role of tax gatherer on Lismore was undertaken by the hereditary keeper of Moluag's bachuil. The principal sanction of the Church was the threat of excommunication, which carried great weight in the thirteenth century. Later, we shall see that laymen and priests alike became less deferential and did not hesitate to defy the authority of the bishop.

However, the financial viability of the diocese was compromised by the fact that the revenues of several parishes had already been alienated, to support one or other of the many monastic houses that had been established in the twelfth century. This was a universal problem across Scotland. The income of two parishes in Kintyre (Kilcalmonell and Kilkerran) had been appropriated by Paisley Abbey and at least part of the resources of Kilfinan, Glassary and Kilmun were also destined for the Cluniac monks. Whithorn had Kilcolmkill (Kintyre) and Kilmodan; Kilwinning in Ayrshire had Knapdale; Iona had Kilchenzie and part of Muckairn, and the Augustinians at Inchaffray in Perthshire drew support from Kilmorich, Inishail and Muckairn. The monks of Saddell had the surrounding parish of Kilkivan. Over and above these appropriated teinds, David I granted his income from legal activities in Kintyre jointly to Holyrood and Dunfermline.[33]

This diversion of property and revenues to prestigious religious houses reflects the fact that the Church had national calls on its resources: building and maintenance of great cathedrals and abbeys to the glory of God, including music, religious art and costly vestments; the university training of senior clergy, including those who would become lawyers and civil servants, in support of the crown (there were few educated men outside the Church); and the many costs of running an extensive administration, including frequent travel to Rome – not to mention the onerous taxes imposed by the Vatican. Much of this was, of course, paid for by exploiting abbey and cathedral endowments in the form of land, buildings, mineral resources, fisheries, wool sales etc. In due course, the Bishop of Lismore appropriated the Argyll parishes of Kilmichael, Kilchousland, Kilmarow,

---

33   *Origines*, p. 1.

FOUNDATION AND EARLY YEARS OF THE DIOCESE

Kilberry, Dunoon and Kilbride, as mensal parishes (i.e. supporting the bishop's 'table') to support the cathedral clergy and the wider life of the diocese. This was in addition to the quarter of all parish teinds that, in principle, should have been devoted to the running of the diocese. In 1243, Alexander II 'compassionating the poverty of the bishoprick of Argyle, granted to the bishop the church of Killean in Kintyr with all its lands and other pertinents'.[34] Altogether the income to the diocese from teinds (according to the 'Old Extent' valuation, finally replaced in the 1270s by Bagimond's revaluation, Chapter 6) was a very modest £51 13s 4d; and it has been estimated that, across the dioceses of Argyll, Ross and Caithness, the yield of teinds was around 2 shillings per square mile, compared with up to £3 10s in parts of Angus, reflecting differences in economic activity and income from endowments.

When a parish had been appropriated, for example by one of the abbeys, the title of parish rector, and part of the income of the parish, would form the benefice/prebend granted to a priest (prebendary) who became a canon (member of the chapter of the abbey). In many cases, the prebend provided the support for the rector's further education. Under these circumstances he was normally non-resident, and the diocese installed a vicar, normally a less educated priest (see below), who would be paid a very modest salary to fulfil the duties of the parish. The complexity of some of these arrangements can be gauged from the agreement for Kilcalmonell (West Kintyre):

> In 1262, Alan bishop of Argyle confirmed to the monks [of Paisley] the church with its chapels, to be converted to their own use, saving the vicar's portion in that church, as in other churches of the diocese, and saving to the bishop the fourth part of the church which was acknowledged to belong to the bishop's table, and the right of the bishop and other ordinaries in all things.[35]

As we shall see later, Bishop Martin (of Argyll, 1342–87) ran into very serious trouble a century later, when he attempted to divert appropriated parish income to meet the costs of his cathedral.

---

34 *Origines*, p. 22.
35 *Registrum Monasterii de Passalet*, p. 27.

A related problem for the bishop was the issue of patronage: the right to appoint rectors and vicars of appropriated parishes. Although he was ultimately responsible for maintaining the quality of the clergy in the diocese, the bishop had only limited control of most appointments, which were actually in the hands of major landowners and monasteries. This could lead to serious disagreement and, in at least one case, the involvement of the Pope in dislodging a vicar incorrectly assigned to Kilkerran (Campbeltown) parish:

> In 1299, on Thursday after the feast of St Simon and St Jude, in a case litigated between the abbot of Passeley [Paisley] and Laurence Bishop of Argyll, in the High Church at Glasgow, before Sir Robert the treasurer, and Sir Robert Stampet, a canon, commissioners of the bishop of St Andrews, who was constituted by the Pope sole judge in the matter, there appeared Master Nicholas, rector of the church of St Modan, procurator for the bishop of Argyle, and Venald a monk of Paisley for the abbot, when the case was settled as follows:- The bishop's procurator admitted that the presentation to the vicarage of the church of St Querin in Kentyir belonged to the abbot of Paisley, and promised on his oath that Sir Angus, who acted as vicar, should resign the vicarage into the bishop's hands, and that the resignation, sealed with the bishop's seal, should be placed in the hands of the monks before the feast of St Andrew the apostle, and the abbot's procurator also promised on oath that on receiving the resignation the monks should present Angus the chaplain to the vicarage.[36]

The Lords of the Isles exercised the rights of patronage in the deanery of Morvern and in their landholdings in Kintyre, as part of their increasing political control of the west. For example, in 1388, Donald, Lord of the Isles, who had installed his chaplain Benedict John Andrew (Bean Johannes Andree) as rector of Kilmonivaig in Lochaber, petitioned Pope

---

36 *Registrum Monasterii de Passalet*, p. 13. This extract shows the distinction drawn between graduate clergy (Master) and senior churchmen without university education (Sir/Dominus).

Clement VII at Avignon to have him appointed dean of Lismore.[37] In due course, the high-flying Benedict was promoted to be bishop, in a period when the Lords of the Isles took a close interest in appointments on Lismore (in addition to the diocese of Sodor, based at the cathedral at Peel on the Isle of Man). It is likely that chaplains such as Benedict, engaged to say daily Mass for the lord's family, were part of the Gaelic Learned Orders (specialists in poetry, history, law, music, medicine, art and fine craftwork), maintained in the households of the lords and other leading families in the West Highlands up to the early seventeenth century.

The development of this very complex system of financing the Church as a whole, which was normal practice across Europe, had two important consequences in Scotland. First, the diversion of funds away from the parish meant that there was little investment in church and manse, and a severe limitation on the support that the parish could provide to the needy; as long as Mass was being said, the more prestigious institutions of the Church had little interest in the care of more isolated communities. There certainly was no intention that the people should benefit from religious education – the avoidance of eternal damnation was sufficient for the masses. Secondly, there evolved two distinct classes of priest. On the one hand, according to Church protocol, the 'dignitaries' of the cathedrals (see Chapter 5) and the rectors of appropriated parishes (the prebendary priests) were supposed to be either university educated or 'of noble birth' or both.[38] On the other hand, the parish vicars, recruited from the peasantry as they usually were, may have been required only to be able to read the service books in Latin, and to be sufficiently competent in accounting to manage the teind.

The education system was geared to provide these two classes of priest. In the more populous east and south of Scotland, a few sons of 'good' families might learn to read, count and write Latin at burgh grammar schools before going on, in their early teens, to university at Oxford or Cambridge, or further afield in Paris, Orléans or Bologna, possibly even

---

37 Burns (2021), para 172, p. 89.
38 But see, for example, the petition of Robert, King of Scots, October 1394, to Pope Benedict XIII at Avignon, where he recommends his 'relative David de Spalding' for a canonry at Aberdeen 'notwithstanding defect of age, being in his 15th year, and notwithstanding constitutions regarding non-graduates and rules of the Pope's chancery' (Burns (2021), para 259a, p. 135).

Toledo, Salamanca or Salerno, where they studied language, law and philosophy. University-level education was not available in Scotland until 1413, at St Andrews. The link with the law school of Bologna in the thirteenth century was particularly important in ensuring that Scottish canon lawyers were personally familiar with popes and senior members of the curia during the perilous years of the War of Independence (Chapter 6).

Of the students supported at university by benefices as rectors of parishes, many would be expected, on their return, to fill senior posts at the cathedrals and abbeys, or in the service of the crown, rather than to do the humble work of the parish priest. It seems likely that promising candidates from the West Highlands would have fed into this system, although it is not clear to what extent the Gaelic Learned Orders provided relevant education. There certainly was training in medicine, by hereditary groups of doctors, in touch with developments on continental Europe.[39]

It is likely that, in the West Highlands, vicars were drawn from the class of tacksmen (major tenants) and provided with elementary education in the parish organised by the bishop. As vicars of this kind were fully rooted in the community, there would have been strong motivation to retain the, admittedly frugal, income within the parish from generation to generation. Across the diocese of Argyll, a significant proportion of the clergy were illegitimate and, in spite of the rule of celibacy, some of these were sons of priests.[40] There is evidence of a limited degree of 'hereditary priesthood' of this kind on Lismore (Chapter 9).

The Drowning of Bishop William and the Intervention of King Alexander II

The death of Bishop Harald in the early 1230s exposed the weakness of the new bishopric. No new bishop came forward, possibly because the diocese had yet to form an effective chapter of canons (see Chapter 5) to elect a successor, and Argyll came under the care of Bishop Simon of Sodor. On 7 July 1236, Pope Gregory IX wrote from Reate, north of Rome, to the Bishop of Moray to relieve Bishop Simon of this responsibility:

---

39 See, for example, Bannerman (1998).
40 In supplications to the Pope for benefices, such candidates were commonly described as 'being born of a priest and an unmarried woman'.

Our venerable brother, the Bishop of Sodor, has humbly made request that we should deign to relieve him from the burden in this respect on him incumbent, since formerly [in the case of] the Bishopric of Lismore, which in consequence of the evil of the time had come to great poverty, the Apostolic See had taken [it] to itself, to grant '*in commendam*'; and in consequence of the frequent infirmities of himself, he is unable to exercise the 'cure' of both [dioceses]. And so to his prayers we being disposed to move do to thy fraternal relation to us commit, so far as relates to the said bishop, that thou, releasing him from the 'cure' and the anxiety of the Church of Lismore, do cause to be provided for the said Church by Canonical election (of) a suitable person to be bishop and pastor.[41]

In due course Bishop Andreas de Moravia (Moray) arranged for his chancellor, William, to be installed as bishop on Lismore in 1239 but within three years he had drowned, leaving the diocese leaderless for another decade. In what seems to have been his only recorded achievement, in 1240 William received from Ewen MacDougall of Argyll: 14 pennylands in the south-west quarter of Lismore: Barnaray (Bernera); 2.5 pennylands of Achacendune (Achinduin); 5 of Tyrchulen; 2 of Tyrknannen; 1.5 of Tenga; one of Drumchulochir; and one of Craganas (Craignich).[42] In spite of this, the bishopric was still very short of resources, as evidenced by King Alexander II's grant of the church, lands and 'other pertinents' of Killean to the bishopric three years later.[43] The grant included five pennylands associated with Killean and Kilmarow. Because it was founded later than the other dioceses and monasteries, which had pre-empted the available resources, the estimated annual income of Argyll by the late thirteenth century (Bagimond's Roll – see Chapter 5) at £280 was similar only to Caithness (£286), and much lower than most of the other dioceses (St Andrews £8,023, Glasgow £4,080, Aberdeen £1,610, Moray £1,418, Dunkeld £1,206, Dunblane £607, Brechin £441, Galloway £358,

---

41 *Journal of the Manx Museum*, Vol. 23, p. 308: <www.isle-of-man.com/manxnote book/jmmuseum/d175.htm>.
42 *Origines*, p. 164. The charter appears to be incorrectly dated in *Origines*; see Turner (1998).
43 *Origines*, p. 22.

Ross £351). Inadequate finance would be a problem for all of William's successors.

These long vacancies between bishops might suggest that the MacSorleys were failing to provide the necessary political support to the fledgling diocese, and it seems clear (from the king's plan to move the bishop to Kilbride on the mainland, see below) that no start had been made in building a cathedral for the bishop (see Chapter 7). It is difficult to interpret this neglect in the face of the foundation by Duncan MacDougall of a community of Valliscaulian monks at Ardchattan in the 1220s (although Ranald MacSorley and the king may have been more important, see above). King Alexander II was concerned about the state of the Church in Argyll (for example, the lack of progress in building a cathedral), but by the 1240s he was also minded to bring the independent MacDougalls, now led by Duncan's son Ewen, under his direct control.

In the summer of 1249, at the height of his powers, King Alexander sailed for Argyll with a great fleet and a full court retinue, but when he arrived at Kerrera, Ewen MacDougall was not present to do homage. He had just returned from the court of the King of Norway (from whom he held his western islands) but, when the King of Man was drowned at Orkney on the way home from his marriage, Ewen had been dispatched to Man to keep control in the meantime. In the face of such insubordination, Alexander moved to deprive him of lands and castles, including the new state-of-the-art fortress of Dunstaffnage. Shortly afterwards, the king suddenly sickened and died on Kerrera. The fact that his son, Alexander III, aged only eight years, was formally crowned king around a hundred miles away only a week later, on 13 July, suggests that the king's death may not have been unexpected.

In the royal retinue was Clement, Bishop of Dunblane, the king's counsellor and, later, one of the guardians of the young Alexander III. He had papal authority to fill the Argyll vacancy. He and the king had had ambitions to transfer the bishopric to the mainland; and before his death, the king had granted to the diocese the parish church of St Bride the Virgin in Lorn, as a mensal church with its lands and other pertinents. The apparent intention was that the new cathedral should be built in the parish, at the ancient Kilbride church site near Lerags, south of Oban (later the burial place of the MacDougalls). In the minority that followed, the transfer appears to have been overlooked, but the following years were to see important changes fuelled by Clement's energy.

5

The Coming of the Dominicans

The appointment of Bishop Clement to deal with the crisis affecting the bishopric of Argyll had lasting implications. Clement had experience of reviving a moribund diocese (Dunblane), but he was also a senior statesman, close to the crown, favoured by the papal curia, and able to exert political leverage to bring about change. At least as important was the fact that Clement was a friar of the Dominican Order of Preachers, the 'shock troops' of Christian orthodoxy against heresy, already well known through their role as preachers for their competence in languages, and unlikely to find Gaelic an impediment in their work.

The Dominican Order of Preachers

The continuing cycle of renewal of monasticism brought into being, in the early thirteenth century, two major orders of friars (not monks): the Dominicans and the Franciscans, each promoting the ideals of the ascetic life, free of material possessions, but with the remit to live in the world and preach the gospel in the language of the people. A priest from the diocese of Osma in northern Spain, Dominic de Guzman (*c.* 1170–1234) was sent to Languedoc in southern France around 1207 as part of a peaceful campaign to convert the Albigensians or Cathars from their heretical beliefs. This work, involving preaching, teaching and debating in the vernacular rather than Latin, was overtaken in 1209 by the violence, torture and executions of the Albigensian Crusade (1209–29), led by Simon de Montfort. This crusade destroyed most of the Cathar communities.[44]

---

44 But see Le Roy Ladurie (1990).

Guzman's order of mendicant friars, based on the teachings of St Augustine, was formally recognised by the Pope in 1216. From the start, the Dominicans ('Blackfriars' in the British Isles) valued university education, producing a steady stream of teachers and theologians, most famously Thomas Aquinas. Because of their commitment to maintaining competence in a range of languages for preaching, they played an important part in international diplomacy; for example, Dominican friars acted as interpreters in the exchanges between Scotland and Norway, leading to the Treaty of Perth in 1266 and the ceding of the Hebrides to the Scottish crown. However, their language skills were used by the Church for more sinister purposes: in 1230, Gregory IX instituted the Papal Inquisition to counter Cathar and other heresies, and torture was officially sanctioned after 1252. Dominicans were recruited as principal inquisitors in Italy and Spain up to the nineteenth century, but there is no evidence that they fulfilled this role in Scotland. Officially sanctioned to support themselves by begging, they soon became the papal tax collectors. Dominicans were clever, articulate and very much in the world.

Clement, Bishop of Dunblane (d. 1258)

The Dominican movement spread rapidly across Europe, with the first community of friars in the British Isles established at Oxford by 1221, only five years after the original foundation of the order. King Alexander II was a particularly enthusiastic supporter, financing the establishment of friaries in Edinburgh, Aberdeen, Perth, Stirling and Elgin between 1230 and 1233, and at Inverness, Berwick, Ayr and Glasgow in the 1240s. Based in urban centres, and open to society, Dominican friaries became important centres for the political and church life of the country, and as residences for the king when he was touring the country. Until the assassination of James I at the Dominican Priory in Perth in February 1437, it was the preferred venue for the royal court, parliament and national Church councils. Noble families such as the Earls of Argyll lodged at Dominican houses in Stirling and Glasgow when travelling to court.

Although little is known about the early years of Clement,[45] subsequent events make it plausible that he was from Scotland (but probably not a native Gael). He was a student at Oxford when the Dominicans burst on

---

45 Duncan (2004).

the scene, and joined the order in the 1220s. By 1233, following success in settling Dominican houses in several Scottish towns, he had been appointed Bishop of Dunblane, the first of the Blackfriars to achieve such status in the British Isles.

Consecrated by Bishop William Malveisin of St Andrews at Stow, near Galashiels, on 4 September 1233, he inherited a diocese that had been vacant for three years, without a functioning chapter or cathedral. It was also on the brink of financial collapse, with most of the diocesan revenues appropriated by other religious houses or diverted by powerful laymen. He displayed great diplomatic skills in negotiation with the abbeys of Coupar Angus, Culross, Lindores, Cambuskenneth and Arbroath, and other houses, for the recovery of some of the income, and resisted the proposal that the bishopric should be based at Inchaffray. He also faced a serious challenge from Walter Comyn, Earl of Menteith, one of the most powerful men in the kingdom, whose establishment of a new monastic house on Inchmahome threatened to drain a major fraction of the revenue of the diocese. In these years before Clement had aligned himself with the Comyn faction, he succeeded in reaching a compromise, confirmed by a visit to Rome between 1235 and 1237, during which Gregory IX commissioned the bishops of Glasgow and Dunkeld to investigate the alienation of Dunblane's lands to the Earl of Strathearn and the Earl of Menteith. With improving finances, Clement was able to start work on a cathedral at Dunblane.

Clement was becoming one of the most powerful men in the kingdom, inferior in influence among churchmen only to Bishop Gamelin of St Andrews. In 1247, Pope Innocent appointed him papal tax collector, with the remit to collect one twentieth of all ecclesiastical revenues within Scotland to finance the Seventh Crusade (1248–54), which resulted in a series of crushing defeats by the Muslim forces. In the 1240s, he was a leader in the successful campaign to canonise Queen Margaret, the ancestress of Alexander II. This can have done him no harm in his relations with the king, and when, in 1248, the Pope appointed the bishops of Glasgow and Dunblane to fill the Lismore vacancy, Clement worked closely with Alexander, accompanying him on his punitive raid into Argyll the next year. Described by Matthew Paris as the 'indiscreet bishop of Strathearn, a friar to wit of the order of the Preachers',[46] Clement was at the king's side when he died suddenly at Kerrera.

---

46 Vaughan (1986), p. 194.

In the years up to his own death in 1258, Clement was at the heart of the power struggle in Scotland between the parties of Alan Durward (a leading noble of Gaelic descent and for some time Justiciar of Scotia) and the Comyns (the Earl of Menteith, the Earl of Buchan and the Lord of Badenoch). His natural place was with the Comyns because of the action of Durward in driving Bishop Gamelin of St Andrews out of his diocese and into exile in Rome. Clement became a guardian of the young King Alexander III in 1251, on the dissolution of the Durward guardianship, but he and the Comyns, in turn, were dislodged in 1255, under pressure from Henry III of England (father of Alexander's young queen). The fact that the Comyns were banned from taking part in government for seven years did not prevent them from 'liberating' the young king from his guardians on Loch Leven and installing him, under their influence, in Stirling Castle in 1257. Meanwhile Pope Alexander IV had provided decisive support to Bishop Gamelin, and Clement's last act in 1257, shortly before his death, was to obey his instructions to excommunicate Alan Durward and the other king's councillors 'with striking of bells and extinguishing of candles'[47] at the abbey church of Cambuskenneth.

The Dominican Bishops of Argyll (1250–1387)

Clement had a profound and lasting influence on the bishopric of Argyll, initiating a line of Dominicans as bishops: Laurence (1262–99); Andrew (1300–42); and Martin (1342–87), although Clement's own appointment, Alan de Carrick (1250–62), was not a friar. Yet another Dominican, Finlay, became bishop in the fifteenth century (1419–26). These were members of the Scottish elite, university graduates, members of the ruling class, but also, by family background, fluent in Gaelic. They were members of an order that had recent experience of dealing with heresy and irregularity in a pastoral community in the south-west of France, which in some respects was not unlike Argyll; they would have had little patience with any residual elements of the Early Church on Lismore, nor with any outright pagan practices that might have survived (such as the Beltane fire festival). It can be assumed that, at least in the time of Laurence, firm discipline would have been imposed on society in general, and preaching and teaching would have been a priority in a diocese that had been neglected for

---

47   Cockburn (1959).

decades. The risk that the Church ran in appointing men of this calibre was that they could, and did from time to time, think for themselves. Bishops Andrew and Finlay became embroiled in the politics of their day, both suffering exile, and Martin came close to excommunication as a result of his financial dealings (see Chapters 6, 8 and 9).

If, under Harald and William and during the subsequent vacancy, the bishopric had drifted along without establishing a firm foundation, and apparently without real engagement on the part of the MacDougalls, things were to change after 1250. Clement's influence at court ensured that Lismore gained powerful allies and loyalties. The new bishop, Alan de Carrick, was the son of Duncan, Earl of Carrick (d. 1250), descendant of the Gaelic princes of Galloway, but the family was forming a close relationship with the Anglo-Norman Stewards. At this time the political influence of the Stewards, later to become the Royal Stewarts (sometimes written as Stuarts), was advancing into Argyll, and, as Lords of Badenoch, the Comyns were establishing a power base in Lochaber. Ewen de Ergadia (Ewen MacDougall of Argyll), in disgrace because of his failure to attend the king at Kerrera, and pinched between these two powerful families, was obliged to cooperate with the government of Scotland. After the restoration of his lands around 1260, he remained a staunch supporter of Alexander III and ally of the Comyns. Later, his son and heir, Alexander (named after the king) married a daughter of the Lord of Badenoch, aligning himself closely with the Comyn and Balliol families, with fateful consequences. Possibly the most important result for the diocese was that at least three members of the MacDougall family, Laurence, Andrew and Martin (each styled 'of Argyll'), trained as Dominican priests in preparation for becoming Bishop of Argyll. Clearly, the MacDougalls were taking a closer interest in their bishopric, and moving to control its affairs.

Alan de Carrick (Bishop of Argyll 1250–1262)

Alan was almost certainly a younger son of Avelina, daughter of the High Steward of Scotland, and Duncan, 1st Earl of Carrick. His eldest brother Neil or Nigel, 2nd Earl, in turn, was married to Margaret, daughter of Walter, 3rd High Steward of Scotland, but he was influential in his own right, being one of the king's councillors from 1255.

Alan first appears in the records as rector of Straiton in Ayrshire and Kirkemannen (probably Kilkivan) in Kintyre. His brother John held the lands of Straiton, whose parish revenues had been granted to Paisley Abbey, and Alan would have received his parishes through the influence of the Stewards, founders of the Cluniac abbey. Without surviving records from his diocese, most of what we know about Alan after he became bishop in 1250 comes from records of his dealings with Paisley. It is tempting, but probably unfair, to think that he was more interested in the abbey than in his own cathedral. There is no evidence that he played a part in the wider political life of Church or state, although the charter of 1256 (Plate 5) shows that, in common with other Scottish bishops, he had contact with the diocese of Durham.

In 1253 and 1261,[48] he confirmed earlier grants to Paisley of the parishes of Kilkerran and Kilcalmonell in Kintyre, although ensuring that the monks did not acquire 'the vicar's portion' or the (mensal) quarter of the income, which was to be devoted to the support of the Bishop of Argyll. In a similar grant of Kilfinan (deanery of Glassary) in 1250, the bishop also reserved the right to 'the pasture of twelve cows, and forty rigs belonging to the vicarage'.[49] In 1261, he became involved in resolving a complex lawsuit between Paisley and Malcolm, rector of their church at Kilkerran. Malcolm had entered into an unusual agreement with the abbey, promising to provide a 'stone' of iron each year, but had failed to deliver. In a formal legal process, he and the abbot submitted themselves 'to the determination of bishop Alan, who ordained that in order to complete Malcolm's absolution from the non-payment of the debt down to the day of the bishop's decision, he should pay one pound of wax or sixpence yearly at Paisley during the holding of Glasgow fair'.[50] The impression that Alan was a trusted ally of the Cluniac monks is confirmed by his role, in collaboration with William de Bodington, Bishop of Glasgow, in carrying out an audit of Paisley charters.[51]

Lists of witnesses to the Paisley grants and other records show that Alan had a small chapter of priests to support him in administering the diocese. A fully fledged set of cathedral canons would include the four 'dignitaries':

---

48 *Origines*, p. 13.
49 *Origines*, p. 49.
50 *Origines*, p. 13.
51 *Registrum Monasterii de Passalet*, p. 134.

Dean	the senior administrator, normally chairing the chapter
Treasurer	the manager of the property (the 'treasure') of the diocese, but not necessarily the finances
Chancellor	responsible for correspondence, library and education
Precentor/Chanter	responsible for ritual and music

supported by:

Archdeacon	the spiritual deputy of the bishop
Official	responsible for dealing with all offences against canon law by clergy and the lay population (in practice chiefly sexual matters, but also involving the payment of teinds, contracts etc.)

as well as varying numbers of ordinary priests/canons (normally entitled to a prebend/benefice from one of the parishes of the diocese) who were rectors of those parishes and served in rotation in the cathedral. At least by the middle of the fourteenth century, the prebends were held by the rectors of the parishes of Glassary, Kilberry, Kilmodan and Kilmartin, joined later by Kilcolmkill.

It took several years to establish 'standard' arrangements on Lismore. From a charter of 1240,[52] it is known that, before Alan's time, the chapter consisted of:

Archdeacon of Argyll: Sir Christino

Dean of Lismore: Gillemoluoc (devotee of Moluag)

Official of Argyll: Sir Daniele

Dean of Glassary: Sir Maluine

---

52 Duncan and Brown (1957), p. 219.

Dean of Lorn: Sir Johanne

Dean of Kintyre: Sir Gillecund

with five prebendary canons:

Therthelnac Makdouenald

Gillecolm MacGillemichell (devotee of St Michael)

Dunedall Makgilascop

Kennach MakGillemichell

Giliso Macmollrenni

but it is apparent from the crisis after the drowning of Bishop William in 1242 that the chapter at that time was not capable of nominating a successor without help from outside. Deans of Christianity (rural deans) had been appointed to represent the bishop in Kintyre, Glassary and Lorn, but apparently not Morvern. These deans disappeared in later years as the diocese became more organised.

Records for the thirteenth century are very scanty, but lists of witnesses in the Paisley records show that, during his time as bishop, Alan was supported by, at the least, a dean (Sir Gillemelnoc), archdeacons (Sir Cristin, Gilbert), and officials (Sir Daniel, Maurice), a dean of Glassary (Sir Maluine), and at least one simple canon (spelling of names varying). The fact that several of the members of the chapter had local names has been taken as evidence for a continuation of the Céli Dé community on Lismore, well into the fifteenth century (see Chapter 9 for the problems encountered by Bishop George Lauder). In this regard, the diocese of Argyll should not necessarily be seen as an 'outlier' in Scotland (note the persistence of Céli Dé at St Andrews, and elsewhere in the former Gaelic heartland). One other feature of the Lismore chapter is that, in contrast to the bishop, the dignitaries were generally not graduates (and so addressed as Dominus/Sir rather than Master).

The poverty of the diocese may not have justified a dean, a chancellor and a treasurer, although the role of archdeacon was filled fairly continuously throughout the life of the Catholic diocese. The fact that, in the early years of the cathedral, the Mass in Scotland seems to have been primarily *said* rather than sung would explain the absence of a precentor (see the summary of the statutes of *c*. 1240, Table 4.3). At some point and up to 1371, the right to provide the precentor was held by the Prior of Ardchattan, and the Abbot of Saddell held responsibility in 1395.[53] However, lists of this kind must be treated with caution. Although the next bishop, Laurence de Ergadia, is known to have been very active on the national and European stage, we know little about his chapter, possibly because of the scarcity of surviving lists of witnesses. Watt and Murray (2003) have concluded that Argyll did not have a full collegiate chapter until the second half of the fourteenth century. All that can be said for Bishop Alan is that he did have a body of active clerics which was capable of nominating a successor immediately on his death, under the supervision of the Bishop of Sodor, and of transmitting their decision to the Pope. Their consultations must have been facilitated by the fact that Laurence was a MacDougall family member, presumably expressly trained to succeed.

Cathedral Ritual

Although a start may have been made on building the cathedral during Bishop Alan's time (Chapter 7), the church must have been a modest affair, where services were conducted daily by members of the chapter (including prebendary canons from the parishes attending on rotation) or the Lismore vicar. The overarching structure was 'the Divine Office', the daily ritual of Matins and Lauds (at sunrise), Prime, Terce, Sext, None, Vespers (at sunset) and Compline; each involved scriptural readings, other readings such as lives of the saints, prayers and responses, possibly also psalms and hymns. The Mass books or breviaries providing the material for these offices were handwritten in Latin, commonly illuminated, and it appears that there was no standard format across the Church in Scotland before the arrival of the printing press in the early sixteenth century.

The separate celebration of Mass could be conducted communally or by a single priest. It is known that the form of the Mass known as the Salisbury or Sarum Use had been adopted in the Glasgow, Moray, Dunkeld, Ross and Aberdeen dioceses by 1250, although handwritten missals evolved to accommodate variations, for example, readings about local saints. It is likely that the Sarum Use would also have been used on Lismore. The

---

53 McGurk (1976), p. 57.

highest form of Mass for Easter and special saints' days included the formal Kyrie (Lord have mercy . . .), Gloria, Credo, Sanctus and Agnus Dei, probably spoken rather than sung at Lismore at this time, interspersed with readings, prayers and a sermon. The service culminated in Communion and the Benedictus. At other times, a simpler, more abbreviated format would be adopted. Some idea of the possible variations in the rite, and the attention to detail, can be gained from an entry in the St Andrews synodal statutes of 1225–1559:

> Once a day in every church before the *Pax Domini* is said in any Mass, whether it is for the dead or any other Mass, let it be said, with prostration and the ringing of the bell, the prayers for remission of sins: *Paternoster*, *Deus venerunt*, *Levavi*, and the collects for the king and the bishop, and for the troubles and perils of the church; and when these have been finished let there be said *Kirieleyson* thrice, *Paternoster . . . et ne nos*; afterwards these prayers, *Exurgat Deus*, *Domine salvum me fac*, *Fiat pax*; the collect *Deus in cujus*, and in that collect let there be added 'for our king and queen and their children'; the collect *Deus qui caritatis dona*; the collect *Ecclesie tue quesumus Domine preces*, etc. Now when the celebrant has come to the participation of the body and blood of our Lord, if he must celebrate a second time on the same day – which is not lawful for any priest to do unless there is an urgent necessity – let him not take the wine, or the water which after the consecration is poured out to rinse the chalice . . .[54]

In view of the general poverty of the diocese, and the discipline that would have been exerted by successive Dominican bishops, it is unlikely that costly vestments were a feature of the early years of the Argyll diocese. In the 1240s, the statutes of the Scottish Church provided a guide to correct practice:

> We further ordain that rectors and vicars of churches, as well as those who are placed in dignities as priests and clerics in holy orders, shall be becomingly clothed – as in the bearing of their

---

54   *Concilia Scotiae*.

minds so also in their bodily attire. Let them not wear red or green or striped clothes nor clothes conspicuous for too great shortness. Let vicars also and priests have outermost garments without openings; let them wear the proper tonsure so that they may not offend the sight of the beholders, whose model and example they ought to be. But if after being warned by their ordinaries they will not amend their ways, let them be suspended from office and underlie ecclesiastical discipline.[55]

As we shall see later, the Lismore canons seem to have been more gorgeously attired in later years.

---

55 *Concilia Scotiae.*

6

The MacDougall Bishops during the Wars of Independence

Laurence (1262–1299) and Andrew (1300–1342)

It can be argued that, over the lifetime of the Catholic diocese of Argyll (1200–1560), Laurence was the only incumbent to fulfil the role of bishop in terms of the vision of the Church. A member of the local ruling family, highly educated and living through the relatively peaceful years of the maturity of King Alexander III, he was able to play a full part in the life of the national Church and parliament, and to take his place among senior clergy in at least one international council. There is growing evidence that he was also responsible for the major phase of building of the cathedral on Lismore (Chapter 7).

However, this period of relative calm was not to last. Laurence died at a time of great national confusion, with Edward I, King of England, moving to take control of Scotland after deposing King John Balliol; and civil war festering in the west between the MacDougalls on the one hand, and the MacDonalds of Islay and the Campbells of Lochawe on the other. To make matters worse, 1250 had marked the end of the favourable 'Medieval Climate Anomaly', when countries surrounded by the North Atlantic had benefited from warm, dry conditions, and the start of several decades of cooler, wetter summers and severe winters, resulting in frequent famine years and outbreaks of livestock disease. This undermined the subsistence economy of the country, and severely affected the tiend income of the diocese.[56] This was only the prelude to the onset of the 'Little Ice Age' from around 1300.

---

56 Oram (2014a, b).

Laurence's successor, Andrew, found himself isolated politically within a national Church that had moved decisively against the Balliol/Comyn faction, and within a family that maintained its opposition to Robert Bruce. Going into exile in England with the defeated MacDougalls after 1308, Andrew was able to return to Scotland after Bannockburn (1314), but does not seem to have acted on the national scene after around 1318 until his death in 1342.

Laurence de Ergadia (Bishop 1262–1299)[57]

The title 'de Ergadia' (of Argyll) signifies that Laurence was a member of the family of the MacDougall Lords of Lorn. His dates indicate that he could have been a son of Ewen (died around 1268) and brother of Alexander (died around 1310), sent abroad to study in preparation for taking control of the 'family' bishopric on Lismore. At the time of his appointment to the diocese, he was a consecrated priest and a member of the Dominican Order of Preachers.

The transfer of authority from Alan to Laurence was far from smooth. Three voting delegates chosen from the diocesan chapter elected Laurence, presumably with the 'active encouragement' of Ewen MacDougall, and the dean (unnamed but possibly Sir Gillemelnoc) was sent to the papal curia for confirmation of the appointment. The records of Pope Urban IV indicate that this was withheld because of a technicality; it is tempting to speculate that this was because of the suspicion that the MacDougalls had exerted undue influence in the choice. Whatever the cause, Urban eventually issued a mandate to Gamelin, Bishop of St Andrews, and Richard de Inverkeithing, Bishop of Dunkeld, to arrange the consecration if they found Laurence fit for the post. Because of the invasion of King Håkon of Norway in 1263, this did not take place until 31 March 1264.

The MacDougalls were now at the height of their powers. Having recovered his lands and castles from Alexander III around 1260, Ewen played a leading part in the 1263 emergency, taking a major risk in refusing to provide military support to King Håkon of Norway, his feudal overlord for the Western Isles. Instead, he tried to act as an intermediary between the Norwegians and the Scots. It is a tribute to his standing with Håkon that he was released unharmed, although suffering the temporary confiscation of his property. With the withdrawal of the Norwegians

---

57 Watt (1977).

after they experienced a reverse at Largs (caused by unseasonably severe weather in October 1263), and the death of Håkon, Ewen regained his possessions, but with a greatly enhanced reputation with his Scottish overlord. From this time onwards, he acted to align the MacDougalls more clearly with the ruling class of mainland Scotland; in marrying his son Alexander to a daughter of John Comyn, Lord of Badenoch, and Eleanor Balliol, sister of the future King John, he placed his family at the centre of the power structure of Scotland.

For Laurence, it was important that the Comyns dominated not only the politics of Scotland in the second half of the thirteenth century, but also the Church. In fact, the two arenas were inextricably intertwined. At least two of the three bishops of St Andrews, Gamelin (1255–71; Chancellor of Scotland 1250s) and William Fraser (1279–97; Guardian of the Kingdom from 1290), were firmly within the ruling Comyn party, while William Comyn of Kilconqhar was Bishop of Brechin from 1275 until the 1290s. In the north-east, the Cheyne family worked closely with their relations, the Comyn Earls of Buchan; Henry le Chen (Cheyne), as Bishop of Aberdeen (1282–1328), acted as a Balliol supporter ('Auditor', the formal title of those selected to take part in the process of selecting a new king) in the 1291–2 competition with Bruce for the Scottish crown ('The Great Cause', see below). Over the period, the bishops of Dunblane, Dunkeld, Galloway, Ross and Caithness were also inclined to support the Comyn/Balliol interest. It is tempting to judge from his later activity as a patriot defying Edward I that Robert Wishart (Bishop of Glasgow 1271–1316) was not so aligned, but he was able to work within the existing political structure (as a Guardian of the Kingdom from 1290, and a judge in the Great Cause).

As Bishop of Argyll, Laurence could move comfortably within this network of relations and contacts. Possibly his greatest challenge was to act even-handedly in a diocese where his own family dominated in one part, Lorn, but their great rival, Angus MacDonald of Islay, was in possession of Kintyre and Morvern. Laurence is recorded as a witness to charters by Bishop Gamelin of St Andrews at Loch Leven in 1268 and, at the Dominican house in Ayr in 1269, he confirmed the rights of Paisley Abbey to the churches of Kilkerran, Kilcalmonel and Kilfinan in Argyll, reserving a quarter of the revenue for the support of his diocese and the vicar's stipend. In 1270, he was at Paisley Abbey, witnessing charters, and attaching his seal. This was a sign of progress, as previous bishops had, at times, lacked the authority of an official seal. Other records of his acting as a witness include Dryburgh and Holyrood (1268) and Paisley up to the year of his death. By 1274 he was sufficiently respected to be appointed by Pope Gregory X, along with the bishops of Aberdeen and Moray, to examine the qualifications of William Wischard (Wishart) for the bishopric of St Andrews, and to consecrate him if he was found to be fit. Gregory must have been satisfied with the outcome, because, in the following year, he entrusted Laurence and Robert de Prebenda, Bishop of Dunblane, to resolve a dispute between Robert Wishart, Bishop of Glasgow, and his clergy; and the three bishops of Argyll, Moray and Aberdeen were charged with consecrating Archibald Herok as Bishop of Caithness.[58]

Meanwhile, as many as six Scottish bishops had travelled to France to attend the Second Council of Lyons (7 May–16 July 1274), joining an impressive congregation of several hundred clerics and secular diplomats; the presence of Argyll, Dunblane, Glasgow, Sodor and St Andrews is confirmed by their seals attached to acts of the Council.[59] The unfortunate Matthew, Bishop of Ross, also attended but died during the proceedings. The business of the council was to negotiate a union between the Eastern and Western Churches (resolving the 'Great Schism' between Constantinople and Rome) and to organise and finance a new crusade to the Holy Land. Laurence would have been pleased that they also found time to confirm papal approval of the Franciscan and Dominican orders (the Dominican Thomas Aquinas had expected to be present but he died en route for Lyons). After minor alteration of the Nicene Creed, the proposed union of the Churches was approved, but it later met with opposition from senior members of the Eastern Church and was never achieved. Pope Gregory pressed for a crusade in 1278, and it was agreed to finance it by exacting a tithe of 'all the benefices of Christendom' for six years. There would be a full remission of the sins of those who agreed to take part in the crusade.

It was Pope Gregory's intention that the new tax should be based on a fresh valuation of the income of the Church, and he appointed Master Baiamund de Vicia, canon of Asti in northern Italy (otherwise Bagimund) to oversee the work in Scotland.[60] At a council Baiamund called at Perth

---

58 Dowden (1912); Watt (1977).
59 Watt (2000), p. 96.
60 Watt (2001).

in August 1275, the bishops opposed the idea, suggesting that, if they paid for seven rather than six years, the tithe could be based on the existing old valuation (the *Antiqua Taxatio*). Baiamund took their proposal back to Rome but it did not find favour with the Pope, who wanted a realistic account of the finances of the Church across Europe. The resulting valuation for Scotland, known as Bagimund's Roll, which underlined the poverty of the Argyll diocese, with its poor history of endowment, became the basis for future taxation. Although enthusiasm for Gregory's crusade faded with his death in 1276, the tax collecting continued and the proceeds were spent in Italy.

Following the papal decision to govern the Church in Scotland directly without the intervention of an archbishop, the bishops had been empowered from 1225 to call provincial councils without the need to consult higher authority.[61] It appears that these councils became a regular feature of the life of the Church in Scotland, possibly annual events, but there are few records of their proceedings or lists of representatives. Laurence did not achieve the distinction of some colleagues (principally the bishops of St Andrews and Glasgow), who became royal councillors or Guardians of the Kingdom, but in his later years he must have been one of the most experienced members of the provincial council; by 1290, his service of 26 years, including a great deal of work done directly for Rome, was exceeded only by Archibald of Moray and Henry of Galloway (each 37 years).

There are traces of Laurence's activity after 1280. In 1281, he and Robert, Bishop of Dunblane, were authorised to legitimise the marriage of Mary MacDougall, daughter of Ewen, Lord of Lorn (sister of Alexander, possibly even of Laurence himself) to Hugh de Abernethy. This was necessary to secure the Abernethy inheritance for their son Alexander but it was very late in the day, as both parties were around 50 years of age. Hugh was destined to die in prison in 1293, following the murder of the Earl of Fife. Laurence confirmed the possession of Kilfinan Church by Paisley Abbey in 1269[62] and, after 1286, Thomas de Dundee, the Bologna-trained subdean of Glasgow, audited the charters of the abbey on his behalf. In 1294, he was witness to a charter regranting Kilkerran to Paisley by Alexander, Lord of Islay, the heir of Angus MacDonald, which appears to have been signed at the Cluniac Abbey of Crossraguel in Ayrshire, in

61 Watt (2000).
62 *Origines*, p. 50.

the heart of Bruce country;[63] the cosignatories included the Earl of Carrick (Robert Bruce, the future King Robert I). Here, in a period of great peril for the kingdom, described in the following sections, Laurence was dealing with two of the MacDougalls' greatest rivals.

Laurence's last recorded commission from the Pope was to act as intermediary between the Abbot of Iona and the Bishop of Sodor in 1289. By 1299, nearing death, he required a proctor, Master Nicholas, rector of the parish of St Modan, to represent him at Glasgow in a court case over the wrongful possession of Kilkerran Church (see p. 50). However, possibly the most important act in his entire career was his involvement with the Treaties of Salisbury and Birgham (1289/90), which were to have such an impact on the future of the kingdom and its Church (see below), as well as on the life of his successor as Bishop of Argyll.

The question arises whether, with so much travelling and so many duties for the national Church, the king and the Pope, Laurence had much time to devote to his own diocese, beyond defending its property. Charter entries (Chapter 7), which refer to the 'fabrick of the cathedral church of Argyle' in 1314, and *ecclesiam nostrum cathedralem* in 1327, indicate that there was a building which could be called a cathedral on Lismore at that time. Bearing in mind that Bishop Andrew was absent in exile between 1309 and 1315 (see p. 79) and that Scotland had been sporadically at war from the early 1290s, including conflicts between rival families in the west, the building work probably took place during Laurence's time as bishop. As we shall see in Chapter 7, this conclusion is supported by evidence of building in stone elsewhere on Lismore, radiocarbon-dating of mortar and a national enthusiasm for erecting great churches across Scotland in the years of peace under the mature King Alexander III. Clearly, Laurence was an active bishop both at home and abroad.

Treaties of Salisbury and Birgham 1289/90: Their Consequences for the Kingdom and its Church

During the reigns of Alexander II and Alexander III, a unified kingdom of Scotland, able and willing to hold its own against much stronger neighbours, had started to develop out of its disparate components. Even some of the dominant families, originally Anglo-Norman and still holding

63   *Registrum Monasterii de Passalet*, p. 128.

lands in England, were becoming more closely identified with Scotland; and the Church, although dominated by monastic orders from continental Europe, was united against the ambitions of successive archbishops of York. Suddenly, on the night of 18 March 1286, this achievement was undermined by the accidental death of Alexander III, aged 44, in the prime of life, but with no surviving children. His infant granddaughter Margaret, the 'Maid of Norway' was the sole heir to the throne: young, female, far from robust and living abroad. In the event of the failure of Alexander's line, members of the Balliol and Bruce families had the strongest claim, based on their descent from David I, and the Balliols had strong connections by marriage with the dominant Comyns.

An emergency parliament at Scone appointed six Guardians of the Kingdom. Three (Alexander Comyn, Earl of Buchan; John Comyn, Lord of Badenoch; and William Fraser, Bishop of St Andrews) represented the Comyn/Balliol interest, and two (James, the Steward of Scotland; and Robert Wishart, Bishop of Glasgow) favoured the Bruces. The sixth was Duncan, Earl of Fife, the premier earl of Scotland, whose alignment is not clear. In spite of the involvement of Stewart and Wishart at the heart of government, the Bruces, led by Robert, 5th Lord of Annandale (the 'Competitor') and his son Robert, Earl of Carrick (respectively grandfather and father of the future king, Robert I), raised a rebellion in the south-west, taking control of royal castles. Faced with the challenge of securing the succession and governing the country in the interregnum, the Guardians sought the support of their powerful neighbour, Edward I of England, who was, at that time, occupied in trying to secure his possessions in Gascony.

Diplomatic negotiations with Norway and England proceeded slowly but, by November 1289, the Treaty of Salisbury was agreed between envoys of the three counties. Margaret was confirmed as the successor; she was to travel from Norway during 1290, when she would be six years of age; and the Guardians were to ensure stability within Scotland (and, if they failed, she would stay in England). However, an important concession was made to Edward: that he had the right to interfere in Scotland's affairs if the need arose. Although a marriage between Margaret and Edward's son, also Edward, was not specifically included in the treaty, Edward proceeded to arrange papal approval of the match. Meanwhile, there had been important developments in Scotland with the death of two Guardians: Alexander Comyn, the most experienced politician in the kingdom, and the Earl of Fife, who was ominously murdered by agents of Hugh de

Abernethy (although husband of Mary MacDougall, and clearly in the Comyn/Balliol party). As a result, the treaty was signed for Scotland by the bishops of St Andrews and Glasgow, John Comyn and Robert Bruce, 5th Lord of Annandale.

This agreement by the envoys was confirmed by the Community of the Realm of Scotland (the bishops, earls, abbots and barons) at a parliament at Birgham in Berwickshire in March 1290. Both Bishop Laurence and Alexander de Ergadia were present to sign the letter of agreement sent to Edward. The subsequent Treaty of Brigham, concluded in July, repeated the terms of the treaty, affirming the independence and integrity of Scotland and its 'rights, laws, liberties and customs', but also included the agreement that Margaret should marry Edward (the future Edward II). This treaty, in turn, was ratified at Northampton in August. How the independence of Scotland would have been maintained by a King of England married to a Queen of Scotland was never tested, because Margaret died in September on her way to Scotland.

Even before her death, Edward had already acted to exploit his licence to interfere in the affairs of Scotland, appointing Anthony Bek, Bishop of Durham, as his lieutenant in Scotland and instructing the Guardians to defer to him. This was an important warning to the Church in Scotland, raising the spectre of the renewal of the claim of York to exercise authority over the Scottish bishops, and undoubtedly contributing to the developing nationalism of the Church, which played a pivotal part in the eventual triumph of Robert Bruce.

The consequences of the Treaty of Birgham, played out during the remainder of Laurence's life up to his death in 1299, are well known. Edward took control of Scotland in 1291, occupying its castles, summoning the ruling class and clergy to do homage (although there is no evidence that Laurence did so in person), and establishing the legal process (the 'Great Cause') which eventually decided on John Balliol as the rightful successor rather than Robert Bruce the 'Competitor'. Edward's subsequent domination of King John, including the annulment of the Treaty of Birgham, led to the resumption of power by the Comyns and a comprehensive defeat in 1296 at the hands of the English army, followed by a royal progress by Edward through the east of Scotland as far north as Elgin. King John was deposed and most of the leading men of the kingdom, captured at Dunbar, were taken off into captivity in England. William Wallace and Andrew Moray emerged to lead the opposition to Edward, winning a stunning victory at Stirling Bridge in 1297, but Wallace's career as Guardian of the Kingdom came to an end after defeat at Falkirk in 1298. By 1299, the year of Laurence's death, the fortunes of Scotland were at a very low ebb.

However, there were developments within the Church that had implications for the future, reducing the Comyn/Balliol grip on the Church, creating a group of patriots that coalesced around Bruce, and eventually leading to the isolation of the bishops of Argyll. Matthew Crambeth (d. 1305), a close colleague of Robert Wishart, became Bishop of Dunkeld in 1288, and from 1295 his skills as a diplomat were used to great effect as ambassador to the French king. In 1294, Master Thomas Dalton of Kircudbright (d. *c*. 1324/1326), a supporter of the Bruce family, was appointed to the vacant bishopric of Galloway, in spite of opposition from King John. Even more important, with the death of William Fraser during the Guardianship of Wallace, Master William Lamberton (d. 1328), chancellor of Glasgow Cathedral, was elected Bishop of St Andrews and consecrated by the Pope in Rome in 1298. Lamberton was to prove a courageous patriot, later enthroning Bruce as king in 1306 and undergoing many hardships, including imprisonment in irons in England and later excommunication. Lamberton's ally in securing his appointment, Master Nicholas Balmyle (d. *c*. 1319/1320), the official of St Andrews, acted as Chancellor of Scotland from 1301, becoming Bishop of Dunblane in 1307. Around the same time, the Church enjoyed the benefit of the improbably named Baldred Bisset (1260–1311), rector of Kinghorn, one of the outstanding canon lawyers of the age after lengthy study at the University of Bologna.[64] A master of propaganda, Bisset ensured that Scotland's cause was effectively presented at Rome. It should not be forgotten that many of these roles could not have been fulfilled without the skill of Scottish shipmasters, who shuttled clergy safely to and from continental Europe across the North Sea.

Events in the West (1286–1299)

If the events across Scotland were not sufficiently confusing, the continuing rivalry between the two MacSorley families (the MacDougalls and the MacDonalds) for dominance in the west, and the rise of the Campbells of

---

64 Goldstein (2004); Goldstein (1991).

Lochawe, make it almost impossible to disentangle their various motives and actions. At times, as shown by the career of Alexander MacDonald, this rivalry cut across the Balliol/Bruce divide. The resulting insecurity in Argyll would have made it difficult, at times, for the ageing Bishop Laurence to fulfil his duties, but his action in signing a charter of Alexander MacDonald of Islay in 1294 indicates that his office required him to act in a non-partisan way.

In 1286, Alexander MacDougall was securely in the Balliol party, married to a daughter of John Comyn, Lord of Badenoch and Lochaber. He was in a very powerful position, possessing Ardnamurchan, Morvern, Duror, Glencoe, Mull, Tiree and Lorn, including Benderloch, Appin and Lismore. Alexander's rival in the west, Angus Mòr MacDonald of Islay and Kintyre, had played an equivocal part in the invasion of 1263, just managing to retain his lands after the withdrawal of Håkon. His natural alignment remained in the west and with Ireland, and he married a member of the rising Campbell family. The relationship between the MacDougalls and the MacDonalds was complicated by the surprising marriage of Alexander, elder son of Angus, to Juliana, daughter of Alexander MacDougall.

The rivalry was played out on the national scene. In 1286, Angus Mòr and his son Alexander MacDonald joined a group of landowners from Ireland and south-west Scotland to sign the Turnberry Band, an agreement of mutual aid signalling his membership of the Bruce party. Angus took no part in the proceedings surrounding the Treaty of Brigham and died around 1292. The Records of the Parliament of Scotland mention that 'Letters of Alexander of Argyll and Alexander and Donald of the Isles, on 29 December 1291 [to Edward I] promised to keep the peace between them in their lands until the next parlement at Berwick in September 1292'.[65]

In appreciation of his support as an auditor in the 'Great Cause', in 1293 King John Balliol appointed Alexander MacDougall as the first Sheriff of Argyll, based at his castle of Dunstaffnage, with authority to guard the peace from Ardnamurchan to Islay. With James the Steward assuming the sheriffdom of Kintyre, there was no official role for the MacDonalds. At King John's Scone parliament in February 1293, MacDougall was commanded to summon Angus, Lord of Islay (possibly already deceased), and others in Argyll, to do homage to the new king (John),[66]

65   RPS, A1292/6/1.
66   RPS, A1293/2/3.

but the MacDonalds, true to their earlier pattern of behaviour, would not attend parliament, instead appealing directly to Edward I against the MacDougalls. The ensuing conflict in the area led to the death of Sir Colin Campbell, the kinsman of Angus Mòr, at a confrontation between Campbell and MacDougall forces at the 'String of Lorn' (between Scammadale and Loch Avich) in 1294; then a dispute between the MacDougalls and the MacDonalds over Juliana's marriage portion on Lismore resulted in King John being summoned to court in England.

Everything changed when John Balliol was deposed and Edward took direct control of Scotland. Alexander MacDougall, staying faithful to his Comyn kinsmen, was captured at the Battle of Dunbar in 1296 and imprisoned for several months at Berwick. The Earl of Menteith was instructed to take the castles and property of Alexander and his son John Baccach. Alexander MacDonald, now Lord of Islay, sought favour with the English king and was rewarded with the return of Kintyre, which had been confiscated on the orders of Balliol. Under military pressure from Alexander MacDonald and his allies, John Baccach MacDougall submitted to Edward, and remained his supporter for the remainder of the War of Independence. This did not stop his brother, Duncan, from an abortive rising against the MacDonalds in 1297; it is possible that Duncan's father (Alexander MacDougall) was released from prison by Edward at this point to control events. In the continuing fighting between the rival dynasties, Alexander MacDonald was killed around 1299, to be succeeded by his younger brother Angus Og, who became a lifelong supporter of the Bruce faction.

At the time of Bishop Laurence's death in 1299, therefore, Scotland was defeated but not fully occupied, the MacDougalls had submitted to Edward and were at liberty, but the MacDonald/Campbell alliance in support of Bruce would, in the future, be in the ascendancy.

Andrew de Ergadia (Bishop 1300–1342)

After only three out of twelve bishops of the Church in Scotland had done homage to Edward I in 1296, he decreed that only English clerics could, in future, be appointed to benefices in Scotland. As we have seen with the consecration of Bishop Lamberton of St Andrews in 1298, the Church showed great skill in subverting Edward's will. Much of the credit must be given to Boniface VIII (Pope 1294–1303), whose 1299 bull declared that Scotland was under his protection, and that Edward's occupation of the kingdom was illegal. His support may well have arisen out of a personal relationship with Baldred Bisset, as they had both studied law at Bologna. It is known that Bisset was in Rome between 1299 and 1301 as part of the delegation sent by the Guardians to secure the Pope's support for the independence of Scotland. With the death of Boniface in 1303 and the transfer of the curia to Avignon, Scotland lost an important ally; later popes were to prove much less helpful.

The diocese of Argyll fell vacant in 1299, at a time when the MacDougalls had submitted to the English crown. Edward proposed an Englishman, Reginald de Chen, as candidate for bishop, but the dean and chapter on Lismore (probably with the support of Alexander MacDougall) had the confidence to defy him, and nominated Andrew de Ergadia, a second Dominican priest and member of the MacDougall family. With the permission of the head of his order, Andrew travelled to Rome for confirmation and consecration by Boniface late in 1300.

After his return, in 1304, we find Andrew as bishop receiving a charter at the hands of 'Eugenii de Ergadia', Lord of Lorn, Benderloch and Lismore confirming and extending the landholding of the diocese in the south-west of Lismore. This took place at the MacDougall castle of Achychendone (Achinduin) in 1304. In view of the fact that Alexander MacDougall was Lord of Lorn at the time, Eugenii is likely to be an error of transcription, with the name of Ewen, the original donor to Bishop William, being carried over from 1240.[67] The five and a half pennylands to be added to the mensal lands already devoted to the support of the cathedral and its clergy were Pennyng-Scanghache, Tyrfeirlake, Achychnahunsene and Geyle. None of these townships is easily identifiable today (although the second could be Tirfuir, near the cathedral site) but it is known from a post-Reformation charter from Andrew, Bishop of Argyll[68] that the cathedral lands then extended over Bernera, Achinduin, Frackersaig and Craignich, occupying as much as a fifth of the island.

The unstable political equilibrium since 1299/1300, under the domination of Edward I, was overturned decisively by the murder of John Comyn of Badenoch by Robert Bruce in the church of the Greyfriars in

---

67 Turner (1998), p. 649.
68 Charter of 1629 to William Stirling of Auchyle. Ecclesiastical Papers PFV 15, part 1. Argyll Archives, Inveraray.

Dumfries, and the subsequent enthronement of Bruce as King of Scots by Isobel of Fife and Bishop Lamberton in Scone just over a month later, on 27 March 1306. The MacDougalls, kinsmen of the Comyns, remained loyal to successive kings of England, whereas the MacDonalds aligned themselves with Bruce during his flight after the disastrous Battle of Methven, and were staunch supporters up to and beyond Bannockburn. It had looked at first as if the MacDougalls had made the right decision. During Bruce's retreat from Methven in June 1306 his depleted forces collided with the MacDougalls led by John Baccach at Dalrigh near Tyndrum. Bruce narrowly avoided annihilation and capture, losing his famous charm stone, and became a fugitive in the west, where he survived only because of the support of MacDonald and Campbell allies. John Baccach moved a large body of his men to the south-west of Scotland to help counter the uprising in 1307 (see Chapter 4) but, by adopting guerrilla tactics, Bruce began to turn the tide, driving his enemies and the English garrisons from much of southern and eastern Scotland. A crucial factor in his success was the death of Edward I in 1307. By 1308/9 Bruce was ready to challenge his MacDougall enemies, marching into Argyll and defeating their forces by bold tactics at the Pass of Brander. Their major strongholds, including Dunstaffnage, fell within the following months with the help of MacDonald allies. John Baccach, an ailing spectator at the defeat at Brander, remained a resolute enemy of Bruce, even though his father, Alexander, is known to have attended the parliament presided over by King Robert at St Andrews in 1309. Soon after, both men fled to England and the protection of Edward II. Alexander MacDougall died in 1310, but John was given command of the English fleet on the western seaboard based in Ireland, capturing Man from the Scots. He died in Kent in 1316 on a pilgrimage to Canterbury.

These events placed Bishop Andrew in a difficult position. The last decade had brought about major changes in the Church in Scotland, which found itself not only in opposition to the English Church and king, but also out of favour with the papal curia, now in Avignon. The conflict between Scotland and England was seen as a distraction from more important political problems in Europe, and papal ambitions for a crusade against the Turks, who were threatening Constantinople. Several of the senior clergy in Scotland were in serious trouble. Robert Wishart of Glasgow had been released from imprisonment in England in 1308 to travel to the papal curia to defend himself against a range of charges; these included the claim that he had absolved Bruce of the sin of murdering John Comyn, even though Bruce had been excommunicated by Clement V. Wishart was not able to return to Scotland until after Bannockburn, a blind and worn-out old man. William Lamberton of St Andrews had been released from prison in England, after submitting to Edward and paying a substantial fine, on condition that he remained in the diocese of Durham; by 1310, he was working his way back into the life of his diocese and, in 1312, he returned to live in Scotland. David of Moravia, Bishop of Moray, was in exile in Norway, accused of abetting Bruce in the Comyn murder.

Nicholas de Balmyle (Bishop of Dunblane), Chancellor of Scotland in 1301, William Sinclair (Bishop of Dunkeld), David de Moravia (Bishop of Moray) and William Lamberton (Bishop of St Andrews) were trusted allies of the new king, and the bishops of Ross, Brechin, Aberdeen, Caithness and Sodor had submitted to Bruce by 1310. Only Thomas de Dalton, Bishop of Galloway and originally a chaplain to the Bruce family, was of doubtful loyalty, owing to the fact that he was under the authority of the Archbishop of York. Probably under the leadership of Abbot Bernard of Arbroath (who is credited with drafting the later Declaration of Arbroath), around the time of the 1309 parliament at St Andrews, the bishops, abbots, priors and clergy issued a 'manifesto' in support of King Robert's right to the throne.

Belonging to a family that was opposed to Bruce, Andrew, Bishop of Argyll, was out of step with his peers in the Church, and he chose to abandon his flock and follow his family rather than his colleagues. Departing from Scotland with Alexander and John MacDougall, he came under the protection of Edward II by April 1310, receiving financial support from the king up to 1314.[69] There is documentary evidence that he was active as a senior clergyman at Durham and York during his exile. Protected from any form of punishment for his treasonable conduct by his clerical rank and the authority conferred by his original consecration by the Pope, he was able to return to Scotland soon after Bannockburn to attend the Cambuskenneth parliament on 6 November 1314.

Meanwhile the Lordship of Lorn was divided up by Bruce among his supporters, with Sir Arthur Campbell installed in the former MacDougall stronghold of Dunstaffnage. How this affected the MacDougall Bishop

---

69   100 shillings, and 'a prest of 10 marks' three months before Bannockburn: Carmichael (1948).

of Argyll is not known, although it can be argued that the decline of the bishopric can be traced back to the defeat at the Pass of Brander and the loss of a powerful sponsor. In the next two or three years after his return, Andrew's name appears on charters and he attended parliaments in Dundee and Ayr. His activity in support of his fellow Blackfriars reveals one role of the Church in punishing legal defaulters. He witnessed the terms of the 1314 grant by Gilaspec Maclouchlan in Argyll, from the income of his lands in Strathlachlan, to the Dominican house in Glasgow, which dictated that Maclouchlan was 'bound in the event of his failure in payment to give one mark sterling to the fabrick of the cathedral church of Argyle'. After 1318 until his death in 1342, the only trace of Andrew's continued existence is a renewal of the grant of the three churches of Kilkerran, Kilcolmanell and Kilfinan to Paisley, made at Lismore in 1327.[70]

Bishop Andrew appears to have lived out his later years quietly at home, out of trouble, while momentous events unfolded elsewhere in Scotland. By 1319, continued conflict between Scotland and England had caused Pope John XXII to extend the excommunication of Bruce (still in force since 1306) effectively to cover all Scots, and it was only after extensive diplomacy, centred around the Declaration of Arbroath (1320), that relations began to improve. By 1324 the Pope had lifted the excommunication and recognised Bruce as the rightful ruler of the kingdom, which led eventually to the recognition of the independence of Scotland by Edward III in the Treaty of Northampton in 1328. Although this is seen as Bruce's greatest achievement, his death in 1329 plunged Scotland into a new period of turbulence during the minority of his son, David II, including the destructive invasion of Edward Balliol in 1332/3. By the time of Andrew's death in 1342, the 18-year-old king was back from his protective exile in France and taking up the reins of government.

70 *Origines*, p. 14.

The Cathedral of Argyll

Understanding the Cathedral of Lismore, and when it was built, is like tracing the plot in a detective novel. The surviving structure, cut down from the medieval choir, has undergone at least two major refits over the last 250 years, resulting in the present parish church. Most of the clues to the original cathedral have come from knowledge of what the builders found and did to the structure in the second half of the eighteenth century, and around 1896; and the results of the archaeological excavations carried out in the 1950s, and since 2016. Because of its relative simplicity, it has proved possible to develop a reasonable reconstruction of the original building from these clues. Uncovering when and how the Cathedral of Argyll was built is more difficult, in the almost complete absence of documentary evidence from the time of the MacDougall ownership of Lismore as Lords of Lorn. We are forced to rely on knowledge of comparable activities in other places, including building in stone by the MacDougalls elsewhere in the area; the architecture and archaeology of the remains, including radiocarbon-dating of mortar; fragments of documentary evidence; elements of oral history; and some informed speculation.

Lismore Parish Church Today

The parish church building was created out of the choir of the medieval cathedral, standing ruined and apparently roofless around 1750; its appearance today (see cover illustration) is a result of the alterations to the fabric made from that time and during a major refurbishment around 1896. The nave, to the west, had been abandoned by the Reformation, and served as a quarry for local building work.

The rectangular plan of the choir (internal dimensions 15.6m × 7.2m) is retained in the modern building but, according to the Rev. Donald McNicol (minister of the parish from 1766),[71] its walls were reduced in height by 2–3 metres at the time of reroofing; and, in 1896, the floor level was set at 5.3m below the wall head.[72] From this information, it has been estimated that the original wall height of the cathedral choir was 8–9m. Today, with harling on the outside, and plaster and a low wooden dado covering most of the interior walls, there is limited access to the original stonework. None of the window openings is original; they date from either the eighteenth or late nineteenth century.

Refurbished as a reformed church (Plate 6a–c), the focus of the building was moved from the altar at the east end of the choir to the minister's pulpit placed against the south wall. The congregation sat in pews facing the pulpit from three sides, and wooden galleries were attached to the west, north and east walls, reached by an external stair at the east end, and an internal stair at the west. A central communion table, stretching for most of the length of the building from east to west, was a prominent feature, and there appears to have been a 'portable pulpit' or 'preaching ark' which could have been used for outdoor services, stored in the south-west corner. Entrance by the congregation to the main body of the church was through the archway in the west gable, and the minister reached his pulpit by the round-headed doorway at the centre of the south wall (which would originally have been used by officiating clergy to gain access to the choir in pre-Reformation times).[73]

The 1896 remodelling was even more drastic, totally reversing the medieval alignment (Plate 6b and c). A door for the congregation was opened at the east end, the south doorway was closed up, and the minister now enters from a vestry attached to the west gable. The (much smaller) communion table and the pulpit were moved to the west, faced by ranks

---

71 *First Statistical Account of Scotland* (1791), Vol. 1 (Lismore Parish).
72 Although Brown and Duncan (1957) estimated that the 1896 floor level was at least 0.5m above the original floor level, preliminary investigation in 2023 indicated that the gap below the present level and the underlying *solum* is less than 10cm, suggesting that there may have been infilling in 1896.
73 Details from the Erskine Beveridge photographic images: Canmore 23100 (Plate 6 in this book).

Plate 1. Drone image of Lismore Parish Church and its surrounds. (Photograph: Rab Woods)

Plate 2. Excavation of the monastic site, May 2022. (a) Trench revealing the sites of the roundhouse and workshop in relation to the parish church in the background. (b) The entrance to the roundhouse.

Plate 3. Excavation of the cathedral nave, showing the relationship with the parish church (the cathedral choir). (a) Cutting the first sods, August 2016. (b) Recording the west tower, July 2017.

(c)

(d)

Plate 4. Medieval details of the parish church / cathedral choir.
(a) Sedilia.
(b) Piscina.
(c) Closed-up doorway in the north wall, leading originally to the sacristy chapel.
(d) Detail of the north wall doorway, showing a bishop's head.

Plate 5. Charter (1256) from the Bishop of Durham to Alan, Bishop of Argyll, relaxing 40 days of penance 'to those visiting the feretory [portable shrine] of St Cuthbert or the Galilee [chapel at Durham Cathedral], for devotion or prayer, and to those leaving gifts to it'.

(Reproduced by permission of Durham University Library and Collections)

Plate 6. Lismore Parish Church, photographed by Erskine Beveridge in 1882, before the major remodelling of 1896. (a) The exterior from the south, showing the entrance from the west. (b) The interior from the west, showing the east and north galleries, and the communion table. (c) The interior from the east, showing the pulpit, west gallery and the 'portable pulpit', stored in the south-west corner. (Canmore AG1704, 1705 and 1708. Reproduced with the permission of Historic Environment Scotland)

Plate 7. Bishop Lauder arrives in state at his cathedral on 29 August 1452, accompanied by Master Hercules Scymgeour, Parson of Glassary, with the aim of reinstating Scrymgeour as a dignitary of the cathedral (see Chapter 9). Scene from a performance of the play *Banished*, written by Jennifer Baker and performed outside the church on 7 August 2015.
(Reproduced with the permission of Sebastian Tombs (Lauder) and Sarah Campbell (Skrymgeour); photograph: Pauline Dowling)

Plate 8. Seal of George Lauder, Bishop of Argyll, attached to a letter to the Vatican, 5 April 1454, in connection with the proposed marriage of Sir Colin Campbell of Glenorchy, and Jonet Stewart, daughter of John Stewart, Lord of Lorne, who were within the forbidden degrees of consanguinity.
(National Records of Scotland GDS 112/1/8)

of pews separated by a central aisle. The three galleries were replaced by a single gallery on the east wall accessed by an internal stair. At the site of the external stairway, now removed, a porch was erected to protect the east doorway. The bell lantern was moved from the west to the east gable, above the new entrance (compare Plate 6a with the cover illustration).

External Features

In spite of these very extensive works, and the damage to many churches caused at the Reformation, several medieval details have survived. On the outside, there are four buttresses on the south wall, two on the east, and one at the corner of the east and north walls. As these are heavily harled (and have evidently been cut down when the wall height was lowered), few details of the stonework are visible, although some spalling of the harling on the south side reveals that they are built of buff-coloured sandstone. The external moulding surrounding the round-headed doorway in the south wall is original, featuring two carved heads, now very worn and covered with a thick coat of harling. On the outside of the north wall, near the corner buttress, there is a rectangular recess, which has been identified as an aumbry (recess for storing chalices and communion wafers or bread). This is evidence for the existence of an attached sacristy chapel (for the storage of valuable silverware, vestments service books, etc.) to the north, not now visible but originally accessed from the choir.

Internal Features

Within the church, the moulding of the round-headed doorway in the centre of the south wall is relatively undamaged, featuring a pair of stylised heads. Towards the east end are three round-headed sedilia (seats for clergy officiating at Mass) and a small piscina (basin for washing communion vessels, with a drain hole to the outside). The actual seats of the sedilia are invisible below the modern floor (as a result of the latest remodelling). The north wall features a former doorway with a pointed arch, flanked by two carved heads; these appear to represent a bishop wearing a mitre (left) and a tonsured clergyman (right). Although this doorway (to the sacristy chapel) is closed up, and invisible from the outside, cracks in the harling reveal its position. The two doorways, sedilia and piscina are carved from a buff-coloured stone (from one or other of the nearest sources of suitable

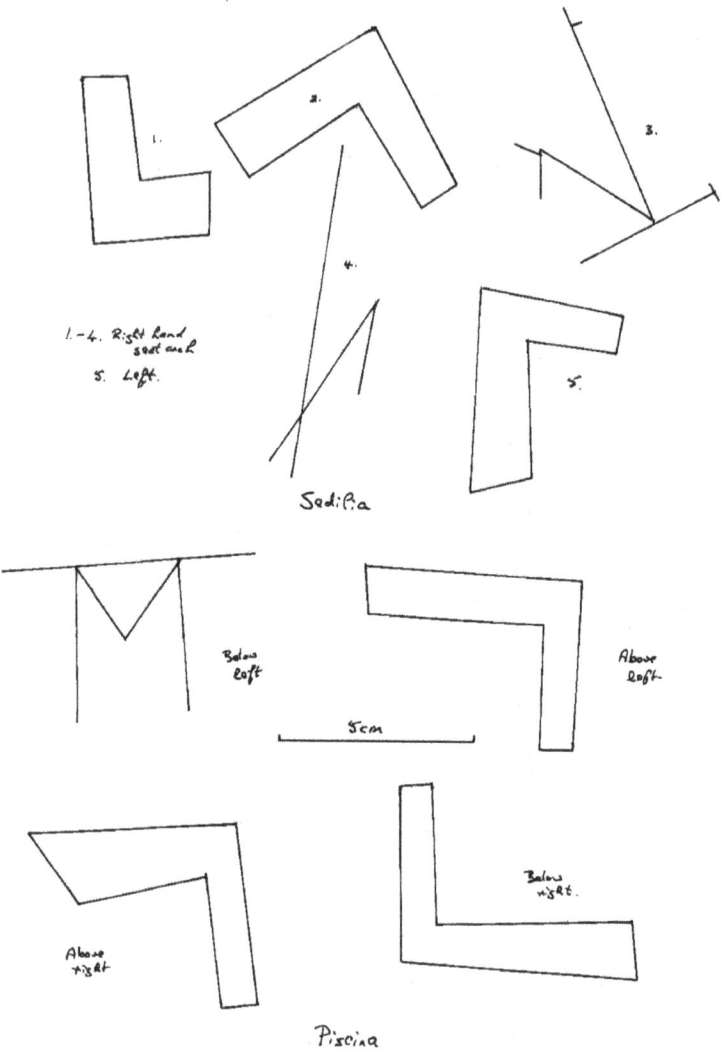

Fig. 7.1 Tracings of the mason's marks on the sedilia and piscina.

stone on Morvern or Mull). Together they display at least 19 mason's marks (Fig. 7.1). Traces of colour show that these features were originally brightly painted. The west wall is pierced by a semicircular (1m) sandstone arch supported on dressed sandstone verticals (2m). Within this arch is a plain semicircular arch (height 2.5m) of green sandstone (apparently from quarries near the mouth of Loch Feochan on the mainland, to the south of Oban), which was revealed by removing plaster in 1956/7. The fact that the verticals do not meet the arch accurately, and the outline of the arch itself is irregular, shows that this is not the work of the original master mason(s). See Plate 4.

Archaeological Evidence

A thorough excavation of the accessible area immediately to the west of the church in 1950–3, and the community-based excavations since 2016 led by Dr Clare Ellis,[74] have revealed the extent of the medieval nave (externally 24m × 9.3–9.4m). Allowing for the thickness of the walls (1–1.2m), this was exactly the same breadth as the choir, and there was no evidence of transepts. The nave foundations were of massive slate and, apart from a drip-course of dressed sandstone at the base, the walls were of rough construction: mixed limestone and whinstone of varying sizes and shapes, with a core of rubble stone, bonded with a sand and seashell mortar (see Chapter 11). Evidence from the footings of the south door indicates that, as for the choir, the detailing around the doorway and windows would have been carved from sandstone. There were buttresses to the north and south near the west end of each wall, and at least one doorway on the south wall of the nave was found, around 1m wide, at 4m from the west end.

The debris within the ruined nave revealed that the building had been roofed with thick slate, but there was no indication of how the nave was floored (and no record for the choir when its floor was raised). However, taking the threshold of the nave south door as a reference level, Brown and Duncan (1957) were able to establish that, in contrast to normal practice, where there are steps up to the altar, the floor of the choir of Lismore Cathedral was around a metre *below* the nave. With a floor even higher than the nave, a small square tower (internal walls 1.2m thick, 2.7m × 2.7m) was attached to the west gable of the nave, slightly to the south of the centre point. Without any evidence of a doorway, it was concluded that its entrance was by a stair within the cathedral. Examination of the masonry where the tower meets the cathedral west wall confirmed that it was a later

---

74   Brown and Duncan (1957); Ellis (2016, 2017).

addition to the building. Reports of the 1950s excavation described the nave as likely to be 'plain and unadorned', but the more recent digs have uncovered a range of carved stones (from the nave area and the nearby spoil heap), showing that the decoration of the building was more elaborate than was at first thought. Some idea of the appearance of the features of the building can be gained from the door and window surrounds in other buildings built by the MacDougalls in the thirteenth century, particularly the chapel at Dunstaffnage.

Several features of the north wall of the choir (doorway, lack of windows, presence of an aumbry) indicate that there must have been an additional chapel to the north of the choir. The existence of such a structure was not fully established in the 1950s excavation, but further work in 1970 found the footing of the west wall of a chapel near the position of the doorway and confirmed that the buttress at the north-east corner had been part of a structure 6.3m in length. Because of the wall surrounding the church, it was not possible to determine the breadth of the chapel.

The 2017/18 dig did expose some stone-built structures within the nave area, which were probably late additions after the nave fell into ruins – possibly even enclosures for stock. An important development was the analysis of charcoal fragments in the original mortar by Dr Mark Thacker (see below).

Fig. 7.2 Reconstruction of the Cathedral of Argyll by Edward Odling. Archaeological investigations have revealed the existence of an additional doorway on the facing (south) wall of the nave. (Reproduced with the permission of Noelle Odling)

Reconstruction of the Medieval Cathedral

There is no way of estimating the original height of the nave but, arguing from similar plain medieval cathedrals in Ireland, Brown and Duncan (1957) proposed that the nave and choir would have been of the same height (Fig. 7.2). They presented an image of the main body of the cathedral as a dark tunnel, with few windows, of uniform height, possibly with a wooden screen to separate choir from nave. The scarcity of carved stones suggested to them that the nave, where the congregation would have stood to receive Mass, was plain and unadorned – in contrast to the choir, whose carved details show traces of earlier painting in red and black. However, this argument is not persuasive in view of the amount of carved stone found in 2017/18, and because it is known that most of the sandstone from the ruined nave was salvaged to build the manse in the 1750s. Large sandstone paving stones in the manse garden are probably from the floor of the nave.

The completed cathedral had a chapel to the north of the choir accessed only through the choir, which would have served as a sacristy (for storing the valuables of the cathedral) and chapter house (where the clergy held meetings). Overall, this was a fairly simple and utilitarian building, to which the later addition of a tower would have added a little distinction. We know nothing about any associated buildings, including the accommodation for the clergy.

The Building of the Cathedral

In the absence of documentary evidence of the actual building work, the following are the only firm pieces of evidence from contemporary records. In 1314, Gilaspec Maclouchlan granted income of his lands in Strathlachlan to the Dominican house in Glasgow, being 'bound in the event of his failure in payment to give one mark sterling to the fabrick of the cathedral church of Argyle'.[75] The first mention of a cathedral at Lismore in the Paisley register of charters is 1327, when the rights to the income from the Kintyre church of Kilkerran were confirmed by Bishop Andrew.[76] In view of the Wars of Independence in the early years of the

---

75 *Origines*, p. 160.
76 *Origines*, p. 14.

fourteenth century and the exile of the bishop along with the MacDougalls (who were opposed to Bruce) from 1309 (Chapter 6), these records indicate that a substantial new building had been erected before the end of the thirteenth century. The fact that King Alexander II had planned to move the bishop to the mainland before his death (Chapter 3) may set a date for the start of building as not before 1249.

The few distinctive features of the building that survive are of little use in dating. The transition from Romanesque (featuring round-headed arches) to Gothic (pointed, as in the north wall doorway) styles of architecture was under way around the end of the twelfth century in Scotland, at the time of the creation of the diocese. Most of the carving work in the choir was already old-fashioned when completed, but the mason's marks may have some value in dating (Fig. 7.1). The stylised letter M on a line, an unusual mark, found on both doors, the sedilia and a stone fragment that is assumed to come from the nave, also occurs on a carved stone from Achinduin Castle, which is known from a charter to have been occupied by 1304,[77] and was probably completed several decades earlier, as part of the chain of coastal stone castles erected by the ruling MacDougalls. It seems that the same master mason or team of masons worked on both the cathedral and Achinduin Castle. The choir also has mason's marks (downward-pointing arrow and set square or boomerang), which are common to Ardchattan Priory, founded in 1230, supporting the idea of itinerant masons moving between Ardchattan, Achinduin and Lismore Cathedral for decades during the thirteenth century, in the service of the MacDougalls.

This places the building of the choir, at least, in the second half of the thirteenth century, and this is compatible with the political realities of the time. Despite poor summers and severe winters between the 1260s and the 1280s, resulting in sporadic food shortages, the years of the maturity of Alexander III (*c*. 1260–86) were a period of stability and relative prosperity for Scotland, reflected in the completion of several great churches, some of which had begun in the peaceful years of Alexander II (e.g. cathedrals at Elgin, Dornoch, Fortrose, Dunblane). Argyll diocese had a strong leader, Laurence (bishop 1262–99), with a national and international reputation (Chapter 6). If building had not already started when he was appointed, he certainly would have set the work in train, and he would have looked to

---

77 RCAHMS Inventory of Argyll (Vol. 2, 1975), p. 171: <https://scotlandsplaces.gov.uk/digital-volumes/rcahms-archives/inventories/argyll-volume-2-1975>; Turner (1998).

his MacDougall relations for financial and practical support. The relative simplicity and utilitarian nature of the cathedral, appropriate for a diocese with limited income from endowments, may have arisen out of the ascetic ideals of the Dominican bishops on Lismore.

Radiocarbon dates from the residual charcoal in the mortar are also compatible with a period of building in the second half of the thirteenth century;[78] the analyses also show that the lime used had been burned from oyster shells (rather than Lismore limestone), using woodfuel including oak, which is not native to the island. Dendrochronological analysis of fragments of the oak charcoal confirmed that one mature tree aged 345 years had been burned,[79] suggesting that, at that time, the mainland woods were in good heart, since the larger trees were not reserved for structural use.

Although the period of building the cathedral is firmly established, several questions remain. The diocese was established around 1190. If the cathedral was not started before the middle of the thirteenth century, then where did the canons perform daily Mass during the first 50 years of the diocese? It is unlikely that any monastic buildings from the Early Church would have survived but, if there was a community of Céli Dé based at Clachan on Lismore in the twelfth century and later (Chapters 9 and 11), then their church (no doubt a simple rectangular chapel of no great architectural merit) might have served the needs of the bishop while his cathedral was being planned and financed. No such structure has been found to date at Clachan; one possibility is that it was incorporated into the later building, although this raises similar issues about how the continuity of cathedral services was maintained. Archaeological investigations around the cathedral have revealed no other medieval buildings, raising the question of where the clergy were accommodated, or the teind stored. It is possible that structures from this period lie under the original manse, its gardens and the adjacent walled enclosure, none of which have been accessible for exploration (Fig. 2.2).

Another related question is why the master masons started work on the cathedral on a site that did not have enough level ground before running into bedrock to the west. Would the bishop, let alone the master masons who left their marks in the choir, have been content with a cathedral in

---

78 Thacker (2020).
79 Thacker (2021), p. 113.

which there were steps *down* rather than up to the altar area? Did this occur because, out of devotion to the memory of Moluag, they began at the site of his original chapel? On the other hand, it should be noted that the altar in Iona Abbey lies below the body of the church.

The Builders

We will never know the names of the stonemasons, carpenters, slaters and general labourers who actually built the cathedral, but there is an oral tradition on Lismore that a foreign master mason, possibly from Italy, died on the job and was buried nearby in the *Uaigh nan Romanach* – Grave of the Romans.[80] This may well be a memory of the itinerant masons who worked across the country in the peaceful years of the thirteenth century. Another local tradition draws attention to the well-engineered track on the island, rising on a gentle gradient from Port na Morlach to Balimakillichan and on to Clachan. This is said to have been the route for hauling sandstone, landed at the port from Morvern, possibly also from Carsaig on Mull, for the masons at work on the cathedral.

The church lands to the east of the cathedral are today very boggy and infested with rushes. However, archaeological exploration between 2018 and 2022 has shown that the area was the site of intense occupation and activity in medieval times (Chapter 2). From the finding of a thirteenth-century coin among traces associated with cooking hearths – iron-working slag, nails, fragments of sandstone and, possibly, signs of small-scale lime burning – it can be concluded that this was where the masons, carpenters, slaters and smiths lived and worked over the decades that it took to build the cathedral. There must have been a great deal of general labouring work for local men for decades, not least quarrying building stone and harvesting timber (Chapter 11).

The Impact of the Medieval Cathedral

There is no way of estimating the original height of the cathedral nave but, arguing from similar plain cathedrals in Ireland, Brown and Duncan (1957) proposed that the nave and choir would have been the same height. When newly built, the cathedral would have been an impressive sight:

---

80 Black (2006), p. 111; Carmichael (1948), p. 93.

by far the tallest building in the neighbourhood, with fresh sandstone details (buttresses, drip courses, window and door details) set against unweathered light-coloured limestone rubble, bonded with white lime mortar (possibly covered by light-coloured lime harling) – altogether a shining lantern, visible from a great distance. The recovery of so many fragments of lustrous phyllite slate from the glebe excavations may tell us that the roof of the choir was even more reflective.

Inside, the choir, for the canons, would have been separated from the nave, for the people, by a rood screen pierced by an arch, and probably around half the height of the building. In view of the very substantial lower wall today, and its apparently original features, it is likely that the screen was stone-built. Above it, visible from both sides, would have hung a large crucifix, the rood. The traces of paint, still visible on the mouldings around the choir doors, the sedilia and the piscina, tell us that the interior of the cathedral must have been impressive, and quite overwhelming for islanders and visitors. See Fig. 7.2.

Burials and Cemeteries

Archaeology has confirmed the tradition that there have been several burial places near the cathedral. This is not surprising in view of the shallowness of the soil. Today, the cemetery to the south, now effectively full, contains burials with a great range of carved gravestones, from the eighteenth to the twentieth centuries.[81] These include significant individuals, including the Gaelic scholar Donald McNicol, the botanist Dugald Carmichael and the folklorist Alexander Carmichael. There are signs of many older burials, most notably the eight West Highland medieval graveslabs, now lifted, conserved and protected in an adjacent shelter. These include fine examples of the Iona and Lochawe carving schools and, although it is likely that they were reused and moved around to suit later needs, they do indicate that the south cemetery area was a prestigious place to be buried in from the thirteenth to the fifteenth centuries. During the same period, there would have been burials within the building; a fine foliated cross (Iona School) with rare tau-headed staves, presumably the memorial of a member of the chapter, was raised to the level of the wooden floor at the

---

81 A.M. White (2009). Transcription of the gravestones in the old graveyard. Privately published.

1896 renovation of the choir (according to Carmichael (1948)). The most recent twentieth- and twenty-first-century burials have been in the new cemetery to the north of the church (Fig. 2.2).

Archaeology has now revealed an older burial ground, below the south cemetery, which had been severely damaged by the construction of the new road in the eighteenth century, and the new manse in the 1970s. Burials that have been radiocarbon dated to the seventh century and the Viking Age (around 1000), within an older boundary wall, have provided the first *concrete* evidence for the presence of the Early Church on Lismore (other than the fragments of an eighth-century cross; see Chapter 2). The finding of many infant burials next to the Sanctuary Stone confirmed the tradition recorded by Alexander Carmichael that this was the burial place for unbaptised children, a practice that continued to the eighteenth century.[82] The site of burial of the foreign master mason has not been identified, but excavation of the nave by Brown and Duncan in the 1950s and by community archaeology in 2016 and 2017 has established that, after the nave had been ruined, its internal area and surrounds had also been used as a cemetery.

---

82 Carmichael Watson Collection, University of Edinburgh. CW106 folio 12r.

Martin – the Contumacious Bishop (1342–1387)

Martin, yet another Dominican friar, presided over the diocese of Argyll over a long period of 45 years of continued political turbulence, involving conflict with (and political interference by) England, and intense rivalry within Scotland between King David II (son of King Robert Bruce) and Robert Steward/Stewart (son of Marjorie, King Robert's daughter; succeeding David as Robert II). International relations were complicated by the papal schism (1378), with rival popes at Avignon (supported by Scotland, France, Spain and the Kingdom of Naples) and Rome (supported by England, Scandinavia and Poland), with the Holy Roman Empire vacillating.

The young King David II had been sent into exile in France for protection when Edward Balliol, son of King John, invaded Scotland and usurped the crown. In 1341, aged 17, he was back in Scotland, but within five years he was captured by the English at the Battle of Neville's Cross. He had to wait until 1357 to be freed, on the promise of payment of an enormous ransom of 100,000 marks, at a time when the economy of Scotland was in deep recession. Each absence allowed the Stewart party to dominate the national scene, and Robert finally succeeded David as King Robert II in 1371, beginning the long Stewart dynasty. Meanwhile, the power vacuum in the west caused by the demise of the MacDougall Lords of Lorn facilitated the rise of the MacDonald Lordship of the Isles, while the Campbells continued to expand their influence from their base around Loch Awe. All of this was happening in a period of continuing poor weather, with serious effects on harvests and the health of livestock, and the unmatched horror of the Black Death pandemic from the 1340s, which has been credited with wiping out a third of the population of Scotland.[83]

Against the odds, despite the eclipse of his MacDougall patrons Martin de Ergadia succeeded as Bishop of Argyll because of the untimely death of a competitor. He is remembered as 'contumacious' (stubbornly or wilfully disobedient to authority), although this reflected his determination to secure the solvency of his diocese in the face of a powerful rival (Paisley Abbey).

Rival Candidates for the Bishopric

A letter from Pope Clement VI from Avignon in 1344 confirming Martin's appointment, provides some tantalising details of the rivalry for the diocese.[84] On the death of Bishop Andrew in 1342, the Lismore Cathedral chapter nominated Martin, who secured the permission of his superior in the Dominican order to set off for Avignon accompanied by a 'proctor' or procurator representing the chapter, to seek confirmation of his appointment by Clement's predecessor, Benedict XII. Meanwhile, Augusio de Congallis (Angus of Cowal) also appeared at Avignon for confirmation, having been nominated by 'the city [or state: *civitas*] and diocese of Argyll'. This has been interpreted to mean that Martin's nomination was not supported by the wider clergy of the diocese, but it may also reflect the confusing national politics of the time, with England interfering.

David II had returned to Scotland from his 'protective exile' in France in 1341 to find John MacDonald of Islay aggressively developing the Lordship of the Isles, which was to dominate in the west for more than a century. As staunch supporters of Bruce in the Wars of Independence, the MacDonalds had been rewarded with some of the MacDougall islands (but not Lismore), and Comyn lands in Lochaber, to add to their heartland of Islay and Kintyre. However, in the confused years of David's minority and the reassertion of the rights of the Balliol family, the MacDonalds had transferred their allegiance to the English crown, and they switched their loyalties over the coming decades as it suited their ambitions. With a major landed interest in the Argyll diocese (in Kintyre and Lochaber), and sharing England's alignment with the

---

83   Oram (2014b).
84   *Registrum Monasterii de Passalet*, p. 283.

exiled MacDougalls, John of Islay was likely to support the candidacy of Martin.

There were, however, other powerful interests in the diocese. In particular, Robert Stewart, regent or lieutenant during David's exile, and future king, held lands in Cowal, and his family were founders of the Cluniac monastery of Paisley, which had major stakes in the Kintyre and Glassary parishes. It is not clear what role Stewart played in one of David's first acts, depriving John MacDonald of Kintyre, as part of a policy to curb his increasing power in the west. In this context, it is possible to see Angus of Cowal as the candidate of choice of the king, the Stewart faction, and the clergy of Kintyre and Paisley Abbey. Angus, a bachelor of civil law, was rector of Dunoeng (Dunoon) and a clerk in the administration of David II. With the title 'de Congallis', he was a close adherent of, if not a member of, the family of the Stewarts.

This was not the only contested Scottish appointment. At the same time, Malcolm de Innerpeffray was at Avignon, competing with Richard de Pilmore for the see of Dunkeld, and it is known from his capture and imprisonment in Berwick that John de Irewyn [Irvine] had been sent home to Scotland by two of the candidates, Martin and Malcolm, to look after their interests. On 16 March 1342, Edward III issued an order from Westminster to free de Irewyn,[85] and he wrote to the Pope in support of Martin, describing him as a member of the family of the ancient Lords of Lorn, and a supporter of the English crown. Decisions were delayed by the death of Benedict XII on 25 April 1342 but, during 1343, Angus also died at Avignon, leaving the way clear for Martin to be confirmed by Clement VI in January 1344. At least half of his fee for 'provision' had been paid by 1346.

Martin was back in Scotland in 1347 at the latest, playing his part as bishop in the Elizabeth More petition (see p. 96). However, it has been suggested that his authority as bishop was undermined by the lack of support of the clergy of the diocese: for official documents in the 1350s, he used his episcopal seal only (without the accompanying seal of the diocesan clergy, which other bishops did use). It is possible, of course, that the diocesan seal had been left at home, or lost.

---

85 *Rotuli Scotiae*, 16 March 1341/2.

Affairs of State

Since around 1150 the most senior position in the royal administration, the chancellorship, had been occupied almost exclusively by churchmen but, in the years just preceding and following the return of David II in 1341, it was held by a layman, Lord Thomas Charteris. The Charteris family, powerful in the Borders, had remained steady supporters of the Bruce interest (William de Charteris was one of the party that murdered John Comyn at Dumfries in 1306). These arrangements were overturned in October 1346 when a rash military adventure led to the death of Charteris and the capture of the king at the Battle of Neville's Cross near Durham. It would be seven years before Patrick de Leuchars, Bishop of Brechin, began his long service as chancellor (up to 1370), but the senior clergy including Bishop Martin were involved immediately in serious affairs of state.

Although King David was 22 and his queen, Joan, 18 at the start of his captivity in 1346, they had been married since childhood but no heir had come forth. David's brother-in-law, Edward III of England, had revived the ambitions of his grandfather, Edward I, to add Scotland to his kingdom, and he now had it in his power to prevent any possibility of an heir (at the least by separating the captive David from Joan). Meanwhile, Robert Stewart had resumed the role of lieutenant, ruling in place of the king. Next in line to the throne, as the son of Marjorie Bruce, he was actually eight years older than his uncle, David II.

Robert Stewart had experienced no problems of fecundity. His difficulties lay in the opposite direction: all of his many offspring were illegitimate; it was generally known that he had had more than one mistress; and he was closely related to two of them, in particular his life partner Elizabeth More or Mure, the mother of four sons and five daughters. Stewart was highly ambitious for himself and his family but there were also important national issues. As the line of succession in Scotland had failed once already, with disastrous consequences, the bishops of Scotland, including Martin, were urgently enlisted by Stewart in 1347 to petition Clement VI to legitimise his union with Elizabeth:

> The kings of France and Scotland, bishops William of St Andrews, William of Glasgow, William of Aberdeen, Richard of Dunkeld, Martin of Argyle, Adam of Brechin, and Maurice

of Dunblane. Signification that although Elizabeth Mor and Isabella Boutellier, noble damsels of the diocese of Glasgow, are related in the third and fourth degrees of kindred, Robert Steward of Scotland, lord of Stragrifis, in the diocese of Glasgow, the king's nephew, carnally knew first Isabella, and afterwards, in ignorance of their kindred, Elizabeth, who was herself related to Robert in the fourth degree of kindred, living with her for some time and having many children of both sexes by her; the above kings and bishops therefore pray the pope that for the sake of the said offspring, who are fair to behold, to grant a dispensation to Robert and Elizabeth to intermarry, and to declare their offspring legitimate.[86]

The petition was granted almost immediately, at Avignon in December 1347, on condition that Robert established 'one or more chapelries' in the diocese of Glasgow. It is not clear how he fulfilled these conditions, but he did marry Elizabeth in 1349, before her death (probably in the early 1350s). This was a crucial event in the history of Scotland, as it established the Stewart dynasty by legitimising Elizabeth's children (Fig. 8.1). Three of her sons were to play prominent roles in the coming decades: John, as Robert III, King of Scots (1390–1406); Robert, Duke of Albany, 'the uncrowned king of Scotland', who acted as regent during the incapacity of his brother and the exile of his nephew, James I; and Alexander, Earl of Buchan (the 'Wolf of Badenoch'), whose acts of destruction and violence in the north included the burning of Elgin Cathedral in 1390.

Meanwhile, endless and convoluted three-sided negotiations began among Edward III of England, David II in captivity in the Tower of London, and the administration of Robert Stewart over the conditions of David's release, including the size of the ransom payment. Because their aims were irreconcilable, these negotiations continued over 11 years, with the bishops of Brechin, St Andrews and Caithness shuttling back and forth between Scotland and the English court. Edward had ambitions to incorporate Scotland into his kingdom; David wished for both his personal liberty and limitation of the ambitions of the Stewarts, even at the cost of a

---

86 Bliss (1896). The prohibited 'degrees of consanguinity', ruling out marriage, according to the Roman Catholic Church, were uncle/aunt with niece/nephew (third degree) and between first cousins (fourth degree).

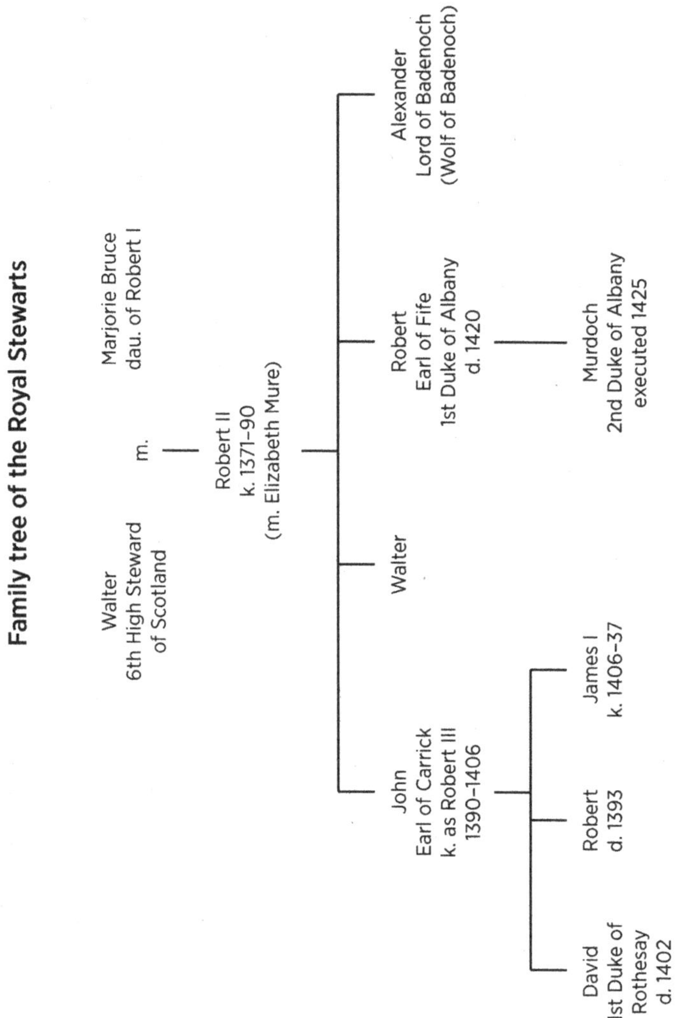

MONKS AND BISHOPS

Family tree of the Royal Stewarts

Walter
6th High Steward
of Scotland

m.

Marjorie Bruce
dau. of Robert I

Robert II
k. 1371–90
(m. Elizabeth Mure)

John
Earl of Carrick
k. as Robert III
1390–1406

Walter

Robert
Earl of Fife
1st Duke of Albany
d. 1420

Alexander
Lord of Badenoch
(Wolf of Badenoch)

David
1st Duke of
Rothesay
d. 1402

Robert
d. 1393

James I
k. 1406–37

Murdoch
2nd Duke of Albany
executed 1425

Fig. 8.1 Family tree of the Royal Stewarts.

Plantagenet king of Scotland; while Robert Stewart, with clear ambitions of his own, had the task of ruling the country and limiting the potential cost of the ransom payments. Part of the delay can be attributed to the outbreak of the Black Death, which reached Scotland in 1349. The epidemic must have paralysed all activity for many months and it certainly compromised the ability of the economy of Scotland to generate the surplus needed to ransom its king.

When the deadlock was finally broken, it was as much a result of events in France as in England. The long-term alliance between Scotland and France meant that Edward, pursuing the twin aims of securing and expanding his possessions in France, and incorporating Scotland into his empire, faced the risks associated with action on two fronts. However, following the shattering defeat of the French army, including a good proportion of Scots, by the English at Poitiers in 1356, and the capture of the French king, Edward had achieved a position of supreme power. He was able to release David II in the knowledge that events in France were, for the time being, under control, and that any threat from the north could be contained by a combination of military and political tactics.

Nevertheless, the terms of the Treaty of Berwick, negotiated in the summer of 1357, were severe: a ransom of 100,000 marks (£66,666 13s 4d) to be paid in equal instalments over ten years, with 20 noble hostages held in England as security. The principal hostage, to be released after the first payment, was John Stewart, the eldest son of the lieutenant. David's earlier proposal that his heir as King of Scots should be one of Edward's sons had, not surprisingly, proved unacceptable to the Stewart administration, and did not feature in the treaty. The Scottish dioceses, in control of a sizeable fraction of the national wealth (estimated in 1366 at nearly £10,000 per annum, see p. 53), were called upon to join the nobles and burghs to meet the ransom payments. On 19 September at Ardchattan, Bishop Martin issued a 'letter patent' appointing Friar Adam of Lanark (a Dominican, later Bishop of Galloway) to act on his behalf in the negotiations about ransom payments; a week later Martin was in Edinburgh in person, joining his fellow bishops in making arrangements for their joint response:[87]

> Letters patent by William bishop of Glasgow, John of Dunkeld, Alexander of Aberdeen, John of Moray, Alexander of Ross,

---

[87] Bain (1887).

[William] of Dunblane, and Martin of Argyll, with the consent of their chapters and the whole clergy of Scotland, appointing William bishop of St Andrews, Thomas bishop of Caithness, and Patrick bishop of Brechin, chancellor of Scotland, their proctors for the ransom of K. David. Append their seals and those of their chapters at Edinburgh. [There is no chapter seal for Argyll.]

Martin's seal is described as:

> Oval, purple, chipped. 3 figures standing in a lymphad [birlinn/galley]. Centre one a bishop with pastoral staff, in benediction. A female saint on either side. Beneath a half figure of a bishop praying.

The Latin inscription, mainly indecipherable, refers to Martin as 'bishop by the grace of God'.

The ransom payments were to be a heavy burden for Scotland, and not discharged until after David's death in 1371. The first instalment was paid in full in June 1358, mainly from the trading resources of the royal burghs, but some of the nobles, particularly the magnates in the west and north, refused to cooperate in assessing their properties and paying their share, as recorded in the record of the parliament held at Scone in July 1366:

> Item, that those rebels, namely of Atholl, Argyll, Badenoch, Lochaber and Ross, and others if there are any, in the northern regions or elsewhere, should be arrested by the king and his armed force to undergo common justice and particularly for paying off the contribution, and otherwise they may be corrected as shall be more opportune for the peace and utility of the community and the kingdom.[88]

MacDonald of Islay does not appear in this list because, as a recognised ally of Edward III, he had been exempted from ransom contributions. The level of the Church contribution was eventually fixed in 1360 when the Pope gave permission for David II to draw one-tenth of clerical income (around £1,000) for three years for ransom payments.

---

88 *RPS* 1366/7/10.

Political Developments in the Diocese of Argyll in the Reigns of David II and Robert II

The political situation in Bishop Martin's diocese was challenging and rapidly evolving. By 1340, John of Islay had come to pose a major threat to the Scottish crown, having extended his authority over an area similar to that of Somerled, his ancestor, and by acting independently on behalf of England, the natural enemy of Scotland. Before Neville's Cross, David II had moved to curb the ambitions of John (MacDonald) of Islay by depriving him of Kintyre but, in his absence in captivity, an alliance developed between the MacDonalds and Robert Stewart, the Guardian of Scotland. John of Islay had originally married Amy MacRuari, thereby achieving a controlling interest in Garmoran (Knoydart, Moidart, Arisaig, Morar, Uist, Barra, Eigg and Rum) but this did not stop him from putting her aside to marry Margaret, the Guardian's daughter, in 1350, and reclaiming Kintyre. With these acquisitions, the Lords of the Isles would be the controlling (political) power in the Argyll diocese deaneries of Morvern and Kintyre for more than a century.

Meanwhile, during his time in the English court, David II had formed a close friendship with the grandson of the exiled Alexander MacDougall, known in the West Highlands as John Gallda ('the foreigner', recognising his upbringing in England). Gallda married David's niece, Joanna Bruce, and one of the returning king's first actions was to restore the Lordship of Lorn, including Lismore, to him in 1358. The deanery of Lorn, therefore, came, at least notionally, under the influence of the king's party, although the seaways in the region were dominated by MacDonald galleys. Before long, John MacDougall was to become as disobedient as his neighbours.

Robert Stewart had strengthened his links with Gaeldom by acquiring a stake in the extensive earldom of Ross through marriage to Euphemia de Ross but, once David II had returned, he retreated to the margins for a time. Other branches of the Stewart dynasty were the most powerful landowners in the deanery of Glassary, but, from around 1360, they began to surrender the responsibility for providing leadership in the area to the rising Campbells of Lochawe, who, in due course, would come to dominate Argyll and the diocese as a whole. The favour shown to the Campbells can be seen in the 1363 grant by Mary Stewart, Countess of Menteith:

to her kinsman Archibald the son of Sir Colin Campbell of Lochaw, the lands of Kilmun in Cowall for the yearly payment of a pair of Paris gloves at Glasgow Fair.[89]

However, the dominance of the MacDonalds in Kintyre and Morvern, the increasing importance of the Campbells in Glassary, and the restoration of the MacDougalls to Lorn did not make for a peaceful diocese. In addition to continuing episodes of famine and outbreaks of both livestock and human disease,[90] and civil war in 1363 between the king's party and its opponents (led by Stewart, the Earl of Douglas and the Earl of March), the 1360s saw King David pursuing all of the major landholders in the west (Stewart, MacDonald, Campbell and even MacDougall) for lawlessness and tax evasion. As across Europe, the insecurity of the times in Scotland (increase of violence, starvation and disease) can be gauged from legislation at the July 1366 parliament at Scone:

> ... no prelate, earl or baron, nor other person of whatever state he be, ecclesiastical or secular, should ride, to the destruction of a district, with a greater household in people or horses than is fitting for his status; and that no one riding through a district should bring lancers or archers with him, unless he maintains them for a reasonable cause, concerning which they are to be held to give their oath upon this question to the king's ministers, under pain of imprisonment of their bodies.[91]

The 'pacification and governing of the highland regions' was the major business of the March 1369 parliament at Scone:

> Concerning which, those chosen by the three communities having diligently discussed upon these points, it was at length delivered and ordained, namely concerning the first point touching the pacification and governing of the highland regions, that [Robert], the lord Steward, and his sons should answer in

---

89 *Origines*, p. 72.
90 For example, 'the plague being so widespread in Scotland [21 November 1380]'. Burns (2021), no. 68a.
91 *RPS* 1366/7/15.

this way for the earldoms of Strathearn, Atholl and Menteith, and for all their other lands and lordships within the highland regions, namely, that they shall make the peaceful and just men living within their said earldoms, lands and lordships to do full justice without delay and prevarication to transgressors, as often and when they can be discovered, and wherever within their said lordships; so also that amends should be made to the complaining parties; and that they may not allow malefactors to be received knowingly henceforth within the limits of their said lordships. And that they should answer for, submit to and apply themselves to our lord the king and his ministers in the matter of collections and contributions and other things that concern their duties. And the said Lord Steward and John and Robert, his sons, promised and undertook faithfully by their oaths to our lord king in parliament to bring about and to hold entirely all and singular the foregoing according to their ability and performance, as far as pertains to them, and under certain penalties imposed upon them in the same place by the king. And that it was delivered similarly that all other lords having lands and lordships in the highland regions, for instance the lords [Thomas], the earl of Mar, and [William, the Earl of] Ross, John de Lorne, Gillespic Campbell and others, should bind themselves in a similar way to all and each of the foregoing for everybody existing or who could in the future come within their lordships, lands and bounds.

That sheriffs and others at present administering lands existing in the hands of our lord king should be wholly answerable for the inhabitants of the said lands, as is set out above.

And they deliver concerning the Islesmen that our lord king ought, either by his own authority or by others having his special power to this end, to compel and force with a firm hand in diverse and convenient places John of the Isles and his sons, and others adhering to him (if formerly they should not be prevailed upon in friendly manner to be reduced to obedience), to come to the king's obedience and stand to law, and undergo services and charges with mainlanders, as they ought to.[92]

---

[92] *RPS* 1369/3/7.

Later in 1369, John of Islay finally submitted to the crown at Inverness, undoing the provision in the Treaty of Berwick that permitted the Lords of the Isles to avoid contributing to the king's ransom.

Another cause of unrest and lawlessness was that, although David travelled widely in the east of the country, holding parliaments from Edinburgh to Aberdeen and doing business in Elgin and Inverness, he showed little interest in the west of the country and never visited the West Highlands. He was inconsistent, at best. As noted by MacDonald:[93] 'This is a huge part of the story of the west *Gàidhealtachd* right through to the modern era. The only "justice" from the crown was occasional punitive expeditions, kidnappings and demands for money separated by long periods of disinterest.' By neglecting to bring the force of his authority into the territories of his opponents, he allowed them free rein to govern as they wished. At the Perth parliament in 1370, it was resolved that the king should address these problems by travelling west and extracting some of the outstanding taxes in kind:

> it seems to them that it is not possible [for] the highland regions to be equal and alike in supporting charges and services to the lowland regions (which are burdened by an increase in the great custom), better than by our lord king disposing himself to undertake a stay, at certain and opportune times, in the highland regions, in which he ought and will be able to have more useful prises [prices] and a better market price, and similarly to pacify the country and to punish malefactors; or otherwise (exempting the lowland regions from charges of this kind for the time), to take barley and marts [livestock] and other victuals which they have in that same place in abundance, namely the highland regions, according to reasonable prises, by the chamberlain [Walter de Biggar] or his deputies, until they shall be equal to the charges of this kind in other regions.[94]

Whether or not David would have acceded to this request, it came too late, as he died early in 1371, leaving the way clear for the Stewart dynasty to assume power.

---

93 I.G. MacDonald, personal communication.
94 *RPS* 1370/2/8.

The remaining 16 years of Martin's bishopric were under the rule of the ageing Robert II, although his son, John Stewart, Earl of Carrick (Robert III from 1390) was effectively in control from 1384. Drawing on his alliance with the Stewarts, John of Islay was able to consolidate his lands in Garmoran and Kintyre, but the most important development for the diocese was the extinction of the male line of the MacDougall Lords of Lorn. John Gallda's two legitimate children, both daughters, had married brothers John and Robert of a cadet branch of the Stewart family (of Innermeath in Perthshire), and so by 1388 John Stewart was Lord of Lorn (Lorn, Benderloch, Appin and Lismore).

Bishop Martin and his Diocese

In his diocese, Bishop Martin was hemmed in by the Lordship of the Isles, and his actions were limited by the power of the Steward and his Campbell supporters on the mainland. The surviving records of the period suggest that, in a time of plague and insecurity, Martin stayed at home for most of his time as bishop. He could hardly have opted out of his two appearances on the national scene (the More petition in 1347, and in relation to ransom payments in 1357), because they were effectively papal business, but the available evidence indicates that, otherwise, he played little part in the administration of the country.

For much of Bishop Martin's time, national affairs were dominated by the bishops of Brechin (Patrick de Leuchars, Chancellor of Scotland 1353–70) and St Andrews (William de Landels, envoy to the English court), but most of the others appeared at parliament when 'the bishops, abbots, priors, earls, barons, freeholders who hold in chief of our king, and certain burgesses from each burgh' (i.e. the 'Three Estates') were summoned. Five bishops (St Andrews, Brechin, Glasgow, Moray and Dunblane) and proxies for three others (Dunkeld, Aberdeen and Ross) attended the parliament at Scone in September 1367 to deal with a crisis in the royal finances associated with the ransom payments; seven (St Andrews, Glasgow, Brechin, Dunkeld, Moray, Dunblane and Galloway) and the procurators of two more (Aberdeen and Ross) attended at Perth in March 1369 to consider 'the pacification and governing of the highland regions' and 'how the Islesmen should be restrained and corrected'. Caithness was not represented, no doubt because of the death of Bishop Thomas, who had acted as an envoy to England in 1357; and the Isles and Orkney were still notionally subject to Nidaros in Norway. It is significant that Martin alone of the Scottish bishops did not attend these sessions devoted specifically to dealing with the turbulence in his diocese. In fact, he does not seem to have been represented at any of the parliaments of David II and Robert II and, unlike his predecessors, he appears rarely as a legal witness, for example in the Paisley Abbey charters.

The rare appearance of Martin or his representatives in national and legal documents makes it difficult to reconstruct his chapter. From the founding of the diocese around 1200 until the fifteenth century, few deans, chancellors and treasurers can be identified, and there is no evidence to suggest that the post of 'official' (chief legal officer) continued after the mid thirteenth century. The responsibility for providing the precentor was carried by the Prior of Ardchattan up to 1371, but the arrangement thereafter is not clear until well into the fifteenth century (MacDonald, 2013). Martin seems to have managed with a dean, an archdeacon and a group of up to ten canons, who were rectors of parishes in the diocese, but we know from the legal process in Glasgow in 1362 (see p. 99) that he did summon all of his clergy to at least one diocesan synod.

Either the bishop was allowed a free hand to appoint his own deputy, or candidates were forced upon him by the local magnates, because two of the deans mentioned in contemporary Church records are described as holding the post 'illegally' (i.e. without papal consent): Roland, son of Lochlan 'for many years' up to 1350; and James Johannis de Tinetur (Tirefour on Lismore?) in 1388, following the death of 'dean Lacham'.[95] The archdeaconry of Argyll, carrying responsibility for deputising for the bishop in Church matters, provided the opportunity for John Dugaldi (MacDougall) to serve the apprenticeship for his elevation to bishop on the death of Martin. In contrast to the deans, there was no doubt about the qualifications of Dugaldi. In 1350 he is listed as a scholar of canon law receiving a benefice in the gift of the abbot and convent of Paisley; and when he was officially appointed as archdeacon in 1366, he is described as advanced in canon law and formerly a Pope's scholar. The income from his benefice as archdeacon, at 40 marks per annum, was not insignificant, and the scramble to secure it in 1387, when Dugaldi succeeded Martin as bishop, is a sign of the times. The papal schism had occurred in 1378, with France, Spain and Scotland adhering to the Avignon popes (commonly

---

95 Burns (2021), no. 172.

called the antipopes) and Northern Italy, England, Ireland and the Germanic states adhering to Rome. Walter Wardlaw, Bishop of Glasgow, created a cardinal shortly after the schism, petitioned Clement VII at Avignon in May 1387 for the archdeaconry of Argyll (ostensibly to meet some of his expenses). However, by November he had died, and the Pope issued a mandate for the appointment of the cardinal's nephew, Alexander Wardlaw, who already held a prebend in the diocese of Glasgow. However, Alexander Wardlaw also died within the year and soon Donald of Islay, Lord of the Isles, would be exercising his influence in arranging for his chaplain David Macmuirechard, the vicar of Lismore, to be archdeacon.[96]

The full list of ordinary canons in the chapter is unknown, but it included two prominent individuals. Known by several names which indicate 'noble birth' (Dugal de Lorne, Dugal de Ergadia, Dugall Petri), the rector of Kilmore parish seems to have been a canon of Argyll and Dunblane, possibly also St Andrews, from 1380 at least. He is known to have studied canon and civil law for three years, and had been the chaplain and secretary of Robert Stewart (son of King Robert II, see Fig. 8.1), who became 1st Duke of Albany. It has been proposed that he was the duke's brother-in-law; as we shall see in the next chapter, the Albany branch was to have an important influence on Argyll diocese. In the same year, the Pope wrote to John de Congallis (John of Cowal, presumably a kinsman of the rival to Martin), rector of Kinlochgoil, noting that he 'is said to have studied canon law at Paris for over three years'. Bishop Martin appears to have made little impact on the outside world but he had at least three well-educated and influential members in his chapter.[97]

Although we know little about the life of the bishop and his chapter, the seventeenth/eighteenth-century Catholic antiquarian Father Richard Augustine has provided a glimpse of how the priests might have appeared:

> Their usual habit reached to the ancles. At divine service in the church they wore a rochet with an amice [*almutium*] placed upon the shoulders, and a surplice with open sleeves, from Easter Eve to the Feast of All Saints [1 November]; and from Hallow Eve [31 October] to Holy Saturday they wore a linen surplice reaching to the ancles, and by peculiar privilege and custom

---

96 Burns (2021), nos 134, 153, 174a.
97 Burns (1976), p. 45.

violet-coloured capes, as appears from the *Iconice Canonicorum Imagines*, printed in 1400, which was to be seen in the choir. They afterwards wore black capes open in front, and under the cape, which was lined with red cloth of silk or silk and wool [*holoserico seu heteromallo*], a linen tunic [*cotta seu phelone*] without sleeves. On the head they wore an amice made of grey fur [*ex griseis pelliculis*], and above it a hood [*capuccum seu mosettam*] which covered the shoulders, with a collar of ermine attached. To the cape was attached behind a train [*cauda repens*] of the same material and colour, which they carried on the left arm. This change was introduced *pro tempore* by Pope Nicolas III [*apud Raynald. Annal. Eccles.*, an. 1278, no. 79]. By a decree of the council of Narbonne [AD 1043] purple vestments were strictly forbidden to clerical persons, lest they should make a boast of worldly pomp. Yet the dignitaries [*senatores*] of this cathedral church were distinguished by the purple, that the memory of the blood shed by them for the gospel of Christ might not perish.[98]

Martin, the Contumacious Bishop

Throughout the lifetime of the pre-Reformation diocese of Argyll it suffered from chronic underfunding. The annual income of the dioceses, evaluated by the 1366 parliament as part of the housekeeping needed to find the resources to pay the annual ransom payment, shows the depth of poverty in Caithness, Argyll and Galloway, with incomes less than a tenth of those of Aberdeen, Glasgow and St Andrews. As a latecomer, Argyll diocese had few endowments and much of its potential income had been diverted to other religious houses, particularly the Cluniac abbey at Paisley. However, its finances were also deteriorating because of the economic decline across Europe following the loss of up to a third of the population to a series of plagues, climate-driven decreases in crop and livestock production, and because the Pope had sanctioned a levy of one-tenth of Church incomes for the king's ransom. Martin needed finance to keep his diocese going but, according to tradition, he also needed money to complete his cathedral: the archaeological evidence is consistent with the building of the western tower in Martin's time.

98 *Scotia Sacra*.

The records of Paisley Abbey[99] bear witness to the diocese's financial problems. John, Abbot of Dunfermline, and Andrew, Abbot of Newbattle, had been appointed by Clement VI as 'commissioners' to look after the interests of the Cluniac monks in Scotland, and it was to them that the monks of Paisley appealed in 1351 for help in restraining Martin, whom they claimed

> occupied and usurped against their will the churches of Saint Colmanel [Kilcolmanel], Saint Queran [Kilkerran] and Saint Finan [Kilfinan], within his diocese, and the tithes and fruits of the same, and was inflicting on them various other grievances contrary to the privileges and liberty of the Cluniac order.

The commissioners were not in a great hurry to deal with the problem as it was at a great distance from their abbeys, and it was not until 11 years later, in 1362, that they, in turn, appointed another body of commissioners from Glasgow diocese (Master John Penny, subdean, and Nigel of Carrotherys, Malcolm Kennedy and Henry of Mundaville, canons) to investigate. They duly summoned Martin to appear at Glasgow Cathedral on 30 May to answer to the charges and 'submit to the law', but he proved to be 'contumacious', defying the summons even though he had actually been in Glasgow for several days up to that date. Accordingly, Martin was suspended from his post by the Glasgow commissioners,

> who then appointed Richard Daurog rector of Kyrkmichael, Walter Rwl vicar of Herskyn, and Thomas of Arthurly vicar of Dalyel, to wait on him within three days after receiving their mandate, to intimate his suspension, and to cite him anew to appear before the commissioners in the cathedral church of Glasgow on the 14th of the following June.

However, by the ninth of June, informal arbitration had resulted in some clarification of the issues, and a degree of agreement was reached. Martin accepted the need to refund to the Abbot of Paisley the fine of 33 shillings and 4 pence he had exacted for non-appearance at the Argyll synod (the abbot claiming his 'privilege of exemption'). However, it became clear

---

99 *Origines*, p. 14.

that the 'sequestration of the fruits' of the parishes had been Martin's response to the lack of repair of the churches, which was the responsibility of Paisley. Martin agreed to 'relax the sequestration' on condition that:

> the monks, as bound, should repair the church, and the bishop should bind those who were engaged to the monks for repairing it to fulfil their engagement on pain of ecclesiastical censure.

The agreement also dealt with disagreements over the appointment of priests by Paisley to parishes in Argyll. The text for Kilkerran reads:

> that the bishop should anew receive and admit to the church the present incumbent by virtue of the presentation of the monks; and that for the future he should not repel but rather benignantly admit the presentation by them to the churches which they held within the diocese of Argyle, provided however that they presented to him as diocesan qualified persons within term of law – the bishop moreover protesting, that by the present agreement he did not in any way prejudice his successors, if and in how far they should think their interests concerned, and promising that he should cause the present agreement to be publicly expounded and proclaimed in the mother tongue in every church and place of his diocese in which there was any question concerning the things premised, the people being assembled either for that or any other purpose.

and for Kilfinan:

> that, if on lawful grounds he should judge the person presented by the monks to the church unworthy or unqualified, he should intimate to them as patrons the vacancy thus produced, that they might present a qualified person to him as diocesan, and that the monks should *hac vice* present to the church the person nominated by the bishop, the right of presentation in future vacancies remaining with them as before.

This was the opportunity to resolve another problem between the bishopric and the abbey.

Between the years 1230 and 1246 Duncan the son of Fercher . . . granted to the monks of Paisley that pennyland of Kilmor which lay on Louchgilp, with the chapel of St Mary built on the same land. [Confirmed 1270.] In 1362 it was arranged between the monks and Martin bishop of Argyle who had encroached on their rights, that he should allow them freely and without imposing any burden to enjoy the land of Kylmor with the chapel of Loucgilp, notwithstanding an inquest which he alleged he had made for his own information without their knowledge; with this addition, that should any one sue them concerning the imposition of any burden on the land of Kylmor Loucgilp, the bishop should do equal justice to both parties, or do his best to make peace between them.

The conclusion from these records could be that, rather than 'contumacious', Martin was diligent in looking after the interests of his diocese and its parishioners, at a time when the teind yields from his diocese were seriously reduced.

9

Into the Fifteenth Century

The Last Dominican (1419–1426) and the First Bishop Without Gaelic (1427–1462)

Martin was followed as Bishop of Argyll by two highly educated lawyers: John Dugaldi, who lived for only another ten years, then Benedict Johannis (otherwise referred to as Beanus Johannis Andree, or Bean, in office from 1397–1419). Papal documents of the time indicate that, in running the diocese, they were assisted by an archdeacon, dean, treasurer and precentor, and a chapter of other canons holding prebends (eight identified by name). In contrast to their successor, Finlay, who became seriously embroiled in politics, these two bishops seem to have remained quietly within their diocese, with no documented appearance on the national scene, although frequently in touch with the antipopes in Avignon.

Their behaviour was understandable in the light of national events. Soon after the appointment of Bishop John in 1387, King Robert II died, to be succeeded by his son John, renamed Robert III (recognising painful memories of King John Balliol). Scotland continued to be a deeply unsettled country with a weak, disabled king and over-powerful subjects (especially John, Lord of the Isles, and the Earl of Douglas) supported by a crowd of ambitious followers. Although the weather may have improved marginally, the Black Death struck again in 1380, possibly once again killing up to a third of the population, and devastating the national economy. The cold, wet, stormy weather again intensified around 1400 and continued through the century, with the return of violence, famine and disease:

[A]ll of these factors fed into undercurrents of discontent among Scotland's noble community, whose levers of political, social and economic power were dependent upon the flow of rents from peasant tenants or the profits from the grain produce, wool, hides and fish of their estates.[100]

King Robert III effectively surrendered the government to two leading rivals: his son and heir David (Duke of Rothesay) and his brother, Robert Stewart, Earl of Fife (created 1st Duke of Albany 1398), the next in line if the royal line failed. The situation became very ugly when Albany and Douglas conspired to bring about the death of Rothesay in 1402, apparently by starvation at Albany's Falkland Castle. As the next in line (yet another Robert) had already died around 1393, the king placed his third and last surviving son, the future James I, under the protection of the Bishop of St Andrews. By early 1406, the young prince, now aged 12, had been moved to the Bass Rock but, embarking for sanctuary in France, his ship was intercepted off the east coast of England. Delivered into the hands of King Henry IV, James was to remain a prisoner at the English court for the next 18 years. This seems to have been the last straw for his father, who died later in the year, leaving Albany in charge of the country as Guardian of the Kingdom, but effectively king. Bishop Bean of Argyll would die before James I returned to Scotland in 1424.

Meanwhile the Lordship of the Isles, now extending over most of the area of Somerled's empire, was approaching the peak of its power and influence, effectively acting as an independent state. This was the achievement of John of Islay (1320–1387), who had secured the lordship by astute political manoeuvring, not least by marrying a daughter of Robert II. Over the coming decades, his successor as lord, Donald, was to sow the seeds of the destruction of the lordship by his ambition to extend its power into the earldom of Ross. Much of the diocese of Argyll was under the control of the MacDonalds, but Lorn, including Lismore, which had been recovered for his family by John Gallda MacDougall, was conveyed in 1388 to Sir Robert Stewart of Innermeath (a kinsman of Albany) when he married Gallda's daughter Janet. Another important development for the diocese was the advance of the Campbells to the north and south of their base on Lochawe. This advance was not only in terms of territory but in

---

100 Oram (2024), p. 76.

their influence on the Church. For example, in 1414 Sir John Campbell, the brother of Sir Duncan Campbell, Lord of Lochawe, was rector of the Church of St Martin at Kilmartin, and a member of the Lismore Cathedral chapter,[101] and Sir Celestine McGillemichael, 'clerk to Sir Duncan', was rector of Kilmelfort. Charter records reveal that Sir Neil Campbell ('of noble birth on both sides') was archdeacon of the bishopric, and second in authority to the bishop for nearly 40 years from 1397. The influence of the founding MacDougalls on the diocese was finally on the wane.

Bishops John (1387–97) and Bean (1397–1419)

There was confusion about the appointment of Bishop John as, during the lifetime of Martin, 'provision to the bishopric was specially reserved to the Pope'.[102] Nevertheless, elected by his chapter, he travelled to Avignon for confirmation as bishop in 1387, appearing in the Vatican records as *Joannes Dugaldi* and elsewhere as *de Lorne*, indicating that he was the last of the priests sponsored by the MacDougalls, who were superseded in Lorn by the Stewarts in 1388, the year after his election. In different documents he is described as having been a Pope's scholar, presumably at Avignon, and 'advanced in canon law'. He petitioned for 'a benefit in the gift of the Abbot of Paisley' in 1350 and, in 1366, when he was already archdeacon on Lismore (income 20 marks), Urban V granted him 'a canonry of Dunkeld, with expectation of a prebend'. The last entry noted that 'the dioceses [of Argyll and Dunkeld] are conterminous: the said John knows the language and idioms of both and speaks them well' (i.e. English and Gaelic).

Bishop Bean was appointed by the Avignon antipope Benedict XIII in 1397. Described as of 'noble birth', he had studied canon law at Paris, and acted as chaplain to Donald, Lord of the Isles. His arrival was a sign of the changed political situation in the diocese. As rector of Kilmonivaig in Lochaber, in the territory of the Lords of the Isles, he had been dean of Lismore Cathedral since 1388[103] but, on his promotion to bishop, he refused to give up the income from the post. This was substantial, amounting to

---

101 *Origines*, pp. 91, 104.
102 Burns (1976), p. 122.
103 Burns (2021), nos 172, 174b, 175, 197, 204a, 207c, 424c, 454; McGurk (1976), pp. 141, 241.

a quarter of the diocesan teind income, the other quarters being held by the chanter, chancellor and treasurer. He remained obdurate in the face of papal disapproval until 1411, when he was finally absolved of the offence but compelled to demit the deanship by Benedict XIII. Previously, after he had been appointed to the deanship of Argyll, he had continued to hold the archdeaconry of Sodor 'without the necessary dispensation'. In 'managing the system' for personal monetary benefit, John and Bean may not have been any more worldly than other contemporary clerics; for example, Henry Wardlaw, Bishop of St Andrews (1403–1440) was simultaneously a canon in Glasgow, Moray and Aberdeen dioceses, as well as (notionally) the precentor of Glasgow and Moray cathedrals.

As highly educated citizens, many trained in the law, senior clergy were expected to attend parliament and general councils when the king was in exile or during a minority. For example, at the important parliament in Linlithgow in 1404, when Albany was appointed lieutenant to the ailing King Robert III, they were represented by the bishops of St Andrews, Glasgow, Dunkeld, Aberdeen and Dunblane; the Prior of St Andrews; the abbots of Dunfermline, Melrose, Scone, Arbroath, Holyrood, Culross, Cambuskenneth, Balmerino; and several other clergy. Most of them were joined by the bishops of Dunkeld, Galloway, Moray, Caithness, Ross and Brechin and the Abbot of Kinloss at the Perth council in 1416, which dealt with the renunciation of Edward III's claim to Scotland. Although bishops John and Bean played no recorded part in these nationally important meetings, or in councils of Scottish churchmen, this does not mean that they were unaffected by the political realities of the time. A letter from Clement VII in Avignon in June 1393 confirming Bean as dean on Lismore was in response to a petition from King Robert III, and it states that the decision was supported by 'Robert Senescali [Stewart], Earl of Fife [later Duke of Albany], true patron of the deanery' and it 'met with the approval of Donald of Islay, Lord of the Isles, true patron of the church'.[104]

The Church was involved with the highly intermarried ruling classes in other ways. Following policies that dated back to Roman law, designed to prevent genetic problems arising out of procreation between closely related individuals, the Pope had to be petitioned to 'dispense' doubtful marriages. The prohibited 'degrees of consanguinity' were uncle/aunt with niece/nephew (third degree) and between first cousins (fourth degree). Between

---

104 Burns (1976), p. 192.

1385 and 1420, the Pope was petitioned to permit several marriages within the Argyll diocese between prominent individuals who were within the prohibited degrees, and to legitimise children resulting from 'irregular' unions.[105] In one case, resolution of the problem was considered to be important in maintaining peace among leading families in Argyll:

> 30 May 1393. Faculty to dispense Hector Macgileom, donzel [young man of high birth], and Mor, daughter of Calen Cambel [Colin Campbell], damsel, of Sodor and Argyll dioceses, from the impediment to marriage arising from the third and fourth degrees of consanguinity. Notwithstanding their knowledge of this impediment, they have espoused themselves to be married, without subsequent consummation, in order to establish peace and harmony among their families and friends, whereas until now there have only been wars, dissensions, murders and other grave scandals.

In another, the legitimising of children of an illegal marriage seemed more important:

> 16 May 1411. To the bishop of Argyll. Mandate to dispense the nobleman Donald MacLachlan to marry anew the noble woman Affrica Negelli, Argyll diocese. Donald and Affrica had contracted marriage per *verba legitime de presente* and had married; but later, after a child had been born, it had been brought to their knowledge that they were related in the fourth degree of affinity as the said Donald had carnally known a certain woman who was related to Affrica in the fourth degree of consanguinity, this invalidating their marriage. The dispensation is granted as above and the child is to be legitimised as are any subsequent children.

Just how complicated the rules of consanguinity could be is illustrated by another 1411 mandate from Benedict XIII, which reveals that the marriage of Devorgall with John Eugenii, which had resulted in at least one child, was 'invalid' because she had previously been married to the

---

105 Burns (1976), p. 188; McGurk (1976), pp. 236–7.

late Peregeret, who had been related in the third and fourth degree of consanguinity to John.

The correspondence also shows that members of the ruling class were seriously concerned about their mortal souls, and the risks of dying unshriven[106] – not an unlikely event in these plague years. In 1397, a petition from 'the nobleman Colin Cambel, Argyll diocese, to choose a confessor *in mortis articulo* [on the point of death]' was granted from Avignon. In 1418, John Steward, knight, Lord of Lorn, kinsman of Robert, Duke of Albany, and Isabella, his wife, petitioned for a plenary indulgence at the hour of death, for a licence to choose their confessor, and for permission to use a portable altar.

Managing the Chapter and the Diocese

As noted in Chapter 8, supplications to Clement VII at Avignon confirm that all had not been well with the chapter in Martin's time, with unqualified candidates occupying senior posts. For example, when Bishop Bean ('nobly born' and a former student at Paris) was appointed to the deanery in 1388/9, he dislodged James Johannis, who had succeeded the deceased Lachlan. Both of these had been irregular appointments. The correspondence also indicates that the archdeaconry was 'unlawfully detained' by David Marcad 'who obtained it by ordinary authority' (presumably by the chapter). In a time of unrest and plague, these may have been opportunities to assert long-standing local ambitions.

Some of the more routine papal correspondence involved the placing of rectors in Argyll parishes, for which a fee would be paid to the papal authorities, but there were several replies to petitions to correct irregular appointments, such as:

> 5 May 1380. To Malachy Ysaach, monk of the monastery of Ardchattan, *o. valliscaul.*, Argyll diocese. Dispensation from illegitimacy of birth, having been born out of wedlock, so that he may exercise all the functions of a monk and even accept the office of abbot, if elected.
>
> 6 November 1395. To Nigel Colini Cambel, rector of the parish church of Katani [probably Kilchattan], Argyll

---

106 McGurk (1976), p. 80; Burns (2021), no. 596.

diocese. Dispensation is granted to Nigel to hold two or three incompatible benefices with power of exchange as often as he pleases, notwithstanding that he had been already dispensed as the son of a married man and an unmarried woman to be promoted to all holy orders, and subsequently he had been provided to the said parish church of Katani, Argyll diocese.

17 July 1403. To Celestine Colini, clerk, Argyll diocese. Indult . . . notwithstanding his defect of birth as the son of a priest and an unmarried woman, from which he had already been dispensed, but the letters of reservation made no mention of his defect of age although he was at that time only 15 years old. The said letters are to be valid as if full mention of this defect had been made, and Celestine although still suffering from a defect of age as he is now only twenty-four years old, is dispensed to hold a benefice with or without cure.[107]

A reply in 1395 provides an example of the use of parish resources for the higher education of priests destined for senior posts:

To John Dugaldi, rector of the parish church of Kylmore [Kilmore], Argyll diocese. Indult for John to receive the fruits from Kylmore and from any benefice he might later obtain, without being bound to residency while studying canon law at a university for three years.[108]

This system ensured that the diocese maintained a body of clergy, many of whom were highly educated as well as being of 'noble birth'; for example, John de Congallo/Congallis [Cowal], rector of the Church of the Three Holy Brethren, Kinlochgoil, had studied for more than three years in Paris.

However, the most serious cases[109] involved Conghan Machabei, who was dismissed from the archdeaconry in 1395 when it was revealed that he had secured the post by bribery; and Celestine Celestini, called MacGillemichael, who was accused in 1411 of 'wasting the goods of the

---

107 Burns (1976), p. 46; McGurk (1976), pp. 56, 105.
108 McGurk (1976), p. 49.
109 McGurk (1976), pp. 57, 243.

church, as well as a notorious concubinary'. The final verdict on Celestine, said to be a 'papal familiar', is not clear, although Bishop Bean was 'forced to make restitution'. The correspondence provides clues to the disturbed nature of the diocese in the absence of a strong central authority. In 1404, the same Celestine Celestini

> had been presented to and peaceably possessed the parish church of St Katani de Lognyghe [Kilchattan], same diocese, a benefice in lay patronage. After its despoilation by powerful laymen he had been presented by the nobleman Colin Cambell, doncel, Argyll diocese, lord of Lochalba [Lochawe], to Bean, bishop of Argyll, for institution in the parish church of St Molrue de Melferth [Kilmelford].[110]

The Pope's mandate of 23 February 1411 shows that while the clergy were competing for the 'fruits' of the diocese, and members of the ruling class were taken up with 'despoiling' their neighbours, with their dynastic marriages, and with the saving of their souls, the cathedral at the heart of the diocese was suffering neglect:

> Mandate to ensure that the first years fruits of all benefices falling vacant within the next two years in the diocese of Argyll should be used to effect repairs to the church despoiled by wars and to buy books and ornaments for it, at the petition of Bean, bishop of Argyll, and despite constitutions to the contrary of Gregory XI and Clement VII which had decreed these fruits should go to the papal treasury.[111]

The serious state of the diocese finances is underlined by the (presumably temporary) sentence of excommunication of Bishop Bean incurred in 1411 'for not paying certain sums of money to the papal treasurer Ludivicus, bishop of Majorca, and other papal officials'.[112] In that year, Bean

---

110 McGurk (1976), p. 125.
111 McGurk (1976), p. 233.
112 McGurk (1976), p. 243.

complained about financial problems caused by wars raging in his diocese, and the appropriation of episcopal lands and revenues by local nobility.[113]

Bishop Finlay de Albany (1419–1426)

Whether or not Bishop Finlay was a member of the wider Stewart dynasty, he was clearly closely aligned with its Albany branch, acting as chaplain to the Earl of Fife (later Duke of Albany) by 1396 and later described as the duke's confessor. Studying at Oxford or Cambridge, and holding a degree in Theology, he became a Dominican friar and gained prominence as Vicar General of the order in Scotland. He was a delegate to the Council of Constance (1414–18), which ended the papal schism between Avignon and Rome and elected Martin V as a unifying pope, based in Rome, and he was a leading player in the subsequent steps in 1418 to reconcile Scotland to the decision. In acting in this way, he must have strained his relationship with the Albany faction, which favoured the Avignon antipopes, but gained favour with the exiled James I, who followed the English position, adhering to Rome. It is a tribute to his diplomacy that he was rewarded with the bishopric and travelled to Italy to be 'provided' by Pope Martin in 1420. At Florence, he paid '5 gold florins, 13 shillings and 2 pence'.

Finlay's alignment may have been important in the progress of his career but it was eventually to prove fatal. As Guardian of the Kingdom, Duke Robert did little to try to release James I from imprisonment in England; indeed, he first devoted his energies to securing the return of his own son, Murdoch, also a captive in England, in 1415. No doubt, he was banking on the death or permanent captivity of James and the ultimate accession of the Albany line to the throne. Duke Robert died in 1420, to be succeeded by Murdoch as Guardian, but the death of Henry V, and growing support in Scotland for the return of James, led to negotiations with the regents of the young Henry VI, culminating in an agreement for the release of James in return for the commitment to pay an enormous ransom of £40,000.

James returned to reign in person in April 1424, after 18 years in the English court, to a country that had been controlled by the Albany Stewarts effectively for 30 years; their family members and supporters dominated positions of power in the country, not least the earldoms (including Lennox, Buchan, Mar, Strathearn, Menteith, Atholl and Caithness). However, soon

---

113 McGurk (1976), p. 233.

INTO THE FIFTEENTH CENTURY 121

after, in August, the crushing defeat of a joint French and Scottish army in France, at Verneuil, removed several of the leading members of the Albany faction and provided James with the opportunity to avenge both the death of his brother, David, Duke of Rothesay, and the actions of the Guardians in preventing his return from captivity. The rebellion against the king by Walter, son of Murdoch, soon led to the imprisonment, and later execution in 1425, of Murdoch and his sons, excepting James Stewart, known as 'the Fat'. He avoided capture, to lead a revolt in Lennox, destroying the town of Dumbarton but failing to capture the castle.

At this point, Bishop Finlay's political instincts seem to have failed, and he threw away any credit he may have accrued with the king arising out of the Council of Constance. Maintaining his alignment with the Albany faction, he provided undefined 'counsel and aid to the traitors', probably encouragement of the men of Argyll to play an active part in the uprising. The revolt was suppressed by a force assembled by King James, and Finlay, accused of treason, fled to Ireland with James 'the Fat'. In the Book of Pluscarden, Finlay is described as 'a culpable abettor against the King's majesty'.[114]

Bishop George Lauder (1427/8–1473/5)

In contrast to all of his predecessors, who were members or supporters of one or other of the great families of Gaeldom, Lauder was supported by the king, newly returned from exile, and looking to reward those who had remained faithful to the crown in the Albany years. In 1406 George's father, Sir Robert Lauder of the Bass, a descendant of a leading Norman family with its roots in the Borders, had played a central role in protecting the young Prince James on the Bass Rock before the failed attempt to secure his safety in the French court. The patronage of the king can be detected in the careers of five of Sir Robert's many sons:

> *William*, Graduate of Paris; Bishop of Glasgow from 1408; Chancellor of Scotland from 1422; and responsible for major building work at Glasgow Cathedral

---

114 *Liber Pluscardensis*, an abridgement of Walter Bower's *Scotichronicon* in Latin and Scots: <https://referenceworks.brillonline.com/entries/encyclopedia-of-the-medieval-chronicle/liber-pluscardensis-SIM_00345>.

Robert of the Bass, Lead negotiator in London for the king's release; Justiciar of Scotland south of the Forth; Governor of Edinburgh Castle 1425–33

James, Justice Clerk under Robert

Alexander, Graduate of Paris; Archdeacon then Bishop of Dunkeld from 1440

George, Bishop of Argyll; Graduate of St Andrews (1417–19)

At the time of his elevation to the bishopric, George Lauder was already comfortably off as permanent vicar of Crail parish in Fife, master of the Hospital of St Leonard's for the old and indigent in Peebles, and feuar of the estate of Balcomie near Crail.

He was Bishop of Argyll for nearly 50 years, matched in longevity only by Martin, serving through the reigns of three kings and the complex fluctuations in the political activity of prominent magnates: James I up to his murder in 1437; James II (1437–60, including a minority up to 1449); and James III (1460–88, including a minority up to 1469). During the early years he was protected by the favour bestowed by the crown on his family, but this did not survive the death of James I. In later years, the diocese came to be dominated by the descendants of Duncan Campbell of Lochawe (Colin, 1st Lord of Glenorchy and, from 1460, the latter's nephew, Colin, 1st Earl of Argyll) who, at times, were in opposition to Lauder. The Campbell family was originally allied by marriage with the resurgent Albany faction, but later adapted to benefit from providing strong support to James II and James III (including the elevation of the senior line to an earldom). Even as early as 1443, during the minority of James II, the king was personally supplicating the Pope in support of 'his kinsman Duncan Cambel of noble race'.[115] By the time of Lauder's death, Campbells controlled territories from the Clyde to Loch Linnhe, including Lismore, and wide areas eastwards into Perthshire, with the associated rights of patronage to many parishes, as well as senior clerical positions. Colin, grandson of Duncan, as Earl of Argyll, was to play a prominent part in the government of James III.

Meanwhile, the patronage of other parishes of the diocese was still controlled by the Lords of the Isles, whose intermittent conflict with the

---

115 Dunlop and MacLauchlan (1983), p. 967; MacDonald (2013), Appendix 1: no. 144.

crown, including at least three major invasions of the mainland by islanders, resulted in general insecurity and widespread violence and 'despoilation'. The Edinburgh parliament of January 1450 refers to 'highlandmen, who before the king's homecoming commonly plundered and slayed one another'.[116] This was at least partly the result of 'war bands', maintained particularly by the MacDonalds, which were difficult to keep under control.[117]

Lauder faced several challenges as a new bishop, not least the fact that he was an outsider. The primary problem was that he had been recommended to the Pope by the king rather than being voted by the chapter. This risked alienating his clergy, who had been sidelined. For example, as late as 1441, 'Dugal [Campbell] of Lochaw, Lic. Dec., a priest in the diocese, questioned the authority of George Lauder, whom he refers to as alleged Bishop of Argyll'.[118] However, there was a more fundamental difficulty. As noted by MacDonald (2013), many of the cathedral clergy, from indigenous (Argyll, possibly Lismore) families (MacFadyen, MacLachlan and MacGillemichael), may well have been descendants of the original Céli Dé community. They would be resistant to the intrusion of clergy from elsewhere, and the diversion of the financial 'fruits' of their benefices from the local economy and their immediate families. Their opposition was fuelled by the fact that Lauder could not communicate or officiate in Gaelic, which was the language of the majority. To add to these issues, the senior clergy on Lismore had not benefited from further education, with the opportunity to experience the wider world.

In spite of this perilous environment, Bishop Lauder seems to have been determined to bring his diocese into line with elsewhere in Scotland, and to introduce allies into the diocese. Soon after his arrival in the early 1430s there were formal complaints about John Arous, described in the papal correspondence as the Queen of Scotland's secretary. He was occupying the perpetual vicarage of Kilcalmonell, although ignorant of Gaelic. His stay was short, but the post was then occupied in 1432 by William Arous, presumably a relation. Both of these priests had been prominent members of the diocese of St Andrews, Bishop Lauder's home country. William lasted only a year ('because he cannot speak Gaelic'), and it is ironic that

116 *RPS* 1450/1/3.
117 Caldwell and Hall (2014), pp. 85–6.
118 Dunlop and MacLauchlan (1983), p. 782.

their successor, John Finlaius Prioris MacPhilip (John Finlari), although apparently competent in Gaelic, was, a year later, accused of 'fornication, dilapidation, concubinage and producing offspring' and had 'rendered himself unworthy of the vicarage of St Colmanel'.[119] Nearby in Kintyre, James Douglas, clearly a Lowlander, appeared as rector and canon at Kilcolmkill.

Serious accusations were made about two other Lowlanders in 'Campbell' parishes. James de Lawdre, vicar of Glenorchy in 1441 (presumably a relation of the bishop), was said to be 'unable fittingly to preach the word of God to the parishioners, hear confessions and administer the sacraments'. Peter de Dalkeith, vicar of Lochgoilhead 1441–2, was accused of being unlawfully 'intruded' by the bishop; of being ignorant of Gaelic; and of neglecting the spiritual life of his parishioners.[120] It is not clear whether he actually took up residence in the parish, as the church is described as 'completely collapsed in its structures, roofs and edifices . . . and destitute of ornaments, books, and other trappings and jewels necessary for divine worship'.[121] Furthermore, in September 1441, he was actually in Rome, trying to assert his appointment to the archdeaconry of Argyll, while continuing to hold the vicarage.[122] His efforts were in vain, as Duncan Campbell of Lochawe acted to ensure that he did not succeed Neil Campbell as archdeacon of the diocese.[123] It is noticeable that none of these clerics, presumably careerists, lasted long in their Argyll posts.

The history of Glassary parish was quite different. Sir Alexander Scrymgeour, landowner in Fife and Perthshire, Constable of Dundee and heritable Standard Bearer for the king, acquired extensive lands in Glassary by his marriage to Agnes de Glassary. In 1427 this was challenged by Duncan Campbell, resulting in a long and ultimately indecisive legal wrangle, but the Scrymgeours maintained their possession, and rights of patronage until the end of the seventeenth century. This led to a long, nearly uninterrupted, line of nine Scrymgeour parish rectors and cathedral canons between the first, James (rector 1421–5, who petitioned the Pope for a vicar to support him because he was 'not learned in the

---

119 Dunlop and MacLauchlan (1983), pp. 48, 306.
120 MacDonald (2013), Appendix A: nos 117, 249, 250, 251, 335.
121 MacDonald (2013), p. 249.
122 Dunlop and MacLauchlan (1983), p. 782.
123 Boardman (2006), p. 144.

language of the country') to Henry and James, who served after the Reformation (1570s onwards).[124] Most of them were graduates of the new university at St Andrews, founded in 1413, and they were Lowlanders without Gaelic.

The various discontents simmering in the diocese finally boiled over on Lismore in 1452, as attested by a chance recording of the events on 29 August 1452 in the *Auchinleck Chronicle*[125] (Plate 7):

> Ane thousand cccc lii. [1452] the xxix [29] day of August, thar was command to the cathederall kirk, master George of Lawder that tyme bischope of Ergyle, fra his castall of Auchindoun, efter that he had bene in the ile of Lesmor that tyme xxx [30] dayis and mair. And thar was in his company, that samyn tyme, master Hercules Skrymgeour person [parson] of Glassar [Glassary], schir Jhon McArthour, and schir Adam his perrische [parish] preist, and Alexander Skrymgeour the personis brothir, and the lordis awne servandis of houshald, and nane utheris, for the lord come for gud trety [treaty] and trastit [trusted] nain evill. This person forsaid brocht ane summondis apon schir Gilbert McLachane, that tyme chanceller of the forsaid cathedrall kirk, and apon schir Morys McFadyane, that tyme thesaurer [treasurer] of the said kirk. The quhilk [which] schir Gilbert and schir Morys gadderit [gathered] all hale the Clanlachane, and all uthiris that thai mycht purches [obtain], and send [sent] to thir men word [told them], that the forsaid bischop come with the forsaid clerk, and put thaim out of that benefice, and to put in the forsaid master Hercules. And thus thai informit the peple wranguisly [wrongly] and begylit [deceived] thaim, for the person [parson] had no thing bot [except] a summondis apon schir Gilbert, and apon schir Morys McFadyin, for a sentence diffinitive that thai gaf [gave] aganis him of his benefice that he had joysit [possessed] peceably xv[15] yer, with schir Gotheray

---

124 MacDonald (2013), Appendix A: nos 4–14.
125 T. Thomson, ed. (1819). *The Auchinleck Chronicle: Ane Schort Memoriale of the Scottis Croniklis for Addicioun; To Which is Added a Short Chronicle of the Reign of James the Second King of Scots* (privately printed); MacDonald (1950), pp. 218–20.

McForsan. Becaus that this summondis was apon his chennonis [canons], the lord passit in proper persoun till haf maid gud tretye. And als fast as this lord with thir personis forsaid come ner the kirk within the quarter of ane myle, the forsaid schir Gilbert and schir Morys come with all the power that thai mycht be, in fere [fear] of were [war], apon the forsaid lord the bischop and his company, and spak till himself richt dispituoslie with felloun [fierce] wordis and scorne, and for dispyte halsit [addressed] him in errische [Gaelic], sayand bannachadee, and dispituoslie reft [pulled] fra him the forsaid master Hercules, and pullit him fra his hors, and brak the lordis belt, and tuke the clerke ande his brother and harllit [dragged] and led thaim away rycht dispytfully, and band [bound] the gentill man and thocht to strik of [off] his hed. And quhen [when] this foull suppres [injury] was done till [to] God and haly [holy] kirk, than the lord wald haf past on his fute [foot] till his kirk, thai stert [stood] befor him, sayand that and he schupe [attempt] to gang thair away, that thai suld sla [slay] him and all that war with him. And thai war all about him, and wald nocht lat hun pas ony gait [way], till he was oblist [obliged] till assolye [acquit] thaim of all thing that than was done thar. And for dreid of his lyf and his mennis he grantit, throw [through] consall [advice] of Rure Alanson and uthiris that war with him. And than thai come with a flyrdome [mockery] and said that thai come for na ill of him ne his childer. And thai held the clerk and his brothir, and on the morne gart thaim swer that thai suld never follow him, nothir [nothing] of summondis, nor of uthir thing that was done to thaim be thaim self na na uthiris, bot held thair bullis [documents] and thair silver and a silkyne twys and all uthir graith [possessions] that thai had that was occht [any] worth, viz. gownis clokis [cloaks] huds [hoods] bannettis [bonnets] and uthir small geir.

This reveals a great deal about Lauder's position. The record of his occupation of Achinduin Castle has been widely interpreted to mean that it was the 'Bishop's Castle', although there is no other documentary evidence to support the idea; it would be more normal for the senior clergy to have had lodging much nearer the cathedral, but perhaps he concluded that he needed greater protection at this time. The chronicle seems to show that Bishop Lauder had not been resident on the island for some time. This complex story and its conflicting messages have been very fully explored by MacDonald (2010). It begins on 23 January 1451, when McLachlane and McFadyane were commissioned by the Pope to investigate allegations of 'perjury and dilapidation and consumption of goods' by Hercules Skrymgeour at his parish of Glassary. Around eighteen months later, Bishop Lauder arrived on the island, apparently to support Skrymgeour in peaceful negotiations over the allegations, but there were suspicions that the bishop intended to depose the Lismore dignitaries. Emotions were running high and the meeting immediately got out of hand, with the serious consequences described in the *Chronicle*. Strangely, there did not seem to be any subsequent disciplinary action against the Lismore canons for their violent actions but, before the end of the year, Hercules was replaced at Glassary by his relative Alexander Scrymgeour. It is significant that Morys McFadyane was still working closely with Lauder in the 1460s.

The *Auchinleck Chronicle* account clearly conveys the deeply held resentment against an 'intruded' bishop, expressed in mockery for his lack of Gaelic, as well as threats, outright violence and robbery. Subsequently, the issue of Gaelic reached the Vatican in 1465/6 when Colin Campbell, 1st Lord of Glenorchy, was acting as ambassador in Rome for James III. He supplicated the Pope to withdraw support for any clerical candidate 'unless he understands and speaks intelligently the language of the greater part of the parishioners'. In view of the assault, it is surprising that it was not until 1462 that an indult (privilege) from Pope Pius II was granted permitting him to live outside the diocese, 'in Glasgow, or elsewhere within two days ride of the diocese',[126] because of continuing armed conflict in the area. Today, it is difficult to grasp the idea that the Bishop of Argyll had to petition a foreign ruler to be permitted to live elsewhere than on Lismore, in his own country.

The Later Life of Bishop Lauder

Lauder may have been resident away from Lismore well before permission was granted by the Pope. As early as 1447, he was given the right to cut timber from the woods of Duncan Campbell of Lochawe for 'the bishop's

---

126 Kirk et al. (1997), nos. 903 and 1105, pp. 265, 329.

building' which has been interpreted as a new house in Dunoon, although there is charter evidence of an episcopal palace in Dumbarton by 1472. In 1447, Campbell also granted him fishing rights on Loch Eck and the River Echaig near Dunoon.[127] Six years later, King James II 'compassionating the poverty of the bishoprick of Argyle, granted to Bishop George the parish church of Dunoon with its tithes and churchlands as a mensal church forever'[128] and, around 1455, the king gave Lauder the custodianship of Dunoon Castle for his lifetime.[129] Plate 8 shows Lauder's seal. By the time of the papal indult, the parish church of St Mary the Virgin of Dunoon was fulfilling the role of diocesan cathedral. Nevertheless, the cathedral on Lismore had not been entirely forgotten:

> In 1451 Sir Duncan le Campbell lord of Lochaw granted to the Friars Preachers of Glasgow, for the repair and maintenance of their buildings, the repair of the ornaments of their church, or other pious uses, twenty shillings Scots yearly from the fermes of the lands of Inchernerusk lying within the lordship of Cowale [Cowal] beside his lake of Lochayk [Loch Eck], the one half to be paid to them at Glasgow Fair, and the other at Martinmas following, and Sir Duncan in the event of his failure to fulfil the grant became bound to pay a mark Scots to the fabrick of the cathedral church of Saint Moloak [Moluag] in Ergyle [Argyll], and half a mark to the collegiate church of Saint Mund [Kilmun] in Cowale.[130]

The move to Dunoon was significant, as Cowal had become the focus of the religious life of Duncan Campbell of Lochawe. In 1441, he was able to enlist the support of the young James II ('being zealous for the propagation of divine worship') and his mother Joan Beaufort (widow of James I) in a supplication to Rome to erect the parish church of St Mound (Kilmun) into a collegiate church.[131] He was following a national fashion of founding new chapels to accommodate a body of clergy to say prayers

---

127 MacDonald (1950), p. 218; MacDonald (2013), p. 80.
128 *Origines*, p. 63; *RMS*, nos 3136 xiv 1453.
129 *Origines*, pp. 63–4; MacDonald (2013), p. 80.
130 *Origines*, pp. 68–9.
131 Dunlop and MacLauchlan (1983), p. 791.

for the souls of departed family members and, in 1442, it was established at Kilmun near Dunoon for a provost and seven perpetual chaplains or prebendaries. This new establishment would have been more significant for the Campbell dynasty than the old cathedral on Lismore. Possessing the lands of Cowal and Dunoon Castle, and with a major stake in the religious life of the area, Duncan Campbell and his descendants (the Earls of Argyll and the Lords of Glenorchy) were to play important roles in the future of the diocese.

It might have been expected that the relocation of Bishop Lauder to safer and more accessible parts would have increased his participation in national activities. In the years that he was, at least notionally, resident on Lismore, his attendance at parliament and general councils at Edinburgh, Perth or Stirling had been poor. He seems to have been present only in March 1430 at Perth, when parliament was taken up with a range of 'housekeeping' issues; in April 1449 at Stirling, when James II took possession of the earldom of Mar for the crown; and in June 1455, witnessing the forfeiture of the powerful Douglases by James II. Strangely, he was absent from Edinburgh in 1462, when the parliament of James III asserted the king's right to appoint clergy below the rank of bishop, forbidding clergy to travel to Rome to be 'provided' with benefices. He also missed the parliament at Edinburgh in October 1467, attended by seven bishops and eleven abbots or priors, which dealt with a major overhaul of the Scottish coinage.

In reality, his poor attendance was not entirely unusual, and not simply owing to advancing years. Over his time as bishop, the Church's parliamentary duties in Scotland were fulfilled mainly by a core group (St Andrews, Glasgow, Dunblane and Dunkeld), some of whom held high offices of state (notably James Kennedy, Bishop of St Andrews); Aberdeen, Brechin and Galloway were less regular (although Thomas Spens, Bishop of Galloway, was for a time Keeper of the Privy Seal); Ross and Caithness attended sporadically; the Bishop of Orkney began to attend from the 1470s, following the transfer of the islands to the Scottish crown, as security for the dowry of Margaret of Denmark, James III's queen; but Argyll and the Isles were almost invariably absent. Towards the end of his long life, Lauder failed to be present at the May 1471 parliament, attended by nine bishops and 15 abbots and priors, which confirmed the conditions of Margaret's dowry.

Bishop Lauder died, aged around 80, between 1473 and 1475, when his successor is recorded as attending parliament. Possibly intimidated by the degree of opposition he met from his own chapter, from the Lord of the Isles, and from the aspiring Campbell family, it appears that he spent the last 20 years of his life quietly in Dunoon or Dumbarton, keeping a low profile and leaving other members of the chapter to maintain the life of a neglected cathedral. It has been argued that his most important contribution to Church and society was his encouragement of the further education of Argyll clerics, particularly at Glasgow University.[132]

---

132 MacDonald (2013), p. 211.

10

The Last Days of Argyll Diocese (1475–1560)

The Diocese in 1475

By the time that Bishop Lauder died (1473/5), the headquarters of the diocese had already, for a quarter of a century, been based in Dunoon rather than on Lismore, and it is unlikely that any of his five Catholic successors spent much time on the island. The move reduced the amount of arduous travel that they had to face if they were to fulfil the full range of their duties, including attendance at parliament. Away from the West Highlands, they avoided the violence and disorder of the *Linn na Creach* (Age of Forays) that broke out after 1483 with the suppression of the Lordship of the Isles, which had maintained order to a degree. Indeed, Bishop David Hamilton ensured his own safety when visiting Argyll by building Saddell Castle out of the stones of the suppressed abbey, between 1508 and 1512 (see p. 1).[133] Papal records and charters[134] indicate that the bishop was supported, fairly continuously, by teams of dignitaries (archdeacon, chancellor, dean, treasurer and precentor), although evidence is lacking for the activities of an Official of Argyll undertaking the legal work of the diocese. The fact that the chancellor of the diocese immediately after the Reformation (Gavin Hammiltoun) was a prominent notary in support of the Lords of Glenorchy, suggests that at least some of the legal responsibilities of the diocese had become part of the remit of the chancellor.

---

133 Canmore ID 38867.
134 MacDonald (2013), Appendix A.

However, although these senior members of the chapter were appointed to the diocese, it appears that many of them, like the bishop, were not resident on Lismore. This is particularly the case for the archdeacons, the spiritual deputies. Out of ten identifiable incumbents, at least four were very busy with important jobs elsewhere. William Elphinstone (archdeacon 1475–80) was, during his period of office, rector of Glasgow University; official of Lothian; commissary general of the archdiocese of St Andrews; a member of parliament in his own right; and involved in a diplomatic mission to France. By 1483 he was Bishop of Aberdeen and by 1488, Chancellor of Scotland.[135] John Campbell (1483–6/7) was shortly to become Bishop of Sodor. Andrew Forman, who only lasted a year (1480), was a high-flying courtier, later serving both the king (James IV) and the Pope, including diplomatic work abroad. By 1501 he was Bishop of Moray. David Cunningham (1489–1509) also served as rector of Glasgow University, and Robert Barry (1509–29) belonged to a prominent Dumbarton family; his son is recorded as a burgess in the town.

Absence was not restricted to the archdeacons. According to MacDonald (2013):

> In the sixteenth century Seumas MacGriogar [James MacGregor] and his son Dubhghall served respectively as dean (1514–1551) and chancellor of Argyll (1558–1576) whilst maintaining continuous possession of the vicarage of Fortingall in Glen Lyon throughout their lives. Judging from the everyday chronicle accounts, it is obvious that both father and son remained principally attached to the ancestral home of their lineage, ministering to their local parishioners in Fortingall, and were infrequent visitors to Lismore.

Although they may have neglected their duties on the island, the MacGregors were busy at home in Fortingall compiling *The Book of the Dean of Lismore*, the oldest surviving example of written Scots Gaelic. Meanwhile, the local families that had monopolised some of the senior cathedral posts since the establishment of the diocese were finally being displaced, although Donald Macfadzen (the last of a line of Macfadzen

---

135 L.J. Macfarlane (1985).

canons) did act as precentor from 1507 to 1511. The Clan MacGillemichael, which had provided numerous rectors and dignitaries of the cathedral in the thirteenth and fourteenth centuries,[136] had disappeared from the scene by 1430, although the unfounded tradition that they contributed a bishop (Robert Carmichael – *an Easbuig Ban*, the Fair Bishop'[137]), possibly in the fifteenth century, may well be a backward look to the dominance of these more junior clergy. It seems safe to conclude that most of the senior clergy of the diocese were based in Dunoon and Dumbarton.

The question arises as to which members of the clergy were actually present on the island to maintain the daily rituals in the cathedral. In principle, this role should have been fulfilled on rotation by the five prebendary parish rectors – the canons. For two of the parishes (Glassary and Kilmodan, in Cowal) the incumbents after 1475 were uniformly Lowlanders, who might well have considered that their duties lay with the bishop at the parish church of Dunoon. Kilmartin parish was occupied by Campbell rectors, who may have shared this approach. On the other hand, the Lords of the Isles had established a tradition of recommending priests to the prebendary parishes in Kintyre (Kilcolmkill and Kilberry) from dynasties of Irish origin, based on Islay (for example the Ó Brolcháins) whose orientation was to the diocese of Sodor. It seems likely, therefore, that the responsibility for maintaining the cathedral services would have fallen heavily on the Lismore parish vicars; for the period up to the Reformation, the four identifiable incumbents were clearly Gaels, and competent in Gaelic: Eoin Mac an t-Sagairt Mac an Mhaoil-Chaluim (1495–6); Maol-Coluim mac Solaim (1496–7); Diarmaid Mac na Ceàrdaich (1531); Alasdair MacThàmais (1544).[138]

In the absence of further endowment, the financial resources of the diocese remained inadequate. The situation was made more difficult by the increased costs of developing and maintaining new bases in Dunoon and Dumbarton, although Bishop Lauder had been granted Dunoon as a mensal parish ('compassioning the poverty of the bishopric'); and the diocese did benefit from subsequent grants, such as the right, from the king, in 1506, to

---

136 MacDonald (2013), pp. 54–5.
137 Carmichael Watson Project, University of Edinburgh. CW113/3; Carmichael (1948), pp. 95–8.
138 MacDonald (2013), Appendix A, p. 337.

take fuel from the Lordship of Cowal moors.[139] Recognising the bishop's difficulties, the Vatican reduced the level of taxation of the diocese by half in 1475.

Under the circumstances, few resources would have been devoted to maintaining the fabric of the cathedral. A papal letter of 1411 had already noted that the building required 'costly repairs' and, in 1512, James IV wrote to Julius II with his (probably overstated) opinion that:

> ... the cathedral of Argyll, inadequately endowed, in a solitary and sterile region, among a people rude and uncultured, and little visited for many centuries by bishops or canons, has fallen into ruin and at present lies deserted ...[140]

It is clear from the report of the investiture of a new archdeacon in the cathedral in 1531, with a reference to his 'stall in the choir',[141] that the king was exaggerating, to give weight to his proposal to transfer the cathedral site to Saddell Abbey on the mainland, in Kintyre, as explained in a letter of 1507 to the Pope's representative in Scotland:

> The diocese of Lismore is very extensive and mountainous, more prolific of worry to the bishop owing to its wild character than of episcopal revenue. He has a difficult job in imposing ecclesiastical discipline upon a rude people, unsettled and not amenable to the law. The present bishop is efficient and watchful, and deserves a wide sphere of government. The episcopal mensa is so exiguous that he cannot maintain his household or meet pastoral charges suitably. James feels justified by the circumstances and the merits of the bishop in appealing to the Pope. The house of Sadaguil [*sic*], once Cistercian and established by the king's ancestors in Lismore diocese, has within living memory seen no monastic life and has fallen to the use of laymen. There is no hope of reviving monastic life: the fruits are barely £9 sterling: it would be most troublesome to recall long-standing alienations. James writes for a commission

---

139 *Origines*, p. 63.
140 *Letters of James IV*, James IV to Julius II, Holyrood, 22 April 1512.
141 McRoberts (1952); MacDonald (2013), p. 78.

THE LAST DAYS OF ARGYLL DIOCESE (1475-1560)

to the Archbishop of Glasgow or other prelate to investigate and, if his Holiness approves, unite the place in perpetuity to the bishopric.[142]

However, the account of the investiture may refer only to the choir of the cathedral, and the nave may well have been neglected. Whatever the exact state of the building, it was clearly on the way to becoming an unusable ruin in the years after the Reformation (see Chapter 11). The proposed move to Saddell did not materialise.

Meanwhile, even in the absence of the senior clergy, the graveyard remained an important destination for prominent individuals from the area. Several West Highland graveslabs on Lismore have been dated to the fourteenth or fifteenth century, and most of them are carved from local slate (see Chapter 7). This tradition persisted well into the sixteenth century, as shown by the memorial attributed to Donald Stewart of Invernahyle (*Domhnull nan ord*, Donald of the hammers – referring to his immense strength) who led the Stewarts at the Battle of Pinkie (1547).

All of this was happening in a period when the Campbells were reaching political dominance over much of the diocese, as well as aspiring to leading roles in the government of the country. By 1470, Colin Campbell, 1st Earl of Argyll, had succeeded to the Lordship of Lorn through his marriage to Isabel Stewart, and following a complex legal process with her uncle, Walter Stewart, to surrender the lordship. He then feued out a third of the area, including a third of Lismore, to his uncle, Colin Campbell, Lord of Glenorchy, in recognition of the latter's marriage to Isabel's sister, Janet. With the lordship came the right as patrons to influence appointments to the posts of dean, chancellor and treasurer of the diocese. There can be no doubt about the seriousness with which the Campbells undertook their religious lives. In 1437:

> Anthonius bishop of Urbino, papal legate in Scotland, granted to Sir Colin Cambel of Glenurcha in the diocese of Argyle license to have a portable altar on which in places suited to the purpose he might cause mass and other divine services to be performed in presence of himself and of his family.[143]

142 *Letters of James IV*, James IV to the Cardinal of St Mark, 1507.
143 *Origines*, p. 144.

He was known as Black Colin of Rome because of three visits to the Vatican in the 1460s as royal ambassador, and he is alleged to have taken part in a crusade against the Turks on Rhodes. The dominance of the Campbells would have an important influence on the men appointed to be bishop over the following decades, and on the Protestant revolution to come.

Robert Colquhon (Bishop 1475–1494)

Bishop Robert, like George Lauder, came from a middle-ranking family that had proved to be staunch supporters of James I. As keeper of Dumbarton Castle, his great-grandfather, Sir John Colquhon, 10th of Luss, had held out against the rebellion of James the Fat and Bishop Finlay in 1425. Sir John's privileged situation, however, changed with the murder of the king in 1437 and the reassertion of the Albany Stewart faction, and they were implicated in his own assassination at Inchmurrin in 1439. However, the Colquhons were back in favour by the 1470s, when Sir John's grandson, also Sir John (11th of Luss, his father having died young), was created sheriff of Dumbarton and keeper of its castle by James III. Bishop Robert was his son.

As a younger son, Robert Colquhon (Raibeart MacCombaich) followed a recognisable career path in the Church, securing the income as rector for two parishes (Luss and Kippen in the diocese of Dunblane) by 1466, which allowed him to matriculate at Glasgow University, achieving his MA by 1470. As a son of the sheriff of Dumbarton and supporter of George Lauder, he was an obvious choice for the vacancy caused by the death of the bishop around 1473. Although not elected by the chapter of the diocese, he was 'provided' by the Pope in 1475, paying a tax of 112 florins and 25 shillings.

Like his predecessors, Bishop Robert's tenure was dominated by financial matters: in the early years he acted to retain the income from his prebend at Luss, and openly contested the will of a fellow cleric in Dumbarton.[144] By the late 1480s, following the example of Bishop Martin in the fourteenth century, he tried to reclaim the income from the Kintyre parishes of Kilcalmonell, Kilkerran and Killean, which had been alienated to Paisley Abbey. For this he suffered temporary excommunication.

---

144 MacDonald (2013), p. 96.

This scrambling for money for his own support and the maintenance of the diocese, and the resulting disapproval of the Vatican, does not seem to have damaged his reputation on the national scene. During the reign of James III (up to 1488), he attended parliament regularly in Edinburgh, taking part in important business, such as:

- the restoration of John of Islay as Lord of the Isles in 1476;
- the confirmation of the vast landholding of the Archbishop of St Andrews in 1479;
- peace negotiations with England in 1482.

In fact, he appears to have been a valued administrator. On 1 March 1483 he was appointed, along with the Archbishop of St Andrews, the Bishop of Glasgow, the abbots of Holyrood and Cambuskenneth, and the Archdeacon of Lothian, to be a Lord of the Articles, drafting legislation for the full parliament. It is surprising that, in a time of national insecurity, the committee gave precedence to giving advice that 'the fredom of halikirk [the holy church] be observit and kepit in tyme tocum' (May 1485).[145] Even though the patron of the diocese, the Earl of Argyll, and the Bishop, soon to be Archbishop, of Glasgow were prominent members of the successful rising against James III, and benefited from the accession of James IV after the Battle of Sauchieburn, Bishop Robert made no more recorded appearances at parliament.

The Last Four Catholic Bishops: David Hamilton (1497–1523), Robert Montgomery (1525–1538), William Cunningham (1539–1553), James Hamilton (1553–1580)

The appointment of David Hamilton marked another step-change in the diocese of Argyll. The last four bishops were all members of powerful families from south-west Scotland: David Hamilton was the brother, and James Hamilton was the son, of the 1st Earl of Arran; Robert Montgomery was the son of the 1st Earl of Eglinton; and William Cunningham was the son of the 4th Earl of Glencairn. This shift of focus towards Ayrshire reflects the political realities of the time. The 4th Earl of Argyll was married to a daughter of the Earl of Arran, and was associated with the

---

145 MacDonald (2013), p. 97; *RPS* 1485/5/7.

rising star of the Campbells of Loudon in Ayrshire. The Hamilton bishops were illegitimate, and Montgomery, too, appears to have needed papal dispensation: for his young age (24) and his involvement in a homicide. Montgomery and James Hamilton had children, some of the latter being by marriage. There were irregularities about their ordination as priests and investiture as bishops, and only the first two (David Hamilton and Robert Montgomery) can be identified as having studied at university. Cunningham was the only Bishop of Argyll not to die in post; in 1553 he resigned to become Dean of Brechin, clearly a more lucrative position. It is unlikely that any of the four were competent in Gaelic, and very unlikely that they visited Lismore. It is difficult to reconcile these developments with the attitude of the Stewart kings:

> In the year 1507 the grant [of Kilmarow parish] was confirmed to David bishop of Argyle by King James IV on account of the singular devotion he bore towards the blessed confessor Saint Moloc [Moluag], patron of the cathedral church of Lismore.[146]

It is clear that the lifestyles of the last bishops fell well below the original ideals of the Catholic Church (Chapter 1). They were part of the political structure of Scotland but were deficient even in this aspect of their duties: the last three are recorded as attending parliament on a single occasion each.

During the careers of the four bishops, a tide of reformation was sweeping through northern Europe, at least partly fuelled by the kinds of abuse of power and resources shown by the clergy, including in Scotland. While Henry VIII was negotiating his own version of divorce from Rome, King James V of Scotland (reigning as an adult from around 1528, after a prolonged and turbulent minority) remained a resolute supporter of the Catholic Church, persecuting priests returning to Scotland from Germany and Switzerland with revolutionary ideas. The most prominent victim of the time was Patrick Hamilton, burnt at the stake for heresy at St Andrews in 1528. The king's religious fervour, recognised formally by Pope Paul III in 1537, did not prevent him from exploiting the Church for his own benefit. With the blessing of the Vatican, his clutch of illegitimate sons were awarded lucrative posts as abbots or priors of at least seven

---

146 *Origines*, p. 22.

religious houses; and he was skilled at diverting Church funds for secular activities.

After the king's death in 1542, the persecution continued under his widow, Mary of Guise, strongly supported by her chancellor, Cardinal Beaton. The burning of George Wishart, a disciple of Calvin, in St Andrews in 1545 led in the following year to the assassination of Beaton, and the occupation of St Andrews Castle by a group of Protestant revolutionaries. They were dislodged by French troops brought in from France by Mary but, surprisingly, were sent to serve in French galleys rather than being executed. Prominent among them was John Knox, who survived to continue his studies in Geneva.

In the following years, the Protestant cause continued to grow, particularly among the aristocracy, with the Earls of Argyll leading the so-called Lords of the Congregation. These were precarious times, involving invasion by both French and English forces, but in August 1560 the Lords and their supporters, including Bishop Hamilton, ensured that the Scottish parliament abolished the jurisdiction of the Pope in Scotland, declared the saying and hearing of Mass illegal, and approved the Calvinist Confession of Faith that had been drawn up by Knox and his colleagues to establish the doctrine and liturgy of the new Church.

James Hamilton continued as bishop for a further 20 years but his position was now a sinecure (Chapter 1). The religious authority in Argyll diocese had passed to John Carswell, who was appointed Superintendent in Argyll, and he devoted himself to developing a Gaelic version of the Reformed *Book of Common Order*, the first published book in Scottish Gaelic. This was important in ensuring that the Reformation took root in Argyll, and he oversaw the introduction of Protestant ministers to Argyll parishes, with arrangements to ensure that they were sufficiently educated. Chapter 12 charts the post-Reformation developments on Lismore and the fate of its cathedral church.

How the Cathedral Affected the People of Lismore

Up to this point, the story has been about powerful and influential men: popes, bishops, priests, kings, leading landowners and warriors. Nothing so far has been about the ordinary men and women who lived on the island close to the cathedral, and were affected by the activities of its powerful clergy. Population growth in Scotland was severely curtailed by the Black Death in the fourteenth century, by frequent periods of famine, and by warfare but, arguing from the demography of Scotland as a whole, it is likely that, by the fifteenth century, there would have been not fewer that 300–400 people on Lismore, perhaps around 50 family units. This chapter attempts to explore the roles and experiences of these families, relying inevitably on some informed speculation, but we owe it to them to try to understand the parts they were required to play, and the wider implications of a cathedral on the island.

Land and People

On account of its fertile and well-drained soils, Lismore was a predominantly arable island up to the mid nineteenth century, a valuable source of grain in a region better suited by its climate and geology to the rearing of cattle. The division of the island into separate townships, many of whose names have persisted to the present time, had already taken place by 1200, each being occupied as a joint tenancy by groups of closely related households. Their buildings – which they had built themselves – were clustered together within the cultivated area, which was managed in runrig, and surrounded by head dykes to keep the cattle out of the corn in the growing season. It was a hard, unrelenting life, not least owing to the physical challenges of rig and furrow cropping. For some, attendance at the cathedral on Sundays and Holy Days must have been a welcome break from their work.

It is not known whether the environmental conditions on Lismore were favourable for the cultivation of wheat during the benign Medieval Climate Anomaly, which ended around 1250; it is certainly known from the archaeological record that wheat crops were grown across the country from the Neolithic Age.[147] However, baron court records from the lowest point of the little ice age in the seventeenth century show that the economy of the island by then relied on growing oats and bere barley.[148] Although these crops had relatively low yield potential (particularly the black oat, *Avena strigosa*), they had characteristics which made them suitable for mainly subsistence farming under unpredictable conditions (for example, stormy weather delaying harvest into the late autumn or winter). On the one hand, oats could be harvested green and matured in the sheaf, while bere crops had the shortest growing season, typically around 100 days from mid May.[149] There was the additional benefit that bere grain was particularly suited to alcohol production, although in many seasons there would have been little or no surplus beyond the needs of the family.

Some of these tenants, in the townships of Achinduin, Frackersaig and Craignich, held their land directly from the bishop, the others from the Lordship of Lorn. Rents were paid in kind, mainly grain, although it was also common at that time in the West Highlands for tenants to be required to provide oarsmen for the lord's birlinn, and they must have been needed for the bishop's boat. This would, no doubt, have been drawn up on the shore under the protection of Coeffin Castle. The island men would also have been called out to fight, when necessary. For example, it is more than likely that Lismore men were represented in the force of 800 that the MacDougalls sent to garrison Ayr in 1307, and among the 2,000 defeated by Bruce at the Pass of Brander in 1308. The tenancy arrangements seem to have become more complicated after 1470, when the Argyll and Glenorchy Campbells feued individual townships to junior members of their families, who may have become resident on the island. Although they

---

147 Bishop et al. (2022).
148 National Records of Scotland (NRS) GD112/17. Court books of bailie court of Disher and Toyer, 1573–1748.
149 Hay (2012).

were effectively tacksmen (intermediate between the owner and the joint tenants) they adopted grand titles of ownership (for example Campbell *of* Cloichlea, Achuran or Balimenach). Tenancy agreements expanded to include, for example, maintenance of the island grain mills, and regular attendance at baron courts on the mainland.[150]

The Teind

In addition to their rent, the townships were required to pay the teind to the Church: an annual tax of 10 per cent of all commercial activity, delivered in kind (grain, meat, hides, fish, eggs) rather than money (Chapter 4). The islanders would also have supplied the clergy with fuel, brought in laboriously in small boats from the woods and peat banks on the mainland, as the island had already exhausted most of its resources. Living near the cathedral and its resident clergy, they would have had very limited scope for evasion, at least up to 1450. Relationships would have been further complicated by the fact that some of the 'dignitaries' of the cathedral, and possibly the vicar of the parish, were from local families (Chapter 9) – with divided loyalties. Alexander Carmichael (1908–9) has speculated that the role of tax collector on Lismore was assumed by the hereditary keepers of St Moluag's bachuil, although there is no concrete evidence for this. Such taxes on the islanders' hard-won resources must have generated a great deal of resentment in the townships, since most of the income would have been spent on the support of the Church rather than the local community and infrastructure. At times, the tenants would have been hard-pressed just to feed their families. As discussed in Chapter 7, although there are no archaeological clues to its location, there must have been a substantial depot near the cathedral for the storage of all this bulky produce.

Building Work

Chapter 7 presents the evidence that there were large-scale building projects on Lismore for at least a hundred years during the thirteenth and fourteenth centuries: not just the cathedral and its associated buildings, but also the MacDougall castles at Coeffin and Achinduin. This activity must have had major effects on the economy of the island and the lives

---

150 Hay and Fryer (2015).

of its people. According to a local legend, a master mason in charge of the cathedral project was from Italy (the *Romanach*, reputed to have been buried out of sight of the building). It is likely that the skilled masons, carpenters, slaters and smiths living and working in the area to the east of the church were members of international teams that moved from project to project across Europe, bringing new styles of architecture; unusual mason's marks that are common to Lismore Cathedral, Achinduin Castle and Ardchattan Priory provide local evidence of these itinerant specialists.

Nevertheless, there would have been an enormous demand for less skilled local labour to provide direct assistance to the craftsmen on site, and to transport the incoming fine sandstone (from Mull or Morvern) for the detailing of windows, doorways and internal features (Chapter 7). One of the surprises from the study of the cathedral mortars has been the extent to which the lime was prepared from shells rather than limestone, reducing the amount of labour required for quarrying limestone, and the amount of fuel-wood required to fire the kilns. Clearly, oysters were a normal component of the diet of islanders. The firewood used to burn the lime (presumably in clamp kilns on the island), possibly in the form of charcoal, was predominantly oak (not native to Lismore), hazel and birch. There can be no doubt that there was a great deal of felling, cutting and transporting to be done, and the forests of Appin must have been devastated by the demand for firewood, which included mature oak trees up to 345 years old. Local labour was probably raised in the same way that fighting forces were recruited, with all able men expected to report for duty after they had sown their crops, and released in the late summer to take in the harvest. Meanwhile, the women would have been left in charge of the townships. It will never be known whether the islanders received any reward for their contributions.

The People and the Mass

In principle, attendance at Mass on Sundays, and on the many religious festivals in the year, was required of all adults, men and women; they stood in the nave, while the priests took part in the full celebration in the choir. With so many prominent clergymen on the island, it is likely that there was a great deal of pressure to attend, although confession, absolution and full participation in Holy Communion would normally occur only once a year. Without regular attendance, confession could be refused and, at a time when life could be precarious, the resulting risk of eternal damnation must have felt real for many. It was also critical for the future of their souls to be protected by the sacraments of baptism, marriage and absolution on the point of death. Arguing from the practice elsewhere in the West Highlands,[151] in addition to Easter, Christmas, Candlemas and St Moluag's Day (25 June) feast days would celebrate the lives of a galaxy of saints: Andrew, Brigid, Columba, David, Donnan, John, Maelrubha, Martin, Mary, Patrick, Peter, Ternan.

On Lismore, the Dominicans were unlikely to have met the scale of heresy that they had been called upon to deal with among the Cathars of south-west France. Drawing on the folklore collections of Alexander Carmichael in South Uist, where Catholicism still persists, the beliefs and practices of the islanders would have been informed by a complex mixture of residual paganism (such as the fire festival of Beltane, and the reverence for holy wells); Early Church traditions (such as the blessing of livestock and boats by Moluag's staff (the bachuil), and devotion to particular saints); and orthodox Catholicism. For the devout, life was regulated by a succession of rituals, incantations and prayers to the saints, from the daily rekindling of the hearth to the smooring of the flame; the sowing of the seed to the harvesting of the grain; the launching of the boat to its safe return to shore.

However, there is some documentary evidence of more serious deviation from Christianity, suggesting that 'trafficking with the Devil' might have existed among the island population. For example, the Argyll Archives record that 'Euphrick Ninichol Roy or Efric Nichol; and Christian Nicean vic Couil vic Gillespie', who were recognised 'white witches' on Lismore, were consulted by those plotting to kill Campbell of Cawdor and the Earl of Argyll in 1592. Later, in 1677, Donald McIlmichael was hanged at Inveraray after a confused confession involving not only the Devil but also fairies. At his trial for horse theft on Lismore, he admitted consulting the Devil on the discovery and disposal of stolen goods, but also described his attendance at Sabbath dances on a fairy hillock where he played the Jew's harp.[152] Whether these were remnants of practices on the island in

---

151 R. Black, 'The Quern Dust Calendar': <www.querndust.co.uk>.
152 Inveraray Sheriff Court Records, mentioned in: A. Campbell (2002); D. Mackechnie (1975).

earlier times or a result of the turbulent religious environment around the Reformation, is not clear.

It is arguable that it took the rigours of the Calvinist Church of Scotland to root out most of these 'errors', but widespread belief in the fairy folk did continue well into the eighteenth century. The persistence of the islanders in holding on to age-old traditions is attested by the parish minister, Rev. Gregor McGregor, in the *New Statistical Account*; describing the surviving base of the eighth-century cross at the top of the ancient graveyard, he notes:

> ... it was at this cross that marriage banns used to be published, and the custom was continued until about twenty or so years ago. The friends of both parties assembled at the cross, to the number of perhaps forty or fifty people, on Sabbath morning, and it did not signify whether there was a sermon in the church or not; the clerk issued the proclamations amid the huzzas of the company, after which they all retired to the public-house, and spent the remaining part of the day in drinking, and frequently concluded the scene with a battle. Happily, the last incumbent [Rev. John Stewart, minister 1802–37] succeeded in abolishing this unseemly practice.[153]

Archaeology has revealed one Roman Catholic practice that persisted well into the Protestant era: the burial (apparently secretly) of unbaptised infants (stillborn or premature) in a mass grave outside the normal area of Christian burial.

How the People were Controlled

Throughout the second half of the thirteenth century and most of the fourteenth century, the bishops of Argyll, normally resident on Lismore, were Dominican friars, from an austere order that was experienced in dealing with heresy and committed to limiting the potential for the commission of sins among the population. However, towards the end of this period the behaviour of the clergy themselves was deteriorating, with the widespread incidence of sexual liaisons and illegitimate children, as well as the general scrambling for money and posts. What were the

---

153 McGregor (1845), p. 223.

effects of these developments on the township families? Were they cowed by the iron fist of the Dominicans or were they defiant, living their lives according to their own standards?

One of the first tasks of the early bishops would have been to come to terms with the resident Céli Dé monks, who were orthodox in their beliefs but had a tradition of independence of central Church authority. The three *Kil* place names on Lismore (Kilcheran, Kilandrist and Killean) have been cited as evidence of early monastic centres. If this is correct, then these communities of monks would have been embedded in island society for centuries, even part of a hereditary priesthood, as found elsewhere in Scotland. Although forming important bridges between the people and the cathedral chapter, clergy from the island community would have faced crises of loyalty.

Pre-Reformation bishops were expected to maintain consistorial courts where the archdeacons would have dispensed justice in a range of civil areas including inheritance and matrimony, as well as being able to control society through the sanctions available to the Church (in extreme cases, excommunication). This was in addition to the activities of the legal officers appointed by the landlords – for example, the 'sergeandry' duties of the tackholder at Achuran in the 1540s, on behalf of the Earl of Argyll.[154] At times, especially in the thirteenth century, the Church and civil authorities would have been able to call on the help of forces billeted in the two castles to maintain order.

However, the single 'eyewitness' account of the behaviour of islanders, in the *Auchinleck Chronicle* (Chapter 9), makes it clear that they were far from overawed by these authorities. Indeed, the MacLachlans and MacFadyens acted as if they were entitled to abuse the bishop's party, both verbally and physically, to steal their possessions, and to imprison Hercules Scrymgeour, even though he had been appointed as a cathedral canon. These events in 1452 could be interpreted as the last resistance of the islanders to the interference in the hereditary priesthood by external authority, although anger at the erosion of Gaelic and the intrusion of Lowlanders must also have played a part. It is probably not surprising that, in 1512, James IV referred to them as 'rude and uncultured' (Chapter 10). Later history provides other examples of the pronounced independence of the Lismore people. The surviving proceedings of the Glenorchy baron courts

---

154 From an unpublished archive curated by Diarmid Campbell, Melfort, Argyll.

(1615–43) from only 60 years after the Reformation, reveal a population resisting regulations laid down by the landowner for the improvement of the land (for example, to introduce some crop rotation; to plant and protect trees; and to keep kailyards) and committing a wide range of offences (theft, using hand querns rather than taking their corn to the estate mill, unpaid debts, shooting game, grievous bodily harm).[155] If the compilers of the *Aberdeen Breviary* (1510) are to be believed, this conservatism has a long history: they record that the islanders were 'indisposed to listen to the teachings' of St Moluag in spite of his spectacular miracles, such as crossing the sea with his team aboard a stone.

Services to the Community

In a well-managed medieval diocese, the bishop and his clergy would have taken responsibility for a range of services to the community. These included elementary education of boys showing academic promise, in preparation for assuming the role of vicar of the parish or possibly as a preparation for more advanced study; basic health care, including maintenance of a hospital for the sick; support for the poor and needy; and hospitality to travellers. There is no documentary support for the existence of any of these services on Lismore. Indeed, I.B. Cowan has found no evidence of a building labelled as a hospital in the Argyll diocese,[156] and the first school on Lismore, in a modern sense, is thought to have been established in the early seventeenth century (although there would have been opportunities for education before this time through the Gaelic Learned Orders in the area).

There remain many unanswered questions about the interrelationships among the clergy themselves. Until the middle of the fifteenth century at least, there was resident on Lismore a body of highly educated men, some of whom had studied in Paris, Oxford or St Andrews, but with competence in Gaelic. They were joined by other, locally based, dignitaries carrying the title of Dominus, which signified a lower level of education. Did these men achieve the literacy, numeracy and competence in Latin needed to satisfy the Vatican as members of the Gaelic Learned Orders that were maintained by the MacDougalls and MacDonalds? This certainly seems to

---

155 Hay and Fryer (2015).
156 Cowan (1995).

be the case for Bishop Bean, who began his career as chaplain to the Lords of the Isles and later studied in Paris.[157] The question remains as to whether there was a pronounced hierarchy among the cathedral clergy.

157 MacDonald (2013), Appendix B.

12

Epilogue
After the Reformation

Although James Hamilton remained as Bishop of Argyll for 20 years after 1560, when the jurisdiction of the Pope in Scotland was abolished by the Scottish parliament, this was in name only, as John Carswell assumed most of the authority and duties in Argyll and the Isles, with the new title of Superintendent.[158] He devoted himself to developing a Gaelic version of the Reformed *Book of Common Order*, the first published book in the language (1567), which was important in ensuring that Protestantism took root in Argyll. He also oversaw the introduction of Protestant ministers to Argyll parishes, and an improvement in their education. Meanwhile, all non-Reformed clergy, including the surviving members of the diocesan chapter, were guaranteed two-thirds of their livings for life.

However, the Presbyterian model of the national Church, without the need of bishops, was not finally established until the 'Glorious Revolution' of 1688, and the replacement of Catholic James II with William and Mary. As Scotland, and the clergy, switched back and forth between Episcopalianism and Presbyterianism, under pressure from the crown, there were up to a dozen more bishops of Argyll, several with very short tenure. The challenges of the time are well illustrated by the experience of Alexander McCalman. After study at university in Glasgow and St Andrews, he was appointed as Presbyterian minister on Lismore in 1660, having to face a situation where the church/cathedral was ruinous and there was no manse or glebe. It is hardly surprising that he was found

---

158 MacKinnon (1932).

to be frequently absent from the island.[159] Following the restoration of the monarchy with Charles II, bishops, too, were restored throughout Scotland in 1661, and the diocese of Argyll was re-established. McCalman converted from Presbyterianism and became both parish vicar and dean of Lismore. It is recorded that he was greatly valued by his parishioners. At the final establishment of a Presbyterian Church of Scotland he declined to change back, but continued to serve unofficially for a further 27 years from his base in Appin.

Witness lists included in legal documents with an official seal show that a diocesan chapter continued in some form, although the members were probably not resident on Lismore. Gavin Hammiltoun, chancellor and precentor of the diocese after the Reformation, also acted as notary for the Lords of Glenorchy; his protocol book at Taymouth records their many property transactions.[160] From time to time there were archdeacons and treasurers. To replace the consistorial courts that had been maintained by Catholic bishops to deal with a range of civil issues, the reformed Church introduced a new system of local commissary courts to resolve legal aspects of marriage, legitimacy, inheritance and debt. By 1571 Archibald Cunningham had been appointed as commissar clerk of Lismore to assume these duties. Diocesan appointments finally ceased in 1688, although the commissary courts continued to 1823.

After 1560 there was a scramble to secure the valuable teinds that had formerly been imposed on society to support the Catholic Church. In a charter of January 1571, the dean and chapter of the Kirk of Lesmoir granted 'the tiendsheaves of lands pertaining to the chantry' to the Lord of Glenorchy and his family 'for three years from Beltane next, and so on for three years at a time, for granter's lifetime', and affixed the chapter seal.[161] This situation continued until James VI annexed the teinds to the crown and granted them back to landowners, with the condition that they be used to support the local clergy and parish schools. In turn, the landowner would simply add the teind to the tenants' rent. By the end of the eighteenth century, the rights to and responsibilities for teinds on Lismore were held by the Duke of Argyll, the Earl of Breadalbane and the Campbells of Airds. Here, as across Scotland, tension continued between

---

159 Hay (2024), pp. 104–6; Carmichael (1948), pp. 123–4.
160 *Origines*: for example NRS GD112/2/94.
161 NRS GD112/51, Ecclesiastical Documents 1456–1912.

these 'heritors' and the parish ministers over the payment of stipends and the maintenance of the church and manse. It would not be until 2000 that the Scottish parliament finally passed legislation to abolish feudal tenure, including teinds.

As early as 1512, when writing to Pope Julius II, King James IV claimed that the cathedral on Lismore was ruinous (Chapter 10), and there are reports from around 1650 that the building was roofless. It is not clear whether this was a result of the alleged burning of the building at the Reformation or by Alasdair MacColla in the 1640s,[162] or simply neglect. It does seem likely that the eighth-century Black Cross had been destroyed by this time by enthusiastic reformers. In 1699, the Argyll synod received an address from the parishioners of Appin

> asking for funds to pay the schoolmaster £80 Scots yearly – the kirk of Appin is wanting a roof and a slate roof is necessary, and a loft for the people – the kirk also wants a bell and as there are two bells in Lismore they ask for the use of one of them *until the kirk of Lismore be built* [my italics].[163]

Meanwhile, the Lismore graveyard remained a prestige site for the burial of prominent locals, as the commemoration of Donald Stewart of Invernahyle (the leader of Appin forces at the Battle of Pinkie in 1547) around 1600 on a reused carved graveslab has shown.

The question arises as to where ministers/bishops such as Alexander McCalman conducted their services. Did they, after the pattern of Covenanting preachers, officiate in the open air (using the portable pulpit?) or sheltered by the surviving walls of the choir? By the mid eighteenth century, the Lorn Presbytery had found the funds for a thorough renewal of the choir as the parish church. The walls were lowered by around 3 metres, the structure was reroofed, and the internal arrangement changed to the norms of the Reformed Kirk, with the pulpit next to the south door, a long communion table at the centre of the area, and a loft built around three sides, accessed from the exterior. This arrangement continued until the refit of the building from 1896 (Chapter 7).

In spite of its turbulent history, the parish church at Clachan, choir of

---

162 Carmichael Watson Collection, University of Edinburgh. Coll-97/CW106/59.
163 Argyll Archives, Inveraray. Bundle 572.

the medieval cathedral, no doubt erected near the site of Moluag's chapel, is the site of an unbroken tradition of Christian worship: 1,500 years from the arrival of the Early Church, 800 years from the establishment of the diocese of Argyll, and nearly 500 years since the Scottish Reformation parliament.

Bibliography

Primary Sources

Anderson, A.O. (1908). *Scottish Annals from English Chroniclers, 500–1286*. London: David Nutt. Cited as Anderson (1908).

Bain, J., ed. (1884). *Calendar of Documents Relating to Scotland Preserved in Her Majesty's Public Record Office, London. Vol. 2, 1272–1286*. Edinburgh: HM General Register House. Cited as Bain (1884).

Bain, J., ed. (1887). *Calendar of Documents Relating to Scotland Preserved in Her Majesty's Public Record Office, London. Vol. 3, 1307–1357*. Edinburgh: HM General Register House. Cited as Bain (1887).

Bain, J., ed. (1898). *Calendar of the State Papers Relating to Scotland and Mary Queen of Scots 1547–1603. Vol. 1, 1547–63; Vol. 2, 1563–9*. Edinburgh: HM General Register House. Cited as Bain (1898).

Bliss, W.H., ed. (1896). *Calendar of Entries in the Papal Registers Relating to Great Britain and Ireland. Vol. 1, Petitions to the Pope AD 1342–1419*. London: HMSO. Cited as Bliss (1896).

Bliss, W.H. and Johnson, C., eds (1897). *Calendar of Entries in the Papal Registers relating to Great Britain and Ireland. Papal Letters, Vol. 3, 1342–62*. London: HMSO. Cited as Bliss and Johnson (1897).

Burns, C., ed. (1976). *Calendar of Papal Letters to Scotland of Clement VII of Avignon, 1378–1394*. Edinburgh: Scottish History Society, Series 4, Vol. 12. Cited as Burns (1976).

Burns, C., ed. (2021). *Calendar of Scottish Supplications to Clement VII and Benedict XIII of Avignon, 1378–1419*. Edinburgh: Scottish Record Society. Cited as Burns (2021).

Concilia Scotiae: Ecclesiae Scoticianae Statuta tam Provincialia quam Synodalia quae supersunt, MCCXXV–MDLIX, Vol. 1. Edinburgh: Bannatyne Club, 1886. Available as: *Statutes of the Scottish Church,*

1225–1559 (ed. and trans. D. Patrick LLD): <https://openvirtual worlds.org/omeka/items/show/435>. Cited as *Concilia Scotiae*.

Dunlop, A.I. and I.B. Cowan, eds (1970). *Calendar of Scottish Supplications to Rome, Vol. 7, 1428–1432*. Edinburgh: Scottish History Society, Series 4, Vol. 7. Cited as Dunlop and Cowan (1970).

Dunlop, A.I. and D. MacLauchlan, eds (1983). *Calendar of Scottish Supplications to Rome, Vol. 4, 1433–1447*. University of Glasgow Press. Cited as Dunlop and MacLauchlan (1983).

Kirk, J., Tanner, R.J. and Dunlop, A.I., eds (1997). *Calendar of Scottish Supplications to Rome, Vol. 5, 1447–1471*. Scottish History Society, Series 4. Cited as Kirk et al. (1997).

The Letters of James the Fourth, 1505–1513 (ed. R.L. Mackie). Edinburgh: Scottish History Society, Series 3, 1953. Cited as *Letters of James IV*.

McGregor, Rev. Gregor (1845). 'United Parish of Lismore and Appin'. In Gordon, J. (ed.) (1834–45), *The New Statistical Account of Scotland*, Vol. 7. Edinburgh: William Creech.

McGurk, F., ed. (1976). *Calendar of Papal Letters to Scotland of Benedict XIII of Avignon 1394–1419*. Edinburgh: Scottish History Society, Series 4, Vol. 13. Cited as McGurk (1976).

Munro, J. and Munro, R.W., eds (1986). *Acts of the Lords of the Isles 1336–1493*. Edinburgh: Scottish History Society, Series 4, Vol. 22.

Origines parochiales Scotiae: The Antiquities Ecclesiastical and Territorial of the Parishes of Scotland. Edinburgh: Bannatyne Club, 1854. Cited as *Origines*.

Records of the Parliaments of Scotland to 1707. University of St Andrews. Cited as *RPS*.

Registrum Episcopatus Moraviensis, e pluribus codicibus consarcinatum circa A.D. MCCCC. Cum continuatione diplomatum recentiorum usque ad A.D. MDCXXIII, ed. C. Innes. Edinburgh: Bannatyne Club, 1837. Cited as *Registrum Episcopatus Moraviensis*.

Registrum Magni Sigilli Regum Scotorum, ed. J.P. Balfour. Edinburgh: HM General Register House 1882. Cited as *RMS*.

Registrum Monasterii de Passalet cartas privilegia conventiones aliaque munimenta complectens a domo fundata A.D. MCLXIII usque ad A.D. MDXXIX, etc. Glasgow: Maitland Club, 1832. Cited as *Registrum Monasterii de Passalet*.

Rotuli Scotiae in Turri Londonensi et in Domo Capitulari Westmonasteriensi Asservati. Vol. 1, *Temporibus Regum Angliae Edwardi I, Edwardi II, Edwardi III*. London, 1814. Cited as *Rotuli Scotiae*.

Scotia Sacra: Ane account of the most renowned churches, bishoprics, monasteries and other devote places from the first introducing of Christianity into Scotland to . . . the severall reformations of religion, ed. R.A. Hay (1700–1707). National Library of Scotland Adv. MS.34.1.8. Cited as *Scotia Sacra*.

Silgrave, Henry (1274). *A Chronicle of English History, from the earliest period to A.D. 1274*, ed. C. Hook (1849). London: Caxton Society.

Sinclair, J., ed. *The Statistical Account of Scotland 1791–1799*. Cited as *First Statistical Account of Scotland*.

Thomson, T., ed. (1819). *The Auchinleck Chronicle: Ane Schort Memoriale of the Scottis Croniklis for Addicioun; To Which is Added a Short Chronicle of the Reign of James the Second King of Scots*. Privately printed.

Vetera monumenta Hibernorum et Scotorum historiam illustrantia, quae ex Vaticani, Neapolis ac Florentiae tabulariis deprompsit et ordine chronologico disposuit Augustinus Theiner, . . . Ab Honorio PP. III usque ad Paulum PP. III. 1216–1547, ed. A. Theiner (1864). Rome. Cited as *Vetera monumenta*.

Secondary Sources

Bannerman, J. (1998). *The Beatons: A Medical Kindred in the Classical Gaelic Tradition*. Edinburgh: John Donald.

Bishop, R. et al. (2022). 'Scotland's First Farmers: New Insights into Early Farming Practices in North-West Europe', *Antiquity*, 96: 1087–104.

Black, D.M. (2006). *A Tale or Two from Lismore*. Glasgow.

Boardman, S. (2006). *The Campbells 1250–1513*. Edinburgh: John Donald.

Brown, A.L. and Duncan, A.A.M. (1957). 'The Cathedral Church of Lismore', *Transactions of the Scottish Ecclesiological Society*, 15(1): 41–50.

Burleigh, J.H.S. (1960). *A Church History of Scotland*. London: Oxford University Press.

Caldwell, D. and Hall, M.A., eds (2014). *The Lewis Chessmen: New Perspectives*. Edinburgh: National Museums Scotland.

Campbell, A. (2002). *A History of Clan Campbell: From Flodden to the Restoration*. Edinburgh: Polygon.

Campbell, D. (2011). 'The Brooch of Lorn', *Historic Argyll*, 16: 60–8.

Carmichael, A. (1908–9). 'The Barons of Bachuill', *Celtic Review*, 5: 363.

Carmichael, I. (1948). *Lismore in Alba*. Perth: D. Leslie.

Cockburn, J.H. (1959). *The Medieval Bishops of Dunblane and their Church*. Edinburgh: Oliver & Boyd.
Cowan, I.B. (1967). *The Parishes of Medieval Scotland*. Edinburgh: Scottish Records Society, Old Series 93.
Cowan, I.B. (1978). 'The Medieval Church in Argyll and the Isles', *Scottish Church History Society Records*, 20(1): 5–29.
Cowan, I.B. (1995). *The Medieval Church in Scotland* (ed. J. Kirk). Edinburgh: Scottish Academic Press.
Cowan, I.B. and Easson, D.E. (1976). *Medieval Religious Houses, Scotland*. London: Longman.
Dowden, J. (1894). *The Celtic Church in Scotland*. London: SPCK.
Dowden, J. (1912). *The Bishops of Scotland: Being Notes on the Lives of all the Bishops, Under Each of the Sees, Prior to the Reformation* (ed. J. Maitland Thomson). Glasgow: J. Maclehose and Sons.
Duncan, A.A.M. (2004). 'Clement (d. 1258), Dominican friar and bishop of Dunblane'. *Oxford Dictionary of National Biography*: <www.oxforddnb.com/view/10.1093/ref:odnb/9780198614128.001.0001/odnb-9780198614128-e-50018>.
Duncan, A.A.M. and Brown, A. (1957). 'Argyll and the Isles in the Earlier Middle Ages', *Proceedings of the Society of Antiquaries of Scotland*, 90: 192–220.
Ellis, C. (2016). Data Structure Report: Excavation on the Nave of Lismore Cathedral, Isle of Lismore. Unpublished, first report. Argyll Archaeology.
Ellis, C. (2017). Data Structure Report: Excavation on the Nave of Lismore Cathedral, Isle of Lismore. Unpublished, second report. Argyll Archaeology.
Fraser, J.E. (2009). *From Caledonia to Pictland: Scotland to 795*. Edinburgh: Edinburgh University Press.
Goldstein, R.J. (1991). 'The Scottish Mission to Boniface VIII in 1301: A Reconsideration of the Context of the *Instructiones* and *Processus*', *Scottish Historical Review*, 70(1): 1–15.
Goldstein, R.J. (2004). 'Bisset [Bissait], Baldred (c. 1260–1311?), ecclesiastic', *Oxford Dictionary of National Biography*: <www.oxforddnb.com/view/10.1093/ref:odnb/9780198614128.001.0001/odnb-9780198614128-e-2475>.
Haddan, A.W. and Stubbs, W., eds (1873). *Councils and Ecclesiastical Documents relating to Great Britain and Ireland*, Vol. II, Part I. Oxford: Oxford University Press.

Hay, R.K.M. (2012). 'Bere Barley: Rediscovering a Scottish Staple', *Review of Scottish Culture*, 24: 126–39.

Hay, R.K.M. and Fryer, L. (2015). 'Island Life in the 17th Century', *History Scotland*, 15(1): 44–50.

Hay, R.K.M. (2024). *Lismore: The Great Garden*. Edinburgh: Birlinn.

Keith, R. (1824). *An Historical Catalogue of the Scottish Bishops Down to the Year 1688*. Edinburgh.

Le Roy Ladurie, E. (1990). *Montaillou: Cathars and Catholics in a French Village*. London: Penguin.

MacDonald, C.M. (1950). *The History of Argyll up to the Beginning of the Sixteenth Century*. Glasgow: W.&R. Holmes.

MacDonald, I.G. (2010). 'The Attack on Bishop George Lauder of Argyll in the *Auchinleck Chronicle*', *Innes Review*, 61(2): 111–36.

MacDonald, I.G. (2013). *Clerics and Clansmen. The Diocese of Argyll between the Twelfth and Sixteenth Centuries*. Leiden: Brill.

McDonald, R.A. (1997). *The Kingdom of the Isles: Scotland's Western Seaboard, c.1100–c.1336*. East Linton: Tuckwell Press.

Macfarlane, L.J. (1985). *William Elphinstone and the Kingdom of Scotland, 1431–1514*. Aberdeen: Aberdeen University Press.

Mackechnie, D. (1975). 'Inveraray: The Beginnings – 1', *The Kist* (Natural History and Antiquarian Society of Mid-Argyll), 9: 2–9. Available at: <www.kilmartin.org/thekist>.

MacKinnon, D. (1932). *John Carswell, 1520–1572: Superintendent of Argyle and the Isles*. Scottish Church History Society, pp. 195–207.

McNeill, P.G.B. and MacQueen, H.L. (1996). *An Atlas of Scottish History to 1707*. University of Edinburgh.

McRoberts, D. (1952). 'An Unnoticed Lismore Document of 1531', *Innes Review*, 3(2): 131–5.

McWhannell, D.C. (2023). 'Croziers of the Gaeltachd', *West Highland Notes and Queries*, 5(9): 6–9.

Màrkus, G. (2009). 'Dewars and Relics in Scotland: Some Clarifications and Questions', *Innes Review*, 60(2): 95–144.

Meredith-Lobay, M. (2009). 'A Contextual Landscape Study of the Early Christian Churches of Argyll: the Persistence of Memory'. PhD Thesis, University of Cambridge.

Ó hAnnracháin, T. and Armstrong, R., eds (2014). *Christianities in the Early Modern Celtic World*. London: Palgrave Macmillan.

Oram, R. (2014a). 'Between a Rock and a Hard Place: Climate, Weather and the Rise of the Lordship of the Isles'. In R. Oram (ed.), *The Lordship of the Isles*, pp. 40–61. The Northern World series, Vol. 68. Leiden: Brill.

Oram, R. (2014b). '"The Worst Disaster Suffered by the People of Scotland in Recorded History": Climate Change, Dearth and Pathogens in the Long 14th Century', *Proceedings of the Society of Antiquaries of Scotland*, 144: 223–44.

Oram, R. (2024). *Where Men No More May Reap or Sow: The Little Ice Age, Scotland 1400–1850*. Edinburgh: John Donald.

Ovenden, S. (2019). 'Geophysical Survey Report, Glebe Fields, Lismore'. Rose Geophysics, RGC19340/GFL.

Scott, W. (1934). *Scott's Tales of a Grandfather* (ed. E.W. Grierson). London: A. & C. Black.

Thacker, M. (2020). 'Dating Medieval Masonry Buildings by Radiocarbon Analysis of Mortar-Entrapped Relict Limekiln Fuels – a Buildings Archaeology', *Journal of Archaeological Method and Theory*, 27(2): <https://doi.org/10.1007/s10816-020-09444-z>

Thacker, M. (2021). 'Modelling Medieval Masonry Construction: Taxa-Specific and Habitat-Contingent Bayesian Techniques for the Interpretation of Radiocarbon Data from Mortar-Entrapped Relict Limekiln Fuels', *Heritage Science*, 9 (113): <https://doi.org/10.1186/s40494-021-00568-3>

Turner, D. (1998). 'The Bishops of Argyll and the Castle of Achanduin, Lismore, AD 1180–1343', *Proceedings of the Society of Antiquaries of Scotland*, 128: 645–52.

Vaughan, R., ed. (1986). *Chronicles of Matthew Paris: Monastic Life in the Thirteenth Century*. Gloucester: Allan Sutton.

Watt, D.E.R. (1977). *Biographical Dictionary of Scottish Graduates to AD 1410*. Oxford: Clarendon Press.

Watt, D.E.R. (2000). *Medieval Church Councils in Scotland*. Edinburgh: T&T Clark.

Watt, D.E.R. (2001). 'Bagimond di Vezza and his "Roll"', *Scottish Historical Review*, 80: 1–23.

Watt, D.E.R. and Murray, A., eds (2003). *Fasti Ecclesiae Scoticanae Medii Aevi Ad Annum 1638*. Edinburgh: Scottish Record Society.

White, A.M. (2009). *St Moluag's Church, Isle of Lismore*. Privately published.

Further Reading

Chapter 1

Buchanan, G. (1958). *The Tyrannous Reign of Mary Stewart* (ed. W.A. Gatherer). Edinburgh: Edinburgh University Press.

Millar, A.H. (1905). *Mary Queen of Scots: Her Life Story*. Edinburgh: William Brown.

Chapter 2

Bede (731). *Ecclesiastical History of the English People*.

Campbell, E. (2000). *Excavations at Dunadd: An Early Dalriadic Capital*. Oxford: Oxbow Books.

Carver, M. (2008). *Portmahomack: Monastery of the Picts*. Edinburgh: Edinburgh University Press.

Clancy, T.O. (2002). 'Celtic or Catholic? Writing the History of Scottish Christianity', *Records of the Scottish Church History Society*, 32: 5–39.

Clancy, T.O. (2003). 'Magpie Hagiography in Twelfth-century Scotland: The Case of *Libellus de nativitate Sancto Cuthberti*'. In J. Cartwright (ed.), *Celtic Hagiography and Saints' Cults*, pp. 216–31. Cardiff: University of Wales Press.

Ellis, C. (2022). *Data Structure Report: Excavation in the Glebe, Isle of Lismore*. Kirk Session and Lismore Historical Society.

Fisher, I. (2001). *Early Medieval Sculpture in the West Highlands and Islands*. Edinburgh: RCAHMS.

Hughes, K. (1976). 'The Church in Irish Society, 400–800'. In D. Ó Cróinin (ed.), *A New History of Ireland: Prehistoric and Early Ireland*, pp. 301–30. Oxford: Oxford University Press.

Hughes, K. (1981). 'The Celtic Church: Is This a Valid Concept?', *Cambridge Medieval Celtic Studies*, 1: 1–20.

Hunter Blair, P. (1997). *Northumbria in the Days of Bede*. Burnham-on-Sea: Llanerch Press.

Lacey, R. (2003). 'The Battle of Cúl Dreimne: A Reassessment', *Journal of the Royal Society of Antiquaries of Ireland*, 133: 78–85.

Lane, A. and Clancy, T.O. (2001). 'The Real Ninian', *Innes Review*, 52: 1–28.

Lowe, C. (2008). *An Early Historic Island Monastery and its Archaeological Landscape*. Edinburgh: Society of Antiquaries of Scotland.

McNamara, C.J. (2021). 'Tracing the Community of Comgall across the North Channel: An Interdisciplinary Investigation of Early Medieval monasteries at Bangor, Applecross, Lismore, and Tiree'. PhD Thesis, University of Glasgow.

McNeil, J.T. and Gamer, H.M., eds (1938). *Medieval Handbooks of Penance*. New York: Columbia University Press.

Màrkus, G. (2008). *Adomnán's Law of the Innocents*. Kilmartin: Kilmartin House Trust.

Marsden, J. (2005). *Somerled and the Emergence of Gaelic Scotland*. Edinburgh: John Donald.

Meek, D.E. (2000). *The Quest for Celtic Christianity*. Edinburgh: Hansel Press.

Ryan, J. (1972). *Irish Monasticism, Origins and Early Development*. Ithaca, NY: Cornell University Press.

Sharpe, R. (1984). 'Some Problems Concerning the Organisation of the Church in Early Medieval Ireland', *Peritia*, 3: 230–70.

Veitch, K. (1997). 'The Columban Church in North Britain, 664–717', *Proceedings of the Society of Antiquaries of Scotland*, 127: 627–47.

Woolf, A. (2007). *From Pictland to Alba: 789–1070*. Edinburgh: Edinburgh University Press.

Woolf, A. (2008). 'The Cult of Moluag, the See of Mortlach and Church Organisation in Northern Scotland in the Eleventh and Twelfth Centuries'. In S. Arbuthnot and K. Hollo (eds), *Fil súil nglais. A Grey Eye Looks Back: A Festschrift in Honour of Colm Ó Baoill*. Ceann Drochaid: Clann Tuirc.

Chapter 3

Barrow, G.W.S. (1973). *The Kingdom of the Scots: Government, Church and Society from the Eleventh to the Fourteenth Century*. Edinburgh: Edinburgh University Press.

Caldwell, D.H. (2014). 'The Kingdom of the Isles'. In D.H. Caldwell and M.A. Hall (eds), *The Lewis Chessmen: New Perspectives*, pp. 71–93. Edinburgh: National Museums Scotland.

Ditchburn, D. (2001). *Scotland and Europe: The Medieval Kingdom and its Contacts with Christendom, 1214–1560*. East Linton: Tuckwell Press.

Duncan, A.A.M. (2005). 'The Foundation of St Andrews Cathedral Priory, 1140', *Scottish Historical Review*, 84: 1–37.

Farmer, D. and Sherley-Price, L., eds (1990). Bede, *Ecclesiastical History of the English People*. London: Penguin.

Oram, R. (2008). *David I: The King Who Made Scotland*. Stroud: History Press.

Oram, R. (2011). *Domination and Lordship: Scotland, 1070–1230*. Edinburgh: Edinburgh University Press.

Skene, W.F. (1886–90). *Celtic Scotland: A History of Ancient Alba*. Edinburgh: David Douglas.

Veitch, K. (1996). 'The Scottish Material in *De dominibus religiosis*: Date and Provenance', *Innes Review*, 47: 14–23.

Woolf, A. (2003). 'The Diocese of the Sudreyar'. In S. Imsen (ed.), *Ecclesia Nidrosiensis 1153–1537: Søkelys på Nidaroskirkens og Nidarosprovinsens historie*, pp. 171–81. Trondheim: Tapir Academic Press.

Chapter 4

Barrow, G.W.S. (2005). *Robert Bruce and the Community of the Realm of Scotland*. Edinburgh: Edinburgh University Press.

Caldwell, D.H. (2022). '1266 and All That: An Archaeological Approach to Understanding the Scottish Takeover of the Kingdom of the Isles', *Journal of the Sydney Society for Scottish History*, 20: 1–16.

Gordon, J.F.S., ed. (1867). *Scotichronicon, Comprising Bishop Keith's Catalogue of Scottish Bishops*. Glasgow: John Tweed.

Grant, A. (1984). *Independence and Nationhood: Scotland 1306–1469*. Edinburgh: Edinburgh University Press.

Henderson, P. (1997). 'Pre-Reformation Pilgrims from Scotland to Santiago de Compostela'. Occasional paper 4. London: Confraternity of St James.

MacGregor, M. (2014). 'Gaelic Christianity? The Church in the Western Highlands and Islands of Scotland before and after the Reformation'. In T. Ó hAnnracháin and R. Armstrong (eds), *Christianities in the Early Modern Celtic World*, pp. 55–70. London: Palgrave Macmillan.

Marsden, J. (2000). *Somerled and the Emergence of Gaelic Scotland*. Edinburgh: John Donald.

Paterson, R.C. (2001). *The Lords of the Isles*. Edinburgh: Birlinn.

Patrick, D., ed. (1907). *Statutes of the Scottish Church, 1225–1559*. Edinburgh: Scottish History Society.

Robertson, E.W. (1862). *Scotland under her Early Kings*. Edinburgh: Edmonston & Douglas.

Starforth, M. (2015). *An Official Short History of the Clan MacDougall*. Glasgow: Bell & Bain.

Watt, D.E.R., ed. (1987–98). Walter Bower, *Scotichronicon*, 9 vols. Aberdeen: Aberdeen University Press.

Woolf, A. (2003). 'The Diocese of the Sudreyar'. In I. Steinar (ed.), *Ecclesia Nidronensis 1153–1537*. Senter for Middelalderstudier, NTNU, Skrifter 15.

Yeoman, P. (1999). *Pilgrimage in Medieval Scotland*. Edinburgh: Historic Scotland.

Chapter 5

Brown, M. (2004). *The Wars of Scotland 1214–1371*. Edinburgh: Edinburgh University Press.

Campbell, M. (1999). *Alexander III: King of Scots*. Colonsay: House of Lochar.

Hinnebusch, W.A. (1966). *The History of the Dominican Order*. New York: Alba House.

Oram, R. (2021). 'The Dominicans in Scotland, 1230–1560'. In E.J. Giraud and J.C. Linde (eds), *A Companion to the English Dominican Province: From Its Beginnings to the Reformation*, pp. 112–37. Companions to the Christian Tradition, 97. Leiden: Brill.

Sellar, W.D.H. (2005). 'Hebridean Sea Kings: The Successors of Somerled, 1164–1316'. In E.J. Cowan and A. McDonald (eds), *Alba: Celtic Scotland in the Medieval Era*, pp. 187–218. Edinburgh: John Donald.

Chapter 6

Barrow, G.W.S. (2003). *Kingship and Unity: Scotland 1000–1306*. Edinburgh: Edinburgh University Press.

Barrow, G.W.S. (2005). *Robert Bruce*. Edinburgh: Edinburgh University Press.

Brown, M. (2004). *The Wars of Scotland 1214–1371*. Edinburgh: Edinburgh University Press.

Grant, A. (1984). *Independence and Nationhood. Scotland 1306–1469*. Edinburgh: Edinburgh University Press.

Paterson, R.C. (2001). *The Lords of the Isles*. Edinburgh: Birlinn.

Chapters 8–11

Ditchburn, D. (2001). *Scotland and Europe: The Medieval Kingdom and its Contacts with Christendom, 1214–1560*. East Linton: Tuckwell Press.

MacDougall, N. (1997). *James IV*. East Linton: Tuckwell Press.

Penman, M. (2004). *David II: 1329–1371*. East Linton: John Donald.

Index

abbot(s) 4–5, 8, 12, 14, 15, 20, 39, 73, 79, 105, 109, 115, 117, 129, 137, 138
  of Iona 71
  of Lismore: *see* Lismore abbots
  of Paisley 50, 60, 106, 109, 114
  of Saddell 63
Aberdeen 19, 104
  Bishop of 22, 31, 68, 69, 79, 96, 99, 105, 115, 129, 132
  Bishop William Elphinstone 132
  Cathedral 31, 40
  diocese/bishopric 21, 22, 33, 46, 51, 53, 63, 108, 115
  Dominican House 56
Aberdeen Breviary 5, 147
Absolution 43, 46, 60, 143, 144
Achinduin 27, 48, 53, 77, 88, 126, 141, 142, 143
Adomnán 3, 5
Aidan 6, 8
Alba 15, 18, 19
Albany Stewarts 97, 98, 107, 113, 115, 117, 120, 121, 122, 136
Albigensian Crusade 56
Alexander I, King of Scots 18, 19, 33
Alexander II, King of Scots 30, 37, 49, 53–4, 56, 57, 71, 88
Alexander III, King of Scots 54, 58, 59, 66, 67, 71, 72, 88

Annals of Tigernach 28
antipopes: *see* Avignon popes
Appin 38, 39, 75, 105, 143, 150, 151
Applecross 5, 10
Aquinas, Thomas 56
Arbroath 33, 57, 79, 115
  Declaration of 79, 80
Ardchattan Priory 30, 36, 38, 54, 63, 88, 99, 106, 117, 143
archdeacon 61: *see also under* canons
Ardnamurchan 28, 36, 38, 42, 75
Argyll diocese/bishopric 2, 7, 21, 24–54
  bishops: *see main entry*
  canons: *see main entry*
  finances 2, 24–5, 29, 46–52, 53, 57, 64, 66, 70, 108–11, 119–20, 133–4, 136–7
  foundation 2, 24–54
  parishes (appropriation): *see main entry*
Arisaig 28, 36, 38, 101
Auchinleck Chronicle 125–7, 146
Augustine, Saint 6, 56
Augustinian abbeys/monks 13, 16, 19, 23, 24, 29, 31, 32–34, 48
Avignon 17, 51, 77, 78, 93, 94, 95, 97, 106, 107, 112, 114, 115, 117, 120

Avignon popes 106, 112, 120
Ayr 27, 56, 68, 80, 141

bachuil (Moluag's staff) 40–1, 48, 142, 144
Bagimond's Roll (Baiamund) 49, 53, 69–70
Balliol family 26, 59, 67, 68, 72, 73, 74, 75, 94
　Edward 80, 93
　John, King of Scots 66, 68, 73, 75, 76, 112
Balmerino (Fife) 115
Bangor monastery, Northern Ireland 2, 5
Bannockburn, Battle of 28, 67, 78, 79
baptism 4, 10, 42, 144
Barra 28, 101
Beaton, Cardinal 139
Beauly 30
Bede (Venerable) 8, 14
Bek, Anthony, Bishop of Durham 73
Beltane (festival) 41, 58, 144, 150
Benbecula 28
Benderloch 28, 36, 75, 77, 105
Benedictine abbeys/monks 8, 13, 16, 19, 22, 29, 31, 32, 39
benefice 45, 49, 52, 61, 69, 76, 106, 118, 119, 123, 125, 129
bere barley 46, 141
Bernera 53, 77
Berwick 32, 56, 75, 76, 95, 104
　Treaty of 99, 104
Birgham, Treaty of 71–3
birlinn 27, 39, 100, 141
Birnie Kirk 22, 40
bishops (Argyll diocese)
　Alan de Carrick 14, 49, 58–62, 67
　Andrew de Ergadia 67, 71, 76–80, 87, 94

Bean/Beanus Johannis
　Andree 50, 112, 113, 114, 115, 117, 119, 148
　David Hamilton 137–8
　Finlay de Albany 58, 59, 112, 120–1, 136
　George Lauder 62, 121–30, 131, 133, 136
　Harald 35, 37, 39, 41–4, 52, 59
　James Hamilton 1, 2, 137–9, 158
　John Dugaldi 106, 112, 114
　Laurence de Ergadia 50, 58, 59, 63, 66–76, 88
　Martin 93–111
　Robert Colquhon 136–7
　Robert Montgomery 137–8
　William 39
　William Cunningham 137–8
Bisset, Baldred 74, 77
Black Cross of Lismore 41, 151
Black Death 93, 99, 112, 140
Blackfriars (Dominicans) 56, 57, 80
Blane (Celtic saint) 41
Bologna 51, 52, 70, 74, 77
Book of Common Order 139
Book of the Dean of Lismore 132
Brechin 15
　Bishop of 14, 20, 22, 68, 79, 96, 97, 100, 105, 115, 129
　diocese/bishopric 21, 31, 33, 40, 53, 138
Brendan (Celtic saint) 41
Bride/Brigid (Celtic saint) 41–2
Bruce family 72, 74, 75, 76, 96
　Robert I, King of Scots 17, 26, 27, 42, 67, 71, 73, 74, 77, 78–80, 88, 93, 94, 141
　Robert, the 'Competitor', 5th Lord of Annandale 68, 72, 73
　Robert, Earl of Carrick 71, 72
Byzantium 4, 17

INDEX

Caithness 15, 19, 22, 120
  Bishop of 22, 31, 68, 69, 79, 97, 100, 105, 115, 129
  diocese/bishopric 14, 21, 34, 40, 49, 53, 108
Calvin 139, 145
Calvinist Confession of Faith 139
Cambridge 51, 120
Cambuskenneth 23, 33, 57, 58, 79, 115, 137
Campbell family 66, 74, 75, 76, 78, 93, 101, 102, 105, 113, 122, 129, 130, 136, 138, 141, 142, 144, 150
  Sir Arthur 79
  Sir Colin of Lochawe, 1st Earl of Argyll 76, 102, 122, 116, 135
  Colin, 1st Lord of Glenorchy (Black Colin of Rome) 127, 135
  Sir Duncan of Lochawe 114, 122, 124, 127, 128, 129
  Earl of Argyll 1, 41, 56, 122, 129, 135, 137, 139, 144, 146
  Sir John 114
Campbell priests/canons 133
  Dugal 123
  John, Bishop of Sodor 132
  Sir Neil 114, 124
candles 46, 58
Candlemas 144
canons 24, 49, 52, 60, 61, 62, 63, 65, 89, 91, 106, 107, 112, 124, 126, 127, 133, 134, 146
  archdeacons 61, 62, 106, 112, 124, 131, 132, 134, 146, 150: Sir Christino/Christin 61, 62; Gilbert 62; John Dugaldi 106; Alexander Wardlaw 107; David Macmuirechard 107; Neil Campbell 114; David Marcad 117; Conghan Machabei 118; William Elphinstone 132

chancellors 61, 62, 106, 115, 131, 135: Gavin Hammiltoun 131, 150; Dubhghall MacGriogar 132
deans 41, 51, 61, 62, 67, 77, 106, 112, 131, 135, 150: Sir Gillemelnoc 62; Lacham 106; Bean 114, 115, 117; Seumas MacGriogar 132; Alasdair McCalman 150; Glassary 60, 101; Kintyre 62, 101; Lismore 61, 62, 101; Lorn 62, 101; Morvern 42, 50, 101
officials 61, 74, 106, 131, 132: Sir Daniele 61; Maurice 62
prebendary (ordinary) canons 52, 60, 61, 62, 63, 65, 89, 91, 106, 107, 112, 126, 127, 133, 134, 146: Dugall Petri 107; John of Cowal 107; James Douglas 124; Scrymgeour family 124-5
precentors/chanters 30, 61, 63, 106, 112, 131: Donald Macfadzean 132
treasurers 61, 62, 106, 112, 115, 131, 135, 150: Morys McFadyane 125; Gavin Hammiltoun 150
see also Campbell priests/canons
canon law 17, 52, 61, 74, 77, 106, 107, 114, 118
Canterbury 43, 78
  Archbishop of 13, 15, 16, 44
Carham, Battle of 14
Carlisle 18
Carmichael, Alexander 9, 41, 91, 92, 142, 144
Carmichael, Dugald 91
Carmichael, Robert (*an Easbuig Ban* – the Fair Bishop) 133
Carsaig (Mull) 90
Carswell, John, Superintendent in Argyll 139, 149
Cathars 55, 56, 144

cathedral ritual (Lismore) 63–5
Céli Dé / Culdees 12, 14, 15, 33–4, 39, 62, 123
celibacy 4, 52
chancellor (of a diocese) 61: *see also under* canons
Chancellor of Scotland 37, 68, 74, 79, 96, 100, 105, 121, 132, 139
Christmas 144
Ciaran/Chiaran/Kilcheran (village) 39, 146
Ciaran (Celtic saint) 41
Cistercian abbeys/monks 13, 19, 22, 23, 24, 28, 30, 31–4, 134
Clachan, Lismore 89, 90, 151
Clement, Bishop of Dunblane 54, 55, 56–9
Cluniac abbeys/monks 13, 29, 31, 48, 60, 70, 95, 98, 109
Clyde 20, 122
Cnoc Aingeal (fire cairn) 41
coarbs 4, 13, 15
Coeffin Castle 27, 48, 141, 142
Coldingham 19, 32
Coldstream 32
Coll 28
Columba, Saint 5, 8, 12, 29, 41, 144
Columbanus (Irish missionary) 5
Comgall, Saint 5
Commissary Court 132, 150
Comyn family 26, 27, 57, 58, 59, 67, 72, 73, 74, 75, 76, 78, 94
  Alexander, Earl of Buchan 72
  John of Badenoch 17, 58, 59, 68, 72, 73, 77, 79, 96
  Walter, Earl of Menteith 57, 58
  William, Earl of Buchan 37, 58, 68
consistorial court 146, 150
confirmation 4, 77, 94, 114
Constance, Council of 120–1
Constantinople 69, 78
confessor *in mortis articulo* 117

Council of the Scottish Churches 44, 56, 69, 70, 115,
Cowal 6, 17, 37, 94, 95, 102, 107, 118, 128, 129, 133, 134
Craignich, Lismore 53, 77, 141
Crossraguel Abbey (Ayrshire) 70
crusades 17, 45, 47, 55, 57, 69, 70, 78, 136
Culkessoch 37
Cum universi (bull) 23, 35
Cumbria 3, 6, 18, 19
Cupar 31, 33
Cuthbert, Saint 14, 28, 43

Dalriada 5, 15
Dalrigh 26, 27, 28
David I, King of Scots 13, 14, 16–24, 31–4, 46, 48, 72
David II, King of Scots 47, 80, 93–104, 106
dean 61, 62: *see also under* canons
deaneries 37, 38, 42, 50, 60, 101, 115, 117
degrees of consanguinity 97, 115, 116
Devil 144
Dewar manuscripts 41
disease/plague 2, 43, 66, 102, 105, 108, 112, 117
Dominican Order of Friars 1, 55–6, 57, 58–9, 64, 67, 68, 69, 77, 80, 87, 89, 93, 94, 99, 120, 144, 145, 146
Dominus/Sir (title) 50, 62, 147
Dornoch 15
Dryburgh 23, 32, 69
Dunadd 11
Dumbarton 121, 128, 130, 132, 133, 136
Dunblane
  Bishop of 14, 22, 54, 56–8, 68, 69, 70, 74, 79, 97, 100, 105, 115, 129

INDEX

Cathedral 40
diocese/bishopric 15, 20, 21, 31, 34, 53, 55, 56–58, 107, 137
Dundrennan 24
Dunfermline 19, 22, 23, 33, 48, 109, 115
Dumfries 14, 17, 42, 78, 96
Dunbar, Battle of 73, 76
Dunkeld 12
  Bishop of 14, 20, 22, 30, 31, 35, 57, 67, 68, 74, 79, 96, 99, 105, 115, 122, 129
  Bishop John Scotus, founding of the Argyll diocese 30, 34–5
  Cathedral 40, 57, 88
  diocese/bishopric 14, 15, 18, 20, 21, 24–5, 30, 33, 35, 53, 63, 84, 114
Dunollie 27
Dunstaffnage, castle and chapel 27, 29, 39, 54, 75, 78, 79, 86
Dunoon 1, 2, 95, 128, 129, 130, 133
  Castle 128, 129
  parish 36, 37, 49, 85, 128
  St Mary the Virgin Church as diocesan cathedral 128, 131, 133
Durham 6, 96
  Bishop of 14, 73
  Cathedral and diocese 14, 19, 30, 60, 79
  pilgrimage/penance 14, 28, 43
Durward, Alan 58
Duthac, Saint 42

Edward I, King of England 27, 66, 68, 72, 73, 75–8, 79
Edward II, King of England 73, 78, 79
Edward III, King of England 80
Elphinstone, William 132
Elgin 22, 56, 73, 88, 97, 104

excommunication 17, 18, 35, 42, 44, 45–6

Falkirk, Battle of 74
famine 2, 66, 102, 112, 140
fasting 4, 8
Fife 19, 78, 122, 124
  Earl of 33, 70, 98, 113, 115, 120
Finan 41
fish 22, 27, 47, 48, 113, 128, 142
Forfar 33
Forth–Clyde line 3, 12, 15, 18, 20
Fortrose 22, 88
Frackersaig 77, 141
fuel 8, 89, 134, 142, 143

Gaeldom/Gaels 20, 23, 31, 35, 56, 101, 121, 133
Gaelic 16, 19, 20, 22, 23, 24, 28, 35, 40, 55, 58, 59, 62, 91, 114, 123, 124–7, 132, 133, 138, 139, 146, 147, 149
Gaelic Learned Orders 51, 52, 147
Gall-Gael 28, 35
Galloway 14, 18, 19, 23, 30, 31, 34, 59
  Bishop of 31, 68, 70, 79, 99, 105, 115, 129
  Cathedral 40
  diocese/bishopric 15, 21, 23, 34, 53, 74, 108
Garmoran 27, 28, 101, 105
Glasgow 56, 71, 106, 109, 127
  Archbishop of 135, 137
  Bishop of 18, 22, 30, 31, 57, 60, 68, 69, 70, 72, 73, 78, 96–7, 99, 105, 107, 115, 121, 129, 137
  Bishop Robert Wishart 68, 69, 72, 74, 78
  Cathedral 1, 18, 23, 31, 40, 50, 74, 109, 121
  diocese/bishopric 15, 18, 20, 21, 34, 53, 63, 108

Dominican House 56, 80, 87, 128
Fair 60, 102, 128
pilgrimage to shrine of
   Kentigern 43
University of 130, 132, 136, 149
Glassary 36, 37, 43, 48, 60, 61, 62,
   95, 101, 102, 124–7, 133
Glencoe 36, 75
Glenelg 36, 37, 38, 42
Glenorchy 36, 38, 124, 129, 131,
   146, 150
Golden Rose 35
graveslabs 2, 91, 135
Great Glen 39
Guzman, Dominic de 55–6

Håkon, King of Norway 67
Halkirk 15, 22
Hamilton, Patrick 138
Hammiltoun, Gavin 131, 150
   protocol book 150
hereditary priesthood 4, 13, 52, 146
heritors 151
Holyrood Abbey 23, 30, 32, 48, 69,
   115, 134, 137

illegitimacy 1, 52, 96, 117, 138, 145
Inchaffrey 31, 48, 57
Inchcolm 19, 33
Insular Church 3–8, 12, 13, 15, 30
Inverness 56, 104
Iona 4, 5, 6, 8, 11, 12, 15, 16, 29,
   30, 31, 34, 39, 48, 71, 90, 91
Islay 27, 28, 66, 68, 70, 75, 76,
   94, 95, 100, 101, 104, 105, 107,
   113, 115, 133, 137
Isle of May 33
Isles, the (diocese): *see* Sodor/
   Sudreyar/the Isles, diocese

James I, II, III, IV, V, VI, Kings
   of Scots: *see under* Steward/
   Stewart dynasty

Jedburgh 23, 32
Jerusalem 18, 43
Jura 28

Kelso 19, 23, 32
Kentigern, Saint 43
Kerrera 54, 57, 59
Kilandrist (Anndraist/Andrew),
   Lismore 39, 146
Kilcheran (Chiaran/Ciaran) 39, 146
Killean, Lismore 39, 146
Kilmun (St Mund) 102
   collegiate church 128–9
Kilwinning 31, 34, 48
Kinloss 22, 23, 34, 115
Kintyre 1, 28, 29, 30, 36, 37, 39,
   48, 49, 50, 59, 60, 62, 68, 75,
   76, 87, 94, 95, 101, 102, 105,
   124, 133, 134, 136
Knoydart 28, 36, 38, 42, 101

Largs, Battle of 68
Lateran councils, Rome 44
Latin 51, 55, 63, 100, 147
Lauder family 121
   Sir Robert of the Bass 121
Law of the Innocents 3
Lennox (region) 18, 120, 121
Lewis 5, 28
Limbo 42
lime burning 89, 90, 143
Lindisfarne 6
Lindores 31, 33, 57
Linlithgow 115
Linn na Creach (Age of
   Forays) 131
Lismore abbots 9, 39
Lismore Cathedral 81–92
   ruined 134, 135
Lismore monastery 2, 8–12, 15, 39
Little Ice Age 66
Lochalsh 20
Loch Leven 15

INDEX

Loch Linnhe 39, 122
Loch Lomond 18
Lord of the Articles 137
Lords of the Congregation 139
Lorn 27, 28, 36, 38, 54, 62, 68, 75, 76, 101, 102, 113, 114, 151
  'Brooch of' 26
  Lords of: *see* MacDougall, Lords of Lorn
  Presbytery 151
Lothian 14, 18, 19, 21, 32–3, 132, 137
Lyons, Second Council of 69

McCalman, Alexander 149–50, 151
MacColla, Alasdair 151
MacDonald, Lords of Islay 24, 29, 66, 74, 75, 76, 78, 94, 101, 102, 113, 123
  Alexander 75, 76
  Angus 68, 70, 75
  Donald 28
  John 94, 95, 100, 101
  Ranald 28, 29, 30, 35, 54
MacDougall, Lords of Lorn 8, 24, 26–30, 39, 40, 54, 59, 63, 66, 67, 68, 71, 74, 76–8, 79, 81, 86, 88, 89, 93, 94, 95, 102, 105, 114, 141, 142, 147
  Alexander de Ergadia 73, 75–8, 79, 101
  Duncan 30, 54
  Ewen de Ergadia 40, 53, 54, 59, 67, 70
  John Baccach 78, 79
  John Gallda 101, 105, 113
MacFadyen (McFadyene, McFadzen) priests 123, 125, 127, 132, 146
MacGillemichael priests 62, 118, 123, 133
MacGregor, Rev. Gregor 145
MacGregor, James and Dubhghall, Fortingall 132

MacLachlan (McLachlane) family 123, 125, 127, 146
MacLea (later Livingstone) family 41
McNicol, Rev. Donald 41, 82, 91
MacRuairi family 27, 28, 101
MacSorley dynasty 14, 24, 27, 28–31, 35, 39, 54, 74
Maelrubha (priest) 5, 144
Malcolm III (Canmore), King of Scots 13, 16, 33
Malcolm IV, King of Scots 31, 33
Margaret, Saint 13, 16, 19, 57
marriage 4, 17, 42, 46, 70, 72, 75–6, 97, 101, 115–16, 119, 122, 124, 135, 138, 144, 145, 150
Mass 4, 42, 43, 44, 46, 51, 62, 63, 64, 83, 87, 89, 135, 139, 143
Man, Isle of 28, 30, 51, 54
mason's mark 84, 88, 89, 143
medicine 16, 51, 52
Melrose 22, 23, 28, 32, 115
Melrose Chronicle 28
mensal parishes 49, 54, 60, 77, 128, 133
Merse 19
metal working 4, 11
missals 63
Moidart 28, 36, 101
Moluag (Moloc/Moloak), Saint 2, 5, 6, 8–12, 22, 35, 39, 40, 41, 48, 61, 90, 128, 138, 142, 144, 147, 152
Montfort, Simon de 55
More/Mure, Elizabeth 96, 98
Morar 28, 101
Moray 20, 22, 24, 30
  Bishop of 22, 31, 37, 40, 52, 53, 69, 70, 79, 99, 105, 115, 132
  Cathedral 22, 40, 88, 97
  diocese/bishopric 19, 21, 22, 33, 36, 53, 63, 115
mortar radiocarbon-dating 1, 80, 86, 89

Mortlach 5, 22
Morvern 28, 36, 38, 42, 50, 62, 68, 75, 84, 90, 101, 102, 143
Mull 5, 28, 39, 75, 84, 90, 143

Nechtan, King of Picts 8
Neville's Cross, Battle of 93, 96, 101
Newbattle 23, 32, 109
Nicene Creed 69
Nidaros/Trondheim 20, 30, 106
Ninian/Nynia, Saint 3, 42–3
Norse 12, 15, 17, 19, 27, 28, 35, 39, 40
North Berwick 32
Northumbria 6, 8, 15, 19, 20
Norway 19, 20, 24, 26, 28, 30, 54, 56, 67, 72, 79, 106

oats, black 141
official (of a diocese) 61: *see also under* canons
Orléans 51
Oswald, King of Northumbria 6
Oswui, King of Northumbria 6, 8
Oxford 34, 51, 56, 120, 147

Paisley Priory/Abbey 29, 30, 31, 48, 49, 50, 60, 62, 68, 69, 70, 80, 87, 94, 95, 106, 108, 109, 110, 111, 114, 136
papal indult 118, 127, 128
Papal Inquisition 56
papal legate 23, 44, 135
Paris 34, 51, 102, 107, 114, 117, 118, 121, 122, 147, 148
Paris, Matthew 57
parishes (Argyll diocese, appropriation) 36, 37–8, 41
  Ardchattan 36, 38
  Arisaig 36, 38
  Dunoon (Lismore cathedral) 36, 37, 49, 128, 133

Eilean Fhianain 36, 38
Eilean Munde 36, 38
Inishail (Inchaffray) 36, 38, 48
Inverchaolan 36, 37
Glassary (Paisley) 36, 37, 43, 48, 61, 95, 124, 125, 127, 133
Glenelg 36, 38
Glenorchy 36, 38, 124
Kilberry (Lismore cathedral) 36, 38, 49, 61, 133
Kilblane 36, 37
Kilbrandon 36, 38
Kilbride (Lismore Cathedral) 36, 38, 42, 49, 54
Kilcalmonell (Paisley) 36, 38, 48, 49, 60, 68, 123, 136
Kilchattan 36, 38, 117, 119
Kilchenzie (Iona) 36, 37–8, 48
Kilchoan 36
Kilcolmkill (Kintyre) (Whithorn) 37, 48, 61, 80, 124, 133
Kilcolmkill (Morvern) 38
Kilchousland (Lismore cathedral) 36, 37
Kilchrenan 36, 38
Kilfinan (Paisley) 36, 37, 48, 60, 68, 70, 80, 109, 110
Kilkerran (Paisley) 36, 37, 48, 50, 60, 68, 70, 71, 80, 87, 109, 110, 136
Kilkivan (Saddell) 36, 37, 48, 59
Killean (Lismore cathedral) 36, 37–8, 49, 53, 136
Killintag 36, 38
Kilmalieu 36, 38
Kilmarow (Lismore cathedral) 36, 37, 48, 53, 138
Kilmartin (Lismore cathedral) 36, 38, 61, 114, 133
Kilkmalie 36
Kilmelford 36, 38, 114, 119

parishes (Argyll diocese) *continued*
  Kilmichael (Lismore
    cathedral)   36, 37, 48
  Kilmodan (Whithorn)   36, 37, 48,
    61, 133
  Kilmonivaig   36, 38, 50, 114
  Kilmore   36, 38, 42, 118
  Kilmorich (Inchaffray)   36, 38
  Kilmory   36
  Kilmun (Paisley)   36, 37, 48
  Kilninver   36, 38, 42, 107
  Lochgoilhead   36, 38, 107, 118, 124
  Moidart   36
  Muckairn (Inchaffray)   36, 38
  Strathlachlan   36, 37, 80, 87
parliament   1, 22, 56, 66, 72, 73, 75,
  76, 78, 79, 80, 100, 102–6, 108,
  115, 123, 129, 131, 132, 137–9,
  149, 151, 152
Pass of Brander, Battle   26, 27, 78,
  80, 141
patronage   50, 119, 121, 122, 124
'pax box'   43
peat   47, 142
penance   4, 5, 14, 42–3, 46
Perth   33, 69, 104, 105, 115, 129
  Treaty of   56
Perthshire   5, 24, 48, 105, 122, 124
Pinkie, Battle of   135
Pict/Pictland   5, 8, 10, 15, 37
Pisa (Italy)   18
piscina   83, 84, 91
Pluscarden   30, 121
Poitiers, Battle of   99
popes
  Alexander IV   58
  Benedict XII   94
  Boniface VIII   76, 77
  Celestine III   23, 35
  Clement V   17, 79
  Clement VI   17, 94, 95, 96, 109
  Clement VII   51, 107, 115, 117,
    119

Gregory IX   52, 56, 57
Gregory X   69–70
Gregory XI   119
Innocent II   18, 57
Julius II   151
Lucius III   35
Paschal II   18
Paul III   138
Pius II   127
Urban IV   67
Urban V   114
Pope's scholar   106, 114
portable altar   117, 135
Portmahomack   10, 11, 12
prebendary (ordinary) priests/canons:
  see under canons
precentor/chanter (of a diocese)   61:
  see also under canons
Premonstratensian abbeys/
  monks   13, 23, 24, 31–4
pulpit   82, 151
Purgatory   42

radiocarbon-dating   10, 11, 12,
  71, 81, 89, 92; *see also* mortar
  radiocarbon-dating
ransom payments   47, 93, 97,
  99–100, 104, 105, 108, 120
Reformation   17, 23, 41, 77, 81,
  82, 83, 108, 125, 131, 133, 135,
  138, 139, 145, 146, 147, 149–52
Renfrew   29
Restenneth   16
Robert I (the Bruce), King of Scots:
  see under Bruce family
Robert II, King of Scots   93, 95–9,
  102, 103, 107
Robert III, King of Scots   98, 99,
  105
Rome   16, 17, 18, 23, 35, 44, 48,
  52, 57, 58, 69, 70, 74, 77, 93,
  107, 120, 124, 127, 128, 129,
  136, 138

Rosemarkie 5, 10, 15, 22
Ross 19, 100, 101, 103, 113
  Bishop/diocese 14, 15, 20, 21,
    22, 31, 34, 36, 40, 49, 54, 63,
    68, 69, 79, 99, 105, 115, 129
Roxburgh 19, 20, 32

Saddell (Kintyre) 1, 28, 29, 30, 38,
  39, 48, 63, 131, 134, 135
sacrament 4, 42, 43, 44, 124, 144
Salamanca (Spain) 52
Salerno (Italy) 52
Salisbury, Treaty of 71–2
Salisbury/Sarum Use (liturgical) 63
Sanctuary Stone (Lismore monastic
  site) 9, 10, 92
Samhuin (festival) 41
Santiago 43
Sauchieburn, Battle of 137
schism in papal authority 17, 69,
  93, 106, 107, 120
Scotia 15, 18, 19, 58
Scotichronicon 30, 121
Scone 19, 33, 72, 75, 78, 100, 102,
  105, 115
Seal, diocese 50, 68, 69, 95, 100,
  128, 150
sedilia (seats for clergy) 83, 84,
  88, 91
Selkirk 19
Silgrave, Henry 32, 39
sin/sinners 4, 42, 43, 64, 69, 79, 145
  mortal sins/souls 42, 117
  minor/venal 42
Skrymgeour (Scrymgeour) family
  Sir Alexander 124
  Hercules 125–7, 146
  Rectors of Glassary 124–7
Skye 5, 28
Sodor/Sudreyar/the Isles,
    diocese 20, 21, 30, 39, 51,
    52–3, 63, 69, 71, 79, 115, 116,
    132, 133

Somerled 24, 28, 29, 30, 35, 101, 113
St Andrews 62, 78, 79, 138, 139
  Bishop/Archbishop of 1, 14, 20,
    22, 23, 35, 50, 57, 58, 67, 68,
    69, 70, 72, 73, 74, 76, 79, 96,
    97, 100, 105, 113, 115, 129, 137
  Bishop Gamelin 57, 58, 67, 68
  Bishop William Fraser 68, 72, 74
  Bishop William Lamberton 74,
    76, 78, 79
  Cathedral 20, 23, 32, 40
  diocese/bishopric 15, 16, 18, 19,
    21, 23, 24, 33, 34, 46, 53, 64,
    74, 107, 108, 123, 132
  University of 52, 122, 125, 147,
    149
Steward/Stewart dynasty 30, 31,
  59, 60, 93, 95, 97, 98, 101, 104,
  120, 136, 138
  of Innermeath, Lords of
    Lorn 105, 113, 114, 117, 135
  James I, King of Scots 56, 97, 98,
    113, 120–1, 122, 128, 136
  James II, King of Scots 122, 128,
    129
  James III, King of Scots 122,
    127, 129, 136, 137
  James IV, King of Scots 6, 43,
    132, 134, 135, 137, 138, 146, 151
  James V, King of Scots 138
  James VI, King of Scots 150
  James the Steward 72, 75
  James 'the Fat' 121, 136
  John Stewart / Robert III, King of
    Scots 98, 99, 105
  Robert Stewart / Robert II, King of
    Scots 93, 95–9, 102, 103, 107
  Robert, Earl of Fife, 1st Duke of
    Albany 107, 113, 115
  Walter, High Steward 29, 59
Stewart, Donald of
  Invernahyle 135, 151
Stirling 23, 33, 37, 56, 58, 74, 129

INDEX

Stirling Bridge, Battle of 74
Strathclyde 14, 15, 18

Tain 42, 43
teind 23, 25, 29, 35, 46–9, 51, 61, 89, 111, 115, 142, 150–1
  Garbal 47
Teviotdale 14, 21
Thomas, Saint 43
Tiree 5, 28, 75
Tirfuir 77, 106
Tironesian abbeys/monks 13, 16, 18, 19, 23, 31–2
Toledo (Spain) 52
tonsure 4, 65, 83
treasurer (of a diocese) 61: *see also under* canons
Turnberry Band 75
Tweed/Tweeddale 14, 18

Uaigh nan Romanach (Grave of the Romans) 90, 143
Uists 28, 101, 144
unbaptised infants 145
Urquhart 22, 27, 33

Vatican 17, 18, 19, 35, 47, 48, 114, 127, 134, 136, 137, 138, 147
Valliscaulian order of monks 30, 54
vestments 46–8, 64, 83, 108
vicars 44, 47, 49, 50, 51, 52

Wales 3, 5, 6
Wars of Independence 26, 52, 56–80, 87, 94
wheat 46, 141
Whitby (Streonshalh), Synod 8
Whithorn 11, 14, 23, 31, 34, 40, 42–3, 48
William I, King of Scots 30, 31, 33, 35
Wishart, George 139
witches (white) 144
Wolf of Badenoch 97, 98

York, Archbishop of 13, 14, 15, 16, 18, 19, 23, 35, 44, 72, 73, 79

ORIGIN

Origin, an imprint of Birlinn Limited.

Head over to our website to find more Birlinn books across, fiction, non-fiction, sport, poetry, children's books, and academic history. You can scan the QR Code below to sign up to our newsletter. Keep up to date with all our new publications, launch events, author interviews, special offers and much more!

Explore Scotland with our app, Scotland-by-the-Book, a new tool for readers at home and around the globe with an interest in Scotland. Scan the QR Code below to find out more: